THE
STORKS'
NEST

THE
STORKS'
NEST

[*Life and Love in the Russian Countryside*]

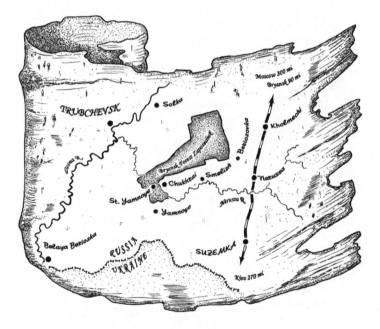

Laura Lynne Williams

WITH PHOTOGRAPHS BY Igor Shpilenok

FULCRUM
GOLDEN, COLORADO

Library of Congress Cataloging-in-Publication Data

Williams, Laura Lynne.
  The stork's nest : life and love in the Russian countryside / by Laura
Lynne Williams.
      p. cm.
  ISBN-13: 978-1-55591-629-9 (pbk. : alk. paper)
  ISBN-10: 1-55591-629-5 (pbk. : alk. paper) 1. Natural history Russia
(Federation)--Gosudarstvennyi prirodnyi zapovednik "Brianskii les".
2. Williams, Laura Lynne. 3. Conservationists--Russia
(Federation)--Biography. I. Title.
  QH161.W55 2008
  508.47'25--dc22

                                    2007042340

Printed on recycled paper in the United States of America by Thomson-Shore, Inc.
Fulcrum Publishing is a member of the Green Press Initiative.
0 9 8 7 6 5 4 3 2 1

Design: Ann W. Douden
Photo credits: © Igor Shpilenok: front cover, i, ii, iv, 96, 241, 242, 289,
306, 308 (top), 309 (top), 310 (bottom), 312 (top), 313, 324
© Nickolai Shpilenok: v (map), 95, 169, 170, 290, 307 (top and bottom), 308 (bottom),
309 (bottom), 310 (top), 311 (top and bottom), 312 (bottom), 314, 327, 328

Fulcrum Publishing
4690 Table Mountain Drive, Suite 100
Golden, Colorado 80403
800-992-2908 • 303-277-1623
www.fulcrumbooks.com

FOR IGOR

Spring

THE ARRIVAL of spring to our tiny Russian village of Chukhrai—population nineteen—means that soon the rutted, ice-covered forest road that connects us to the outside world will become passable. Slowly, the villagers emerge from hibernation. All winter I had observed subtle signs of their existence. Wispy columns of smoke rising from the chimneys of their two-room log cabins. Runner tracks in the snow left from early morning forays in a horse-drawn sleigh to gather firewood. An old man covered from head to toe in torn, dirty, yet warm wadded clothing, sitting on an overturned pail in the middle of the frozen river, his fishing line disappearing into a hole in the ice.

Surrounded on three sides by a strict nature reserve, our village is virtually inaccessible. A narrow forest road leads from the fourth side to civilization. I set out with Igor on an expedition down this road to stock up on supplies, with axe, chain saw, winch, crowbar, and rubber boots in the back of our sturdy Russian UAZ army jeep. It is perhaps the only modern invention other than electricity and television to reach this village. Our neighbors, mostly elderly women widowed half a century earlier, wave us to a stop. I write down their orders.

THE STORKS' NEST

Sacks of rye flour to bake bread. Sugar to preserve berries and make *samogon* (moonshine). Carrot, cucumber, and dill seeds to sow. Chicks to raise for fresh eggs and poultry. All that remains of the village store are a few bricks and chunks of mortar.

My neighbor Olga Ivanovna asks to accompany us so she can pick out a piglet to fatten up for pork and *salo* (salted pig fat, without which it is said no Russian can survive the winter). We pick her up, helping her into the backseat. Although she is seventy-seven years old, I consider her a close friend. She can brew herbal remedies and break a curse. Her stories of growing up in Chukhrai fascinate me, and I enjoy my frequent visits to her house.

We venture down the six-mile lifeline to the next village of Smelizh. Gripping the steering wheel, Igor drives the jeep like an ice cleaver through large, still-frozen potholes in the road. Olga Ivanovna holds on to the passenger seat behind where I am sitting. I hold on to a handle on the dashboard. We brace ourselves for each jolt. The UAZ jeep has earned the national nickname of *kozyol* (billy goat) for the way it jumps about. Farther on, meltwater in deep ruts engulfs the entire front half of the jeep. The engine sputters and water spills into the door wells. A fat tree accosts the side of the vehicle. Next we pull out the chain saw to clear a tree that has fallen on the road.

Igor saws the long pine into three-foot sections and tosses them in the back of the jeep.

Firewood, he says.

I help move the remaining branches aside and, in doing so, snag my pants, ripping a large gash down one leg.

From Smelizh we drive two miles to Krasnaya Sloboda, from which a paved road leads to the district center of

Suzemka, about twenty-five miles away. In this town of seven thousand we find limited produce and foodstuffs at the outdoor market and half-a-dozen respectable stores. For more-substantial needs, we would have to travel more than fifty miles to Trubchevsk, the center of the neighboring district, or make a trip to the provincial capital of Bryansk, ninety miles to the north. But Suzemka's limited selection suits our needs this week. While Olga Ivanovna examines piglets rolling around on the ground in potato sacks, I send Igor to buy me a new pair of pants at the outdoor market.

Size 8, I call after him, and nothing too fancy. Blue jeans and casual tops are my standard attire, although occasionally I will don tight black pants and a slim turtleneck to venture into town.

Outfitted with new $5 black pants, I stock up on supplies: fruit, bread, pasta, cheese, ham, mayonnaise, fresh meat from the market, and beer. We have potatoes, carrots, and beets from the previous year's harvest stored in our root cellar at home. We return to Chukhrai with the piglet squealing in a sack in the back of the jeep. We let Olga Ivanovna out at her house, and Igor carries the sack with the piglet into her yard.

We drive to the end of the village and park the jeep in front of our small wooden house. Igor leans over to the passenger seat to kiss me.

Welcome home, dear, he says in English with his charming Russian accent.

Thank you, I reply in Russian, smiling.

He carries the firewood to the lean-to next to the outhouse while I unload the groceries, piled in boxes and canvas bags. The neighbors come to collect their orders, reimbursing us for the goods and trying to shove additional money for gas into our pockets. We refuse the money, saying we were going anyway, but later they bring us potatoes and *salo*, remarking that they don't like to feel indebted.

Once a lively village of more than three hundred people, today Chukhrai, like so many other villages in the Russian countryside, is on its last legs. The villagers here have never had it easy. There were so many strikes against them: floods, famine, purges, collectivization, war, resettlement, and the absence of a road. Now the only people left in Chukhrai are those who weren't smart or lucky enough to leave. And then there are Igor and me, two naturalists who find solace in the village's remoteness, in its total immersion in the wilderness of the Bryansk Forest, and in each other.

That night I dream I'm back at Cornell. I've overslept and I'm late for Russian. I run into the classroom and everyone stares. I look down to find that I have no clothes on. I dash out the door and up the ivy-covered bell tower that stands at the head of the campus's main square. I look out over snowy Ithaca and the icy Finger Lakes and, for some reason, they look like the frozen floodplain around the village of Chukhrai.

I wake up, relieved my nakedness was only a dream. I think back to my first Russian class, sophomore year. We began by talking about Gorbachev and his efforts to restructure the country, known as perestroika.

I looked blankly at the teacher and asked, What's perestroika?

It was 1988, and though Gorbachev had been in power in the Soviet Union for three years, I was clueless as to what was going on in the country.

Why are you taking Russian? the teacher asked.

His question was fair. If I knew nothing about Russia

and didn't follow current events, why would I bother to learn the language?

So I explained that I wanted to get involved in nature conservation on an international level. I figured that to have an impact on global issues, I needed to work with the world's other superpower, the Soviet Union. That's why I was taking Russian, I said, to build relationships between our two countries on environmental policy, global climate change, and nature conservation.

For the next three years, I took courses on ecology and natural resources, combining them with studies of biology, government, and languages (French and Russian). In all, I learned a little bit about a lot, but knew very little about anything in particular.

The summer after my junior year, I visited Russia for the first time, on a student language exchange to Leningrad State University (now St. Petersburg State University). It was 1990, and the country was plagued by economic depression and food shortages. As privileged foreigners, however, our group was served a hot dog, a boiled egg, and a cup of *smetana* (sour cream) for breakfast each morning at the dormitory. I was a strict vegetarian then, so, unable to stomach breakfast, I was happy to find a bakery around the corner with fresh poppy seed *bubliki,* ring-shaped rolls not unlike bagels. I remember passing a perfume shop on the way to the bakery and being surprised that there was always a long line of puffy-faced men outside. Later I learned that they lined up early each morning to buy cheap cologne, which they then proceeded to consume, as vodka was in short supply.

On group excursions around Leningrad, we were continually buttonholed by *fartsofshiki,* black marketeers peddling Russian souvenirs and offering to exchange money. In a time of new economic discovery, *fartsofshiki* were the predecessors to Russian *biznesmeny* (businessmen, Russified) and the mafia. The young Russian men were handsome, well dressed, smart, and spoke English, so all the girls in our group were immediately drawn to them. They wined and dined us, taking us to hidden-away restaurants and dance clubs, showing us a livelier side of Russian life than that offered by our university classes and historical excursions. One handsome young man named Sergey lavished attention on me, admiring my red hair and freckles. So began my infatuation with Russian men, and, as a side benefit, my Russian conversational abilities improved dramatically. That summer I was bitten by the Russian bug and fell in love with the city, the country, and the wonderfully spirited and hospitable Russians I met.

I invited Sergey to visit me at Cornell during my senior year. When he fixed my VCR, Walkman, and toaster oven while I was at class one day, my admiration for Russian men went a notch deeper. Although Sergey and I parted ways, that didn't stop me from traveling to Russia the summer after graduation to volunteer for a Russian-American park exchange at the proposed site of a Russian national park, two hours north of Moscow. I helped prepare a work plan for the park, which was eventually created in 1997. I fondly remember that experience as the summer of strawberries and champagne, both of which were cheap and plentiful in the small historical town of Pereslavl, where we stayed.

Still in pursuit of my dream of working on global conservation issues, in the fall of 1991 I went to work for a brilliant man named Bill Chandler at a think tank in Washington, DC. He sent me to Warsaw, Prague, Sofia, and Moscow for months at a time to help set up and manage nongovernmental energy efficiency centers, organizations that today are active in formulating energy conservation policies for their countries. The U.S. State Department provided most of the funds for our projects, but the World Wildlife Fund in Washington, DC, also funded the energy efficiency center in Moscow. That's how I met Bill Eichbaum, a vice president of WWF, who sent me to Russia in 1993 to find a Russian compatriot and create a WWF office in Moscow.

I arrived in Moscow in the spring of 1993 to open a representative office for the WWF with my Russian colleague, Vladimir Krever. Russia seemed like an open book to me in terms of conservation opportunities. I was excited to learn that Russia had a vast network of strictly protected natural areas, called *zapovedniki,* covering 1.5 percent of the country. But I felt helpless to stop the preserve system's demise in the face of dwindling government support. With the collapse of the Soviet Union in 1991 and the ensuing economic crisis, *zapovedniki* lost as much as 90 percent of their government funding, putting the entire system at risk. Learning that Russia worked for the better part of a century to create these strongholds of nature that conserve biodiversity through total human exclusion, I began to admire the *zapovednik* system. But *zapovedniki* were now coming under attack. Hundreds of Russian scientists and environmental activists were rising to their defense. I, too, offered my support.

With Vladimir I set out to convince WWF leadership in Switzerland that *zapovedniki* should be the focus of its conservation programs in Russia for the near term to ensure that the system didn't succumb to neglect and economic pressures. Oil companies and mining operations saw *zapovedniki* as areas of untapped mineral reserves. State forestry enterprises were encroaching on old-growth forests, some of which had been protected in *zapovedniki* for more than half a century. Poaching in nature reserves was on the rise due to poverty and high unemployment in rural communities. Without funding, the protected areas were powerless to stop these incursions.

Intrigued with the idea of helping preserve a continent-wide system of unique wilderness areas, WWF leadership agreed to focus its Russia assistance on the *zapovedniki*. Representing the conservation organization in Russia, Vladimir and I solicited grant proposals from *zapovedniki* all over the country. Hundreds of proposals poured by mail, fax, and e-mail into the tiny two-room Moscow apartment that served as our office. The scope of the projects was breathtaking: saving dolphins in the Black Sea or saiga antelopes in the Russian steppe, halting illegal fishing in the Sea of Japan, protecting polar bears in Arctic reserves.

One day a tall, handsome stranger showed up at our door. He was wearing a yellow sweater, bright in contrast with his dark skin and hair. His expression was cheerful and genuine. He introduced himself as Igor Shpilenok, the director of the Bryansk Forest Zapovednik.

Where's that? I asked.

About three hundred miles southwest of Moscow, he said, or eight hours by train.

You could have sent your proposal by fax and avoided the trip, I said.

The closest fax is six hours in the opposite direction, he replied, in Kiev. So it was easier for me to deliver it myself. He smiled and his blue eyes sparkled.

He handed me his proposal and two large black-and-white photographs. One was of four men trying to dig a hopelessly stuck truck out of a muddy depression on a forest

THE STORKS' NEST

road. The other was of him standing in a camouflage uniform surrounded by five women in coats and headscarves who were sitting on a bed of leaves and vegetation amidst tall pine trees. Large buckets brimming with berries stood between the women and Igor.

These women were collecting berries in the nesting grounds of the rare capercaillie, a large forest grouse, Igor explained. The birds need the berries to survive the winter, and these women destroyed the food supply for this colony.

I could tell by the way he spoke about his reserve that he was dedicated to its preservation. I admired the pictures for a moment and then asked, Are you a photographer?

Yes. In my spare time, anyway, he replied.

Of the more than three hundred proposals we received that year, Igor's was the only one requesting funds to work with local people to promote environmental awareness. The other proposals requested funds to equip the *zapovedniki*'s ranger services, provide capacity for scientific research, or boost administrative capabilities. While I realized that these were important aims, I wondered why more of the reserves weren't also looking to build public support in their communities. Under the Soviet regime, it was easy to keep people out of the nature reserves. The government provided funds to arm the ranger services, and people were heavily fined for violating the protected regime. But with government funds reduced to a trickle, in the early 1990s the reserves were forced to fend for themselves. It would seem that working with local communities would be important. But at the time, only Igor had a vision of building a visitor's center and increasing public support for his *zapovednik*.

A few days later, I met with the head of the entire *zapovednik* system from the State Committee on the Environment,

Vsevolod Stepanitsky, to review some of the proposals.

Seeing Igor's proposal in the stack, Vsevolod perked up and said, This is a fine director. He deserves support.

Vsevolod told me that in the 1980s Igor fought for preservation of the Bryansk Forest to save the rare black stork that nests there. When a federal *zapovednik* was created in 1987 as a result of his efforts, Igor was named its first director. Vsevolod believed that Igor, having grown up near where the reserve was created, knew how to reach out to the *zapovednik*'s neighbors and promote conservation efforts in his region.

Hearing about Igor's achievements, I thought back to his recent visit to my office. I admired his modesty while recalling that I was no less taken by his cheery blue eyes and broad shoulders.

Two years passed. WWF funded many of the projects Vladimir and I had reviewed and recommended. One day I received a call from a colleague at WWF-Denmark saying the Danish government was interested in supporting our projects. He asked me to draft proposals for funding two or three reserves in European Russia. Vladimir and I decided that Nizhnesvirsky Zapovednik in the Leningrad Province worked well because of its migratory bird monitoring station, and Oksky Zapovednik in Ryazan Province fit nicely with its rare bison and crane breeding programs. We decided that Bryansk Forest Zapovednik in the Bryansk Province, Igor's reserve, should go in the proposal as well due to its emphasis on environmental education. After doing some research, I wrote a proposal and sent it to WWF-Denmark. Within a few months the project was approved and we received the first installment of funds.

I called Igor to tell him the good news.

I will be the coordinator of your two-year environmental education project, I told him. You will need to come to Moscow to sign the agreement and collect the first installment of the grant.

The excitement in Igor's voice was audible even over the crackling of the phone line. A week later, I arrived at the office late in the morning to find Igor sitting on the old couch in front of my desk.

How long have you been here? I asked.

Oh, for a couple of hours, I guess, he replied shyly.

I am so sorry, I said, I had no idea you were coming or I would have come in earlier.

He dismissed my tardiness with a casual shrug, explaining that he had arrived early on the train and decided it was just as easy to come straight here and wait for me.

I gave him the first installment of the grant and discussed the reporting and accounting procedures. We had tea in the kitchen, and I half jokingly asked him if he wanted a kitten, since one of my two cats had recently had a litter. I was surprised when he agreed to take one. I invited him over to my apartment after work to pick it up.

That evening, Igor arrived with a bottle of Russian champagne, some chocolates, and a red rose. To celebrate the grant, he said. I was surprised and flattered, blushing as I smelled the rose. We sat and talked in my small kitchen, drinking champagne. He engaged me with lively stories about the Bryansk Forest and his village of Chukhrai. I liked him and found myself wishing we had more time, wishing I knew him better. He picked out a solid gray male kitten, saying he'd name it Lorik, after me. Then he left to catch the night train back to the Bryansk Forest, toting the kitten and a wad of cash to start building the visitor's center.

11

THE STORKS' NEST

Over the next two years, Igor used the Danish grant to construct a modern visitor's center, the first of its kind in Russia. The building housed the reserve's offices, as well as a two-story educational center with extensive photo exhibits on wildlife protected in the reserve. The center had a nature library, a slide- and film-viewing room, and a small outdoor amphitheater. During the course of the project, Igor invited hundreds of schoolchildren on excursions to the forest. He made the rare black stork the symbol of the reserve. He placed information stands with his photos of wildlife in train stations and bus terminals around the region to publicize the reserve's environmental importance. By January 1997, the visitor's center was completed, and I attended its inauguration.

I traveled to the reserve by train with Beatrice, my colleague from the Danish Embassy who was attending the ceremony to represent the center's primary sponsor. We spent part of the day exploring the Bryansk Forest with Igor as our guide.

This is one of the smallest *zapovedniki* in Russia, Igor told us, yet there is an incredible abundance of life within its boundaries.

We followed moose tracks and found signs of wolves. Woodpeckers rattled the tall pines above our heads. A huge black stork's nest, empty since summer, tottered on the branches of an ancient oak tree. A singular of wild boars stormed over the snow ahead of us, and we caught glimpses of several roe deer. Igor was a master at bringing our group face-to-face with the reserve's inhabitants. I was amazed that a wilderness area brimming with wildlife had been preserved in this relatively populated region of European Russia.

We drove through the villages surrounding the reserve. The houses were small and decrepit, and most of the residents elderly. Curious eyes peered from behind white lace curtains in dirtied windowpanes as we passed. Smoke rose from the chimneys, since firewood from the forest was used for heat and cooking. Igor said that poaching was a major problem and had nearly wiped out populations of moose and deer in the region because many people living in the villages were unemployed and hunted for food. He believed that the most effective way to reduce pressures from poaching was to work closely with the local communities, explaining the importance of the reserve for regeneration of game populations and involving them in nature conservation. Traditionally this had not been the approach of other *zapovedniki*, which often worked in isolation from neighboring communities.

After the excursion, we attended the inauguration. As the WWF representative, I had the honor of cutting the red ribbon at the ceremony. Russian officials, journalists, and local residents marveled at the beauty of the contemporary educational center with its yellow stucco façade, wooden interior, and beautiful color photographs of local wildlife taken by Igor and his brother, Nikolai, also a photographer. One person stood up and said that neither the visitor's center nor the reserve itself would be here today without the courage and ambition of Igor Shpilenok. I could see that his optimism during desperate financial times in Russia had earned him respect not only from his staff, but from the entire conservation community. Afterward, several journalists asked me for an interview. I was pleased to be in the spotlight, but I found myself wishing I had played a more hands-on role in making this happen.

After the evening banquet, full of toasts to the success of the center, to Igor, to WWF, and to the Danes, Igor drove Beatrice and me to the nearby Nerussa train station to catch the two-hour commuter train to Bryansk, which connected to the overnight train to Moscow. We stood on the narrow platform as the train crawled into the station. Millions of stars peeked out of the dark January sky.

How's the kitten? I asked.

Lorik's great, he said, but now he's a big tomcat, terrorizing all the females.

He must like it out here, I said. I certainly would.

Well, he replied, you're done with this WWF project. Why don't you head up our education program? With your qualifications and fluent Russian, I could pay you one of the highest government salaries. About $60 a month.

I laughed at the ridiculous idea of abandoning my well-paying job at WWF to work in this remote outpost for $60 a month. As the doors to the train sprang open, I gave Igor a peck on the cheek and hopped on the train.

Beatrice and I sat down on the benches of the ancient train car, which was sparse, grimy, and cold. The chilly January air seeped through the cracks in the windows, and the wind whistled over the train cars. We listened to the clickety-clack of the train as it sped down the tracks, occasionally exchanging words. We were both tired and light-headed after the long day and an evening of countless toasts. Beatrice seemed anxious to get back to Moscow, but the thought of returning to the congested capital made me shudder.

At first we were the only passengers, but more people boarded after a couple of stops. In about an hour, a man and an older woman began jumping around at the other end of the car. They pressed the button on the police call box near the doors between the cars and yelled something into it. We couldn't hear what they were saying over the clamor of the wheels on the tracks. I assumed they were drunk and playing around. As minutes passed, they became more and more frantic. The older woman, dressed in a gray overcoat with a shawl wrapped around her head, ran down the aisle to where we were sitting. She asked in a desperate voice if either of us happened to be a midwife.

No, we answered, and looked at each other questioningly.

Then, realizing the meaning of her question, we both jumped up and ran down to the other end of the car, figuring we had to do something to help. A woman was lying on a bench in a pool of blood. Her skirt and coat were lifted to her waist and her stockings pulled down below her knees. A fur hat covered her face. A man in a gray parka with a mustache was jumping up and down next to the woman, gripping his hat to his chest and crying. His eyes were wide with alarm. He was evidently her husband.

A baby's head appeared between the woman's legs. The older woman screamed, and the man covered his face with his hat. No one dared touch it. Without thinking, I took the baby's head in one hand and caught its body with the other as it slipped out. Its skin felt wet and warm to the touch. I turned the baby over to see if it was breathing. Its little face was scrunched up and it looked as though it wasn't. I handed the baby to Beatrice and slapped it on its rear end, like I had seen in movies. We turned it over again and saw that its face was beginning to turn blue. Not knowing what else to do, I wedged my pinky finger down the baby's throat, hoping to clear the clogged passageway. At first nothing happened, so I pushed farther. Then the baby gasped and took its first breath of air, letting out a wail over the din of the train.

I lifted the baby, which we had been holding low between the woman's legs, and realized it was still attached. Beatrice and I looked at each other in a moment of panic. We didn't know what to do with the umbilical cord. I looked around at the other passengers, who were politely curbing their curiosity and looking the other way. I asked one of them for a knife, but at that very moment, the cord detached from inside the mother. One of the passengers handed me a white towel, saying it was clean. I wrapped the baby in the towel together with the cord. I handed the bundle to Beatrice and checked on the mother, who was still lying motionless on the bench. Beatrice asked me if it was a boy or a girl. I realized that I hadn't even looked. Preoccupied with whether or not it was alive, I hadn't noticed the infant's sex. Beatrice unwrapped the towel and reported that it was a baby girl.

We brought the bundled baby close to the mother's face. I lifted up the hat and saw that she was pale and almost lifeless. Beatrice gently placed the bundle next to the woman's head and whispered, It's a girl. She smiled weakly. Beatrice handed the baby to the man with the moustache as we attended to the woman. We got her dressed and helped her sit up. The train was coming to a stop. By this time, two police officers had arrived from the front of the train and announced that an ambulance was waiting at the station. The other passengers turned their attention to Beatrice and me, surprised to hear us speak to each other in English. I wondered what they must think of the two of us, a petite dark-haired Dane and a tall redheaded American having just attended the birth of a Russian baby in a train.

The new father held the baby in the towel, but I suggested he also wrap her in his coat against the cold. He took off his parka and swaddled the baby tightly, covering her face. I opened the jacket a little so the baby could breathe. We helped the woman walk to the exit just as the train stopped at the platform. The doors slid open with a bang, and we ushered the couple out. Then the doors snapped shut. I watched them walk gingerly down the platform, the woman leaning heavily on her husband. I wondered if I would ever see them again.

I stumbled back to my seat as the train lurched forward. Beatrice and I sat down, still not fully realizing what had transpired. It all had happened so quickly. We began to relax and laugh. I pulled out a bottle of liqueur with herbs from the Bryansk Forest that Igor had given me as a souvenir. We opened it and swigged from the bottle, toasting the newborn. It helped us sleep after we transferred in Bryansk at midnight to the six-hour express train to Moscow.

The next day, I called my dad from my Moscow apartment. He was a doctor and, although he hadn't delivered babies since working on an Indian reservation in South Dakota twenty years prior, he'd know if what I did was right.

You did fine, he said. Under no circumstances should you have cut the cord in those unsterile conditions.

I sighed with relief and hoped the baby and the mother were okay.

A month passed and I couldn't get the events of that night out of my mind. Perhaps the baby in the train was some kind of a sign telling me it was time for a change. I found myself thinking about Igor too, and his offer. I had been searching for a way to be closer to nature. Growing up in Denver, Colorado, I was always striving to get out of the city to ride horses, ski, or hike in the mountains. Yet for most of my life, I had lived in bustling, polluted cities. I knew that I was doing important things at WWF; we'd raised nearly $10 million for conservation projects in Russia in the first four years. And I had had a lot of interesting experiences. I'd met Mikhail Gorbachev and

Bill Clinton in Moscow. I'd flown in the British royal jet to the Russian Arctic with Prince Philip, the duke of Edinburgh, who served as WWF's honorary president. I'd traveled to Lake Baikal, the Russian Far East, and other remote corners. But I felt disconnected from nature. The people actually working in the nature reserves—the botanists, the ornithologists, the rangers—they were the lucky ones, I thought. I realized that my Russian colleagues in Moscow had spent years doing research or conservation activities in the field and only came to work at desk jobs in their forties. Ever since I was twenty-one and had graduated from college, I had primarily worked behind a desk. I was beginning to sense that I was ready for something different, to go back to my roots or, more precisely, to let them grow.

I called Igor at the nature reserve.

I've thought about your offer, I yelled over the crackling phone line. Do you still want me to work for you?

I do, he yelled back.

I sensed the enthusiasm in his voice. He explained that having an American at the reserve would help attract the attention and interest of the public. For the next two weeks Igor called me every day to make sure I hadn't changed my mind. I didn't. I wondered if I had made as big of an impression on him as he had on me. I was excited to make this move, to embark on perhaps one of the wildest adventures of my life. I had no idea what I was getting into, but at the moment it felt so right.

Igor found a house for me in Beriozovka, the nearest village to the *zapovednik* office. He asked me to contact the owner's son, who lived in Moscow, to see about buying it. I called the son. He said that his mother, who used to spend her summers in the village, now lived in Australia and had no need for the house. I invited him to my office and, when he showed up the next day, I offered him $1,000 for the house. He agreed, and we signed an informal agreement. He gave me the key. For the first time in my life, I owned a house. I had never seen it.

After completing my assignments at WWF, I moved to the Bryansk Forest in time for spring, packing all my belongings and my two cats, Kosha and her daughter Mysha, in my little Russian Lada car. After an eight-hour drive, I was greeted by Igor at my new house, less than a mile from the reserve headquarters. The yard looked unkempt, but the one-story wooden house was in reasonably good shape and relatively big compared to other houses in the village. It had a kitchen and eating area separated by wooden shelves, a large bedroom, and an enclosed front veranda. The sparse furniture consisted of a wooden table and two slapdash cots made of planks; one served as a bench at the table in the eating area and the other as a cot in the bedroom. Igor had stoked up the great woodstove to warm the house, but he had neglected to open one of its dampers. Smoke fumed out of its many cracks and crannies. Igor asked if everything was okay, and I said yes and walked him out the door.

Although it was late and I was tired, I cleaned the house and washed the floors. I made a bed on the cot with a mattress and sheets I had brought. I would have to carry water in from the village pump thirty yards away and use the outhouse attached to the back of the house, but I didn't mind. Like a wild animal, I felt instinctively at home in the Bryansk Forest.

The next morning I headed out the door for my first day of work. I met an elderly woman on the path in front of my house. She introduced herself as Antonina Ivanovna, using her first name and patronymic (name derived from her father's), as is the custom.

If you need fresh milk, she offered, let me know. I have three cows, so there is plenty of milk to go around.

Thank you, I replied.

The lady who used to live in your house bought milk from me, she added. Now I gather she is off in Australia or somewhere like that.

So I hear, I nodded.

She was a real nice lady, she added. Not many of the Muscovites who come here are nice people, but she was. Anyway, my place is just down the lane. Third house on the left.

I walked down the forest path Igor had told me about to the reserve office, jumping over streams and mud puddles. Igor greeted me warmly and showed me around. He led me to my new office, on the second floor of the visitor's center, where we went over my duties. I was to work with schoolchildren who came to the visitor's center from Suzemka on the commuter train several times a week, as well as any other visitors to the reserve. I was also responsible for relations with the press, providing news and articles to the regional newspapers. Each quarter, I would have to compile the *Zapovednik Scroll*, a two-page insert for the local newspapers in Suzemka and Trubchevsk detailing recent events in the *zapovednik*. That afternoon I got acquainted with the rest of the *zapovednik* staff: the scientists, the rangers, the accountant, the secretary, and the driver. They didn't treat me any differently for being an American, and I was glad for it.

After work I stopped by Antonina Ivanovna's house and

bought a three-liter jar of milk.

It's still warm it's so fresh, she said.

I took it home and drank two glasses of the creamy liquid and poured some in a bowl for the cats. I boiled the rest, as she had suggested, on an electric hot plate in my kitchen so it would keep.

The next day I walked the half-mile trail through the woods from the visitor's center to the Nerussa train station to meet a school group from Suzemka. At the center I showed them slides and a video and took them on an excursion through the nearby woods. I talked to them about general ecological processes, as I had yet to learn the specifics of this forest ecosystem. On the way back to the train station, a boy asked me if they might see a moose.

Well, given that there are more than twenty of us and we are all yelling and screaming, I said, I highly doubt a moose would want to be anywhere near us.

As if on cue, a moose ran across the path not fifty feet ahead of us. I was shocked. The children were ecstatic and yelled, We saw a moose! We saw a moose!

After the excursion, Igor drove me into Suzemka for the annual children's drawing contest that the nature reserve organized at the district library. The drawings were superb and showed that the children in the town's two schools were intimately familiar with the nature around them. Some depicted snowy forest landscapes, while others showed moose, fox, or hare. Although I have loved animals since I was little, I don't think that as a child I ever had such a grasp of what wild animals looked like as the children from this forest town clearly did.

I brought prizes Igor had purchased for the winners, toys and books on nature. We formed a judging committee consisting of the editor of the newspaper, the head librarian, someone from the town administration, one schoolteacher from each of the two schools, Igor, and me. We surveyed all the pictures and chose the top three drawings. Then we gathered the children around and announced the winners and handed out the prizes. Every child got a calendar and animal stickers, so all were pleased.

People started to leave, and the librarians invited the judging committee and a few others to stay behind. In the main room of the library, the six librarians laid out a spread of salami and cheese sandwiches, cookies, and tea. They poured champagne for all the guests. We pronounced toasts to the *zapovednik* and the schoolchildren and exchanged kind words. Then the librarians said good-bye to the judges and the others, pulling Igor and me aside. They invited the two of us into a small office, where they promptly laid out more sandwiches and tea.

A jocund, dark-haired woman produced a bottle of homemade liqueur flavored with coffee that she called Black Prince. We had another drink in a more intimate circle, and Igor proposed a toast to the women. Elena, the head librarian, a small woman with long hair and thick spectacles, smiled and commended Igor for his efforts. I could see that she was enamored of him. The women made us feel like special guests that day.

The next day I was supposed to go to Trubchevsk to hang wildlife photos for an exhibit in the town's historical museum, but the reserve driver was sick and my car was having engine trouble. The secretary told me Igor was out exploring the reserve, so he wouldn't be able to take me. I liked the feeling of uncertainty I had when I called the museum to tell them I wouldn't be coming that day because of unforeseen circumstances, but I would definitely come sometime soon, although I didn't know when and I might not be able to call if the phones were out, so I'd just show up.

Suddenly I had a free day. I sat with the secretary and accountant, chatting and drinking tea. It felt good to have the luxury of time on my hands. The work style in the *zapovednik* was very different from the hectic life I had led at WWF. Here, the weather might impact my work, but one day here or there wouldn't make a difference anyway. There was no phone in my office to distract me. When I needed to make a call, I went to the secretary's office downstairs and, if it was long distance, I had to order the call through the operator, which sometimes took hours. I didn't have e-mail or a fax. I didn't even have a computer, although Igor promised he would get me one soon. With no method of instant communication, things took longer to do here, and that was just the way it was. I was beginning to appreciate this pace of life.

March 8 marked International Women's Day, but as a holdover from Soviet times, the festivities started days before. The women at the Suzemka library invited me to a party on March 7. Igor gave me a car and driver from the reserve to go into town, and it was a good thing because the librarians broke out the Black Prince and I ended up drinking too much. They closed the doors to the library and we sat around a long table in the main room loaded with all kinds of food and homemade cakes. I was amazed at their resourcefulness. After all, they made only $15 a month, and they hadn't received their salaries in over six months due to government shortages. Yet they adorned the table with tomatoes and cucumbers they had canned the summer before, deviled eggs from their hens, homemade sausages, meat dishes, potato salad, fruit compote, cakes, and much more. After our late afternoon lunch, we put on music and danced around the library, just us women. I had a splendid time and was reminded of the innate hospitality of the Russian people, no matter how humble their circumstances. I have always admired this trait. As evening drew near, I said good-bye to all and stumbled out the door into the jeep parked outside. The driver laughed at my condition and took me back to the office. Igor quickly chauffeured me home before anyone else could see the state I was in. To him I must have looked like a loose-limbed debutante who couldn't hold her *samogon*, not the rugged cowpoke from Colorado he thought he'd hired.

The next day I invited the elderly women from neighboring villages to the visitor's center to celebrate Women's Day. While Igor's focus thus far had been mainly children, he wanted to get to know the reserve's mostly elderly neighbors and talk of possibilities for cooperation. Igor and I were pleased when the ladies arrived at the appointed hour with smiles on their faces, decked out in colorful shawls and long, wide skirts.

We drew tea from a samovar and handed out gifts of chocolates along with cucumber and tomato seeds to sow in their gardens. One of the women took out a plastic bottle of murky liquid and offered it to the other women and me. It was sweet and pungent, a homemade vodka steeped in herbs and pine buds.

Igor and I talked to them about the nature reserve and our future plans. We explained that we were looking to find some artisans who could make crafts to sell in the area as souvenirs, providing income both to the local communities and the reserve. They responded that they were too old and their eyes were bad. We suggested visitors might be interested in paying for lodging and food, and they said they couldn't imagine who would want to stay in their drafty old houses. We showed them slides and films about wildlife in the reserve. They enjoyed them immensely and related stories about their own encounters with bears and moose in the woods. Toward the end of the evening they moved the tables aside and danced and sang in front of the fireplace, swinging each other around the room, clapping their hands and stomping their feet.

Soon I was busy making arrangements for upcoming events and projects. WWF had given the *zapovednik* a grant to reintroduce the European bison to the Bryansk Forest. European bison are slightly smaller than the American version and live in forests rather than on open prairies. Bison were hunted to extinction in these parts nearly three centuries ago. Now Igor wanted to bring them back.

We made arrangements to transfer bison from a bison-breeding center in Oksky Zapovednik, 180 miles southeast of Moscow. The bison would arrive in April, which was one month away, so Igor asked me to write a press release and invite representatives of newspapers from Suzemka, Trubchevsk, and Bryansk. I was excited to be part of a rare-species reintroduction program, working closely with scientists and making preparations for the release. It was something I had always dreamed about doing.

That week I also began to arrange the annual March for Parks celebration for the end of April, to coincide with Earth Day. We wanted to organize marches, tree plantings, and environmental contests in Suzemka and Trubchevsk, the two districts in the southern part of the Bryansk Province where the nature reserve is situated. The district governments formed ad hoc committees to help plan the events, including representatives from the culture and education committees, the libraries, and the schools. Igor and I drove to the towns to meet with the committees and determine who was responsible for organizing each activity. Later I met individually with the schoolteachers, librarians, and the editors of the local newspapers to discuss their participation. I was impressed by their commitment to helping promote the *zapovednik* and conservation of the Bryansk Forest.

Although during the day my mind was busy with work, at night, lying in bed in my house, I thought only of Igor. I imagined how he would take me on a sleigh ride through the snowy woods. I pictured him kissing me sitting on a thick mattress of straw. Then we would stop the sleigh and sink into the hay. My excitement was so real my heart would pound against my ribs. Finally I would fall asleep, rising quickly in the morning to skip down the path to work, and to Igor.

In the office I tried to keep things professional and focus on work. But when Igor heard me coughing one morning, he put his hand gingerly on my back, and I felt my spine tingle.

That's a nasty cough you have, he said. I bet I can remedy it in my *banya* (steam bath) in Chukhrai. Would you like to join me later today? he asked.

I eagerly accepted his invitation, and we left work early that afternoon and drove the fifteen miles to his village. The last six miles were down a muddy, rutted forest road. As the jeep bucked and kicked, Igor held the steering wheel tightly with his strong hands, wrapping his long fingers around it. We got stuck in the mud just as the first log cabins of Chukhrai came into view. Igor gently rocked the jeep back and forth, putting it in reverse, then in first gear. The wheels only sank deeper into the muddy slough.

We got out, and Igor asked me to snap branches off nearby willow bushes. He walked fifty feet ahead and found a long log and some boards next to the road, evidently left from the last time he got stuck. He dragged them over to the jeep, propped the log on the board, then wedged it under the metal hub jutting from the center of the front wheel, angling the log perpendicular to the vehicle. He called me over. I tossed my branches in a pile next to the jeep to lend him a hand. We both pressed down on the far end of the log and, to my astonishment, the wheel started to lift. He stepped up on the log, and the wheel lifted even farther. I was amazed at his ingenuity.

Now you stand on the end and I will get off, he said.

What? I am supposed to hold up an entire jeep? I cried.

Here, try, he said. It's leverage. Let the log do the work.

I put a trembling knee on the end of the log, then a foot, and I was standing precariously on the wet, muddy beam. The front wheel lifted a full foot off the ground, leveraged by our weight. Igor told me to stay put as he slowly stepped off the log. The log lifted under me and the jeep descended back into the mud. I could barely keep my balance perched on the slippery wood three feet in the air. Seeing my predicament, Igor retrieved a large sack of potatoes out of the jeep and, pushing the log down with one foot, hung the sack over it near my feet. The jeep went up and held. Igor quickly put one of the boards under the front wheel, which was suspended a foot above the mud. Then he slowly lifted the log up as I hopped off, and the wheel rested securely on the board.

He picked up the branches and pressed them into the

mud under the other three wheels, thrusting them as far as they would go. Then he climbed into the jeep and slowly nudged it forward. The front wheel grabbed the board with its fat treads, and the other wheels held fast to the mats of branches. In an instant we were out of the mud. I hopped in and we drove into Chukhrai, the jeep splattered with the muddy wounds of the battle we had waged to get there.

We motored down the muddy track through the village, passing a cluster of dilapidated wooden houses, all approximately the same small size. Each house had a tall wooden fence surrounding its yard and sealing it off from prying eyes. The timbers were gray with age, and some of the houses were slanted, careening into the earth that had given way beneath them. Several tumbledown outbuildings accompanied each house. Barns, sheds, and outhouses, I guessed.

Igor told me that the houses in Chukhrai were made of natural materials—wood, clay, and moss—all biodegradable. If the roof was left to decay, the houses rotted completely within a few decades, leaving only a low earthen mound. Several such earthen mounds dotted the terrain as we maneuvered the muddy track.

We dipped down into a depression in the road, evidently carved by a stream and filled with stagnant water. There were no houses for several hundred yards.

This depression connects to the Nerussa River when it floods, Igor explained. There are no houses here because the water rises each spring.

We plunged across the fifty-foot-wide channel and emerged on the other side, climbing to higher ground. Three small, run-down houses stood on this spit of land. We dipped into another water-filled depression and emerged once again on higher ground.

The village is situated on three low hills, Igor continued, islands that jut above the flooded lowlands of the Nerussa River in spring.

On the third hill, most of the houses appeared to be abandoned, with the roofs caving in or the walls falling down.

How many people live in Chukhrai? I asked, fascinated that people could live in such isolation.

Twenty, he said. Only eleven of the houses are occupied. The rest are boarded up and the owners dead or gone.

We pulled up to the last house in the village; it was encircled by a gray picket fence. Through the fence, I could see recently planted apple and pear trees protected by carefully braided wicker enclosures. Igor got out and opened the gate, then drove into the tidy yard, parking on the grass right in front of the small house. Beyond the house, a willow towered above an oblong lake. A large nest sat high up in a crook of the tree. I asked Igor what it was.

That's a storks' nest, he said. Soon the birds will arrive for the nesting season.

Does the same pair return to the nest each year? I asked.

Probably yes, he replied, seeming pleased that I was interested. Storks are very loyal birds, he said. They mate for life.

Beyond the lake, a meadow stretched for about half a mile, then ended in a wall of low willow trees. Igor pointed to a row of taller oaks behind the willows and explained that they fronted the Nerussa River. A slight breeze rippled the water in the lake, and the waves glistened in the dying rays of the sun. I stood on the porch stoop for a moment and admired the tranquil scene, taking a deep breath of fresh air.

Igor unlocked the front door, revealing a small entryway

with two doors. The one to the left led to a tiny room that Igor said used to be the *banya*, but it now housed a single bed for guests. The other led into the main house, opening onto a warm and cozy kitchen. The walls of the kitchen were neatly covered with tongue-in-groove planks. A small sink stood in one corner to the right of the only window in the room. Next to the sink, a tall metal safe was topped with a tile surface—a makeshift kitchen counter and cabinet. A wooden table with an electric hot plate stood under the window, flanked by a small refrigerator in the other corner. The opposite side of the room away from the window had a wooden table and four chairs. Planks on the wall held rows of books.

The second room, through a set of narrow double doors painted bright blue, had a comfortable-looking couch, a desk, a wardrobe, a small TV, and an old armchair. A large woodstove, made of bricks and freshly whitewashed, stood in one corner. Floor-to-ceiling bookshelves divided the room into two small rectangular spaces. A raised platform of wooden planks with a mattress on top was nestled in the niche between the bookshelves and the wall next to the stove.

How long have you lived here? I asked.

Since 1991, he said, when I bought the house for $10. Now I split my time between my government-owned house near the reserve office and this house in Chukhrai.

Chukhrai is situated in the *zapovednik*'s buffer zone, on a spit of land surrounded on three sides by the strictly protected area, whereas the reserve's office is a good five miles outside the protected territory. Igor explained that he liked being closer to the *zapovednik* and near the storks, which he photographed each year.

This is actually the second house I wanted to buy in Chukhrai, he said.

The first house Igor looked at in the village didn't come with land, since the owners wanted to keep it for haymaking and a garden. Igor decided not to buy that house and told the owners the day before the agreed-upon date to sign the papers. That night, the house burned to the ground. Evidently, someone in the village did not want Igor to move there and set it afire, thinking he had already purchased the property. Probably a poacher who didn't want Igor as a neighbor.

I learned there are two notorious poaching clans in Chukhrai, both with the last name Presnyakov. One family was nicknamed "Lepen" (thought to mean "wet snowflakes") and the other "Shamornoy" (the local name for the hellebore plant). No one in the village can remember why the families were given these nicknames generations ago. Each family had at least five sons, all of whom once hunted beavers, otters, moose, wild boars, wolves, and anything else that moved, to sell the meat and the pelts. Although the sons had long since moved to Trubchevsk, Suzemka, and beyond, they still returned to Chukhrai on occasion to visit their aging parents and poach a boar or two.

The same week the house Igor nearly bought was set ablaze, a woman drowned in two inches of water at the other end of the village, having fallen facedown in a drunken state into a puddle in her yard. Igor bought the late owner's house from her kin. That house—the one where he now lived— stood on a low rise next to the only lake in Chukhrai and was situated back-to-back with another wooden house, that of the Lepen family. If the poachers were going to burn his house down, Igor reasoned, they would have to burn down their own as well.

This house is better anyway, Igor said, for the lake view.

When Igor bought the house, there were nine abandoned

houses, shacks, and outbuildings on his one-acre piece of land. He told me that before the Germans burned the entire village in the Great Patriotic War—as Russians call World War II—houses stood almost one on top of the other for lack of dry land in the floodplain. One by one, Igor knocked the nine houses down, chopping the timber frames into firewood and burying the shards of window glass, scraps of rubber boots, clothing, and other items found within. He kept two of the houses for a barn and a woodshed. He dug a well and sank cement rings into the ground to keep the dirt out of the water, then fashioned a wooden cover and roof over it. He made repairs to the house itself, jacking up its entire frame and removing rotting logs at the bottom, then laying a brick foundation in their stead. He replaced the old windows and put on a new slate roof. Inside, he chipped the old plaster off the walls and covered them with narrow wooden planks. He laid boards on the floor and topped them with linoleum. In the kitchen, he installed the sink and drain to replace the washbasin and bucket, although he still fetched water from the well. In the main room, he repaired the old woodstove and built the bookcases to wall off the sleeping quarters.

Five years after Igor acquired the house, he dug a giant pit on his land. He fortified the sides with concrete and stuck long cement posts that he'd found near abandoned power lines into the foundation. He obtained two enormous metal doors and installed them at ground level at the edge of the foundation.

We walked to the *banya* to stoke up the fire. In the twilight I could see the pit and metal doors jutting from its bowels.

What on earth are you building? I asked.

A house, he said. The pit will be the basement, and the doors are for the garage.

32

THE STORKS' NEST

But you have a house.

This one will be made out of bricks, he replied.

So you are like the third little pig, I said.

Precisely, he said, laughing.

While the *banya* was heating up, Igor took me to the Nerussa River to listen for beavers, saying he had been observing them each night, trying to figure out how best to photograph the timid creatures. I had seen beaver dams on wilderness trips in the United States, but I had never observed the animals in the wild. Igor said that European beavers differ from those found in North America in that they are strictly nocturnal animals.

Igor explained that beavers had made an amazing come-back in the Bryansk Province in the past half-century. By the early eighteenth century, beaver populations in Europe and Russia sharply declined due to excessive hunting. During the twentieth century, the Soviet government funded wide-scale programs to reintroduce the beaver while simultaneously enacting strict laws against hunting. As a result, beavers became ubiquitous throughout much of their former range. It was one of the greatest reintroduction success stories in the world. Igor said beavers now inhabited every bend in the Nerussa River, from its source to where it joined the larger Desna River.

The ice had just cleared from the Nerussa, and we could see paths where the beavers had carried fresh branches from the riverbank into the water. We squatted over the damp ground under an oak tree to listen. After a while we saw a dim figure moving along the opposite shore and then heard a loud smack. It was the beaver whacking its tail on the water, warning others of danger lurking nearby. Then we spotted another beaver just below us, close enough that I saw its eyes glimmer in the soft light.

After a while Igor said we should go back to the *banya* while it was still hot. He stood up and offered me his hand. As I rose, he leaned down to kiss me. I stepped back to look at his face, hesitating for a brief moment. This is what I wanted, I thought to myself, but what next? Thoughts raced through my head. How could we be together, an American and a Russian, a city girl and a country boy? Then I smiled and pulled Igor toward me, resting against the shaggy mattress of green moss on the trunk of the big oak tree. Suddenly my mind was clear. It didn't matter. I would follow my instincts.

We walked back to the house and entered the *banya*, now hot and steamy and smelling of fresh birch leaves. Igor turned off the light and lit a candle. As we undressed, I shyly covered myself with a towel and Igor politely turned his attention to stoking the fire. We passed through a small washroom into the *parnoye* (steam room), which had two wooden benches and hot rocks on a metal stove. I pulled my red curls on top of my head and tied them into a knot. Igor spooned boiling water onto the rocks. I laid my towel on the bench and sat as steam hissed and rose to the ceiling, then descended in a cloud over us. I breathed in the hot vapor and could feel it unclogging my lungs. In the dim flickering light of the candle, I saw that Igor's body was all muscle and bone, not an ounce of fat on his tall, rugged frame. From a pail of hot water on the floor, he took two brooms of birch branches tied together. He shook out the excess water, telling me to lie down on my stomach. He tossed more water on the rocks, and the steam descended onto my bare back. The candle flickered and cast shadows, exaggerating the curves of my body on the wall. With broad sweeping movements, Igor swung the birch brooms over me. The heat of the steam intensified. He beat my back with the two brooms in a rhythmic manner, moving up and down my body, pausing occasionally to throw more water on the rocks.

Enough, I cried.

I couldn't bear the heat. I ran out into the washroom. Igor poured a tub of water over my head, laughing all the while. I gasped and clutched the door frame as the cool water spilled over my hot body. The water trickled through wooden slats in the floor and seeped into the ground. I rested on the bench in the sitting area near the open door and let the cold night air seep into my burning skin. I was no longer conscious of my nakedness. My head felt light. My back and legs had red blotches on them from the birch broom beating. A weight was lifting off my chest, and I began to breathe freely.

Incredible, I said to Igor. That was incredible.

Back inside, he said. Let's do it again.

My fantasy of us tossing in the cold hay on the sleigh didn't hold a candle to the hot and naked reality of Igor's *banya*.

Every night I would go to sleep in my house in Beriozovka hoping morning would come quickly so I could see Igor's face at the office. At work, Igor would bound up the stairs to the second floor of the visitor's center, his face aglow.

I just had to see you, he said. I missed you last night.

When a ranger walked in the door, Igor's smile quickly turned into a stern crease. He asked me in a sober tone if I had contacted the newspapers about the bison release. Then he looked at the ranger and gave him his tasks for the day. The ranger turned to leave, and, while he was still within earshot, Igor gave me my assignments. Only when we heard the door downstairs close did Igor's lips break into a smile and his blue eyes gleam.

In the evenings after work and on weekends, Igor would take me out to the woods, to get to know the reserve, he said. I was amazed at how at ease he felt in nature. As a child, he had followed his father into the woods when he went hunting for ducks and hares. As a teenager, Igor spent his summers and school vacations trekking through pine stands and wading through alder swamps and floodplain forests near his hometown of Belaya Beriozka. The town is only twenty miles from Chukhrai as the crow flies, on Russia's border with Ukraine. He learned to camouflage himself and walk without making a sound, sneaking up to moose, roe deer, and otters, shooting round after round of film on the camera his grandmother gave him when he was fifteen.

Alone in the woods with Igor, I put my complete faith in him. He would lead me through the trees and around swamps, seeming to know where he was going. I was excited to learn from him, and he was happy to share what he knew. He tried to teach me the names of the trees. The subspecies were different from those I knew in the United States, so I was slow to identify them. I had a particularly hard time with the deciduous trees that had not yet sprouted leaves and the saplings, which all looked alike. As we walked through a meadow, he pointed to ten different waist-high saplings, naming them as we went: aspen, willow, alder, birch. I studied the tiny branches of each one, trying to make mental associations: the birch had more white spots, the alder had a reddish hue. Then he would test me, asking over and over, and I would continually get them wrong.

What's this one? Igor asked, holding the naked branch of a three-foot sapling.

Birch? I hesitantly guessed.

Alder! He threw his arms into the air, then fell to the ground, feigning frustration, crying and laughing at once.

I knelt down beside him and kissed his forehead apologetically. He put his arms around me and pulled me to the ground, and we rolled over and over in the damp grass.

I was falling madly in love. Igor was not like the few other Russian men I had been close to. They were young and reckless and not sure what they wanted from life. They lived for the thrill of the moment, to test the bounds of life with fast cars, drugs, or alcohol. Over time, I realized that the only thing that had attracted me to them was the fact that they were Russian. As I looked deeper, I found we had little in common.

Igor was different. At thirty-seven, he was nine years older than I. He was sincere, determined, and knew what he wanted out of life. He had an established career as a conservation activist and a dream of becoming a full-time nature photographer. A year earlier, he and his wife of seventeen years had divorced. They had married young, Igor explained, and drifted apart, although they chose to remain together until their two sons were nearly grown. He spent a great deal of time with his sons, Petya and Tikhon, then thirteen and seventeen, taking them to the woods, teaching them photography, and investing in their education and well-being.

Igor was optimistic and happy and loved to joke and make fun. At the same time, he was polite and chivalrous and never cursed. I shocked him with the slang that came out of my mouth, Russian *mat* (foul language) I had learned in Moscow. But most importantly, Igor and I shared a passion for all things wild. And we were both committed to spending our lives doing something to conserve nature. For the first time, we each understood that we could do it together with someone we loved.

We tumbled into a euphoric state. For a time, everything else—work, chores, friends, family—faded into the background, and we only saw each other. We would find excuses to spend each day together, exploring the woods or lying for hours in the makeshift bed in Chukhrai. We would talk, laugh, and look deep into each other's eyes. Igor would stroke my shoulders, saying he loved how my freckles blended together there. I would hold his broad cheekbones and angled jaw in my hands. We worried that this first stage of carefree love wouldn't last. When will the second stage begin? we kept asking each other. It had to start sometime.

Although we were happy, not everyone was happy for us. Seeing us together, people at the reserve office started to talk. In fact, my whole village and then the entire Suzemka District started to talk.

People are jealous, Antonina Ivanovna, the milk lady down the road, told me. They don't want you to be happy if they can't be happy. Not with their alcoholic husbands and good-for-nothing sons.

As people gossiped, our tale expanded to new and fantastic heights.

She'll steal him away to America.

She took him from his wife.

She's on a mission from the CIA.

They're planning to bring in the bison so they'll have plenty of meat.

I overheard tidbits of conversation as I approached the village store in Beriozovka one Saturday. When I walked in the door, the cacophony of voices from the older women gathered there suddenly grew silent. They all looked at me.

Rather than have me wait in line with them, thereby cutting their gossip time short, they directed me to the store counter.

Go ahead, you can go ahead. Buy your bread, they urged me.

That afternoon, Antonina Ivanovna brought me a jar of milk, saying she was coming this way anyway, so she figured she would save me the trip. On her way out, she noticed an apple lying in the grass five feet in front of the house. She walked over to the apple and studied it, then found another several feet away, and then a third.

A curse, she said. See the three apples in a triangle? Someone put a curse on the house.

Who would want to do that? I asked in disbelief.

Anyone, she said.

I gasped. We both stood looking over the apples, fixated. Antonina Ivanovna took up a stick and hit the apples out of the way like croquet balls, chanting some words I couldn't make out.

In the evening, Igor came over to my house. I made dinner, chicken and mashed potatoes. It was the first time I had cooked for him. He sat on the wooden cot that doubled as a bench, gawking at me.

What? I asked. Why are you looking at me like that?

You're cooking! I didn't think American women knew how to cook, he said in all seriousness. Later I may have wished he never knew I could cook, but at the time I was happy to indulge him.

Over dinner I told him about the apples and the purported curse.

That's it, he said. You're coming to live with me in Chukhrai. I can't endure another day without you, and I won't risk losing you to some stupid curse.

Some weeks later, we learned that the woman who previously owned my house was killed in a horrific car accident in Australia with her Australian husband and his two sons.

I moved into Igor's small house in Chukhrai, cats and all. Igor; the gray tomcat, Lorik; his two dogs, a black-and-gray mutt and a red dachshund; and his tawny owl all made room for me. We enlarged the bed on the raised platform behind the bookcase by placing a second mattress next to the existing one. Igor retrieved a sign reading EAGLE NESTING AREA— U.S. FISH AND WILDLIFE SERVICE that he had acquired during a park exchange to the United States, and he nailed it to a rafter above the bed. We called it the eagle's nest. I draped a tapestry in front of the nook and threw another over the old couch. I stacked my books next to Igor's on the shelves. His collection was nearly a Russian nature library. Mine consisted of textbooks I still carted around from my studies of ecology, international environmental policy, French, and Russian at Cornell. Works in English by Aldo Leopold, Steinbeck, and translations of Camus and Chekhov mingled with those by Prishvin, Paustovsky, and Seton-Thompson in Russian.

I found a length of fabric in the wardrobe and sewed new curtains for the windows. After I was done, I sat down on the couch and looked around. I saw familiar objects surrounding me, some of which had accompanied me since I was a teenager in Colorado. A marbled clay box I made in pottery class. A picture of me wedged between my best friends, Mandy and Caroline, riding a plastic bucking bull at the National Western Stock Show. CDs of Zeppelin, Dylan, and the Dead. The lanky teddy bear wearing corduroy pants and a suede jacket from my first serious boyfriend at college, perched next to the small round bear my stepmom Pat gave me when he broke up with me two years later. For the first time since I went off to boarding school when I was fourteen and began moving to new living quarters almost every year, I felt like I had my own home.

Igor would wake up every morning at dawn and bring in an armful of wood to heat up the stove. Sometimes he stepped out for a brisk walk in the woods with his camera. He said if he didn't see the sun rise, he felt like he'd missed half the day. I lay lazily under the covers and listened to the crackling of the wood and breathed in the pleasant smell of smoke seeping through the fissures in the brick stove. One morning he returned from his walk to find me still sleeping. He enticed me out of bed with a hot cup of coffee and a poem.

> *I have come to you with greeting,*
> *To tell you the sun has risen,*
> *That with its hot gleaming*
> *Upon the leaves it glistens;*
>
> *To tell you the forest has awoken,*
> *Fully awoken, with every twig,*
> *With every bird it has risen*
> *Filled with the lust of spring;*
>
> *To tell you with that same passion,*
> *Like yesterday, I have come anew,*
> *That my soul with gratification*
> *Is still ready to serve you;*

To tell you that from all around,
A wind blows on me with delight,
And even I don't know that I am bound
To sing—but the song is still not right.

Did you make that up? I naively asked.

No, silly, he said. It's by Afanasy Fet, a Russian poet from the nineteenth century.

You're a hopeless romantic, I said, rising from the cozy lair to kiss him.

The cold air lingered on his cheeks, which were flushed red from his walk. I slid into my slippers and wrapped a robe around me. He held me tightly for a moment as we stood next to the fire. Then I stepped outside, taking in the crisp spring air. The outhouse stood about twenty feet from the house, with a WWF panda sticker on the door. Igor joked that my project had paid for the outhouse.

At least it's environmentally friendly, I said.

There was no toilet seat, just a round hole in the boards and a dark square pit beneath encased with bricks and mortar. I squatted down, leaving the door wide open to take in the view. A cloud of fog hung over the lake. A patch of ice clung tenaciously to the center, but water had eaten away at it on all sides. The snow had retreated, revealing last year's yellowed grasses. The tips of bare willow and birch trees had turned bright yellow and red, filled with the warm juices of spring erupting from within.

The cool spring air woke me like a cold shower. I felt invigorated even before I had had my coffee. I paused outside to watch Igor feed the owl a slice of raw chicken and a mouse from the traps he set in the meadow. The owl took the food and swallowed it in one gulp. Some boys from Suzemka had found it as an abandoned chick in the woods and brought it to Igor at the reserve. It had lived with him the five years since, in a large cage attached to the side of the house outside one of the windows. If we opened the window, the owl would fly inside and perch on the armchair. The bird was quiet during the day, but at night he made a racket outside the window, calling to the other owls and rattling his cage.

I went inside and sat by the warm woodstove to sip my coffee. Igor brought fresh eggs from the hens in the barn and cracked them in a pan with some melted *salo*. The yolks were deep orange and the eggs were splendid, but I pushed the *salo* aside. He stabbed it with his fork and put it in his mouth, saying, You're missing the best part.

Years of fat-free propaganda in America have ruined my taste for lard, I told him.

We spent part of the workweek outdoors in the nature reserve as Igor acquainted me with our surroundings. It was as good an excuse as any not to go to the office, as we couldn't bear to be apart even for a moment. We would spend the morning hours by the river, wading across sandy shoals in our rubber boots. Igor carried his camera around his neck and a tripod under one arm, searching for the right light, the lingering fog over the water, the timid roe deer descending for a drink. He had photographed it all a thousand times, but it was never quite right. The meandering river evoked a fascination in him that could never be sated.

One morning, as we were exploring the banks of the river, Igor offered to take me to meet his parents, who lived at a ranger station on the other side.

That sounds serious, I said.

Don't worry, he replied, they don't know about us yet. And anyway, I know they will like you.

His father first came to the area to help fix up the forest cabin where Igor had lived fifteen years earlier while searching for black storks. His father liked it so much that he quit his job as a typewriter repairman and stayed. When the *zapovednik* was created in 1987, Igor's father signed on as its first ranger. Soon, Igor's mother came to join her husband, retiring from her job as an accountant at a furniture factory in Belaya Beriozka. Igor's father was responsible for patrolling the section on the left bank of the Nerussa River, constituting about a third of the reserve.

I couldn't imagine what his parents were like, willing to live in complete seclusion in the center of the reserve. I thought about my own parents, city slickers who couldn't get by for long without restaurants, theaters, or the gym. We crossed the river in Igor's inflatable boat and debarked on the sandbar on the opposite bank. Three rotting oak posts emerged from the water. Igor told me that a small glass factory once stood here two centuries ago, powered by the waters of the Nerussa. The factory made stained glass windows for churches.

I was intrigued but a bit nervous about meeting Igor's parents as we made our way to the ranger station. The station was a large wooden house that Igor built with government funds next to the ramshackle cabin where he spent summers in his youth. Part of the old cabin's roof had caved in, and the windows lacked glass. A brown-and-white cow occupied one of the rooms, and an old chestnut mare named Anfisa the other. The station and old cabin stood in a large clearing in the forest flanked by a tranquil bowed lake that connected to the river. The river curved around the spit of land; thus, water surrounded it on three sides. Behind the cabin, a swampy

THE STORKS' NEST

forest completed the circle, essentially creating an island of dry ground amid a roadless expanse of floodplain lakes and swamps. Soon the spring waters would flood the entire area except the station itself. The area was known as Staroye Yamnoye, meaning "old hollow," probably for the depression filled by the bowed lake.

I saw that the yard was well maintained. In front of the station, an apple orchard extended out to the high bank of the river. The apple trees had been planted more than a century before and had since gone wild, producing small, sour apples that Igor said only bears could eat. A sizeable garden abutted the other side of the building. A fence made from long poles tied to posts with bailing wire kept wild boars out of the garden. Piles of manure dotted the plot in anticipation of the growing season soon to come. A wooden cross made of thick oak beams stood six feet high on a small, unplowed mound in the center. A hayfield extended for three hundred yards behind the cabin, ending abruptly before a wall of majestic oaks. In the distance, on drier ground, stands of Scotch pines with straight reddish orange trunks reached to the sky.

We walked in the door of the ranger station and the smell of *bliny* (crepes) enticed us into the kitchen. It was Maslenitsa (Shrovetide), the Russian Orthodox festival marking the arrival of spring. *Bliny*, a symbol of the sun, are traditional fare for the week. Igor's father, Pyotr Nikitich, was seated on a stool by the kitchen table in the center of the large, sparse room. Like Igor he was tall and lean, but wore a thick gray beard. Despite his more than sixty years, he was in good shape, walking nearly fifteen miles each day through dense forests and boggy swamps to guard the reserve from poachers.

Igor's mother, Lidya Mikhailovna, came out of the small bedroom off the kitchen to greet us, adjusting the scarf

THE STORKS' NEST

covering her hair. I've got *bliny*, she said, so don't run off.

Igor introduced me, and his parents greeted me kindly, offering me a stool by the table. His mother looked long and hard at Igor, seeming to study the way he watched me, possibly trying to tell if there was something more than a professional relationship between us.

Eat up, Lidya Mikhailovna, Pyotr Nikitich said, pointing to a dish stacked high with *bliny* in the center of the table. He called his wife by her formal name and patronymic, probably for my benefit. Lent starts soon and then you won't be able to eat anything good until Easter. Then he looked at me, saying, I don't fast myself, and I don't go to church, but I believe in God. I am a good Russian Orthodox Christian. That's what's important. Lidya Mikhailovna can fast if she wants, it won't change anything, except maybe she'll lose some of those pounds she gained over the winter. He chuckled, and she shot him a disdainful glare.

Her frame looked slender to me, though her hips were wide. Thin wisps of black and gray hair protruded from beneath the scarf wrapped around her head. Her skin was olive colored and her cheekbones wide, like Igor's. She opened a jar of homemade jam from last year's black currant bushes and brought a bowl of *smetana* from cold storage shelves in the entryway. She made it by skimming the cream off the cow's milk every day and letting it thicken.

Lidya Mikhailovna filled the electric kettle with river water from a bucket and plugged it in. Ten years ago Igor had had the electricity line extended from Chukhrai to the cabin. She sprinkled tea leaves into each of our cups, then poured boiling water over the leaves. The tea leaves floated at the top of my cup for a while and then sank to the bottom, where I had to be careful not to swallow them.

I placed several *bliny* on a plate and spooned jam and *smetana* into the center of the top one. I rolled it up like a burrito and ate it quickly before the filling drizzled out the other end. I ate four *bliny* and was full. Lidya Mikhailovna, who hadn't stopped fidgeting around the kitchen the whole time we were eating, gestured to the low armchair by the great woodstove, offering me the only comfortable chair. She dislodged the hairy black mutt named Charlie from it and moved an armful of coats aside. I shifted from my hard stool to the armchair, glancing up at a stack of blankets folded on a broad shelf atop the large brick stove.

I sleep up there, Pyotr Nikitich offered. It's warmest there, and Lidya Mikhailovna can't poke me from the other room when I snore.

The shelf appeared to be shorter than Pyotr Nikitich, and I thought that his feet must stick out two feet.

I gazed out the window at the large wooden cross standing in the center of the garden. I later learned from Olga Ivanovna, my Chukhrai friend, that two men from the village who served on the front lines during World War II vowed that if they got home alive, they would rebuild the church that once stood here. Only one of them made it home. Because people were prohibited from practicing religion under the Soviet regime and peasants were too poor to build a church anyway, the man put up a cross instead to fulfill his pledge.

Lidya Mikhailovna brought me a handful of pottery shards and old coins.

I found these in the garden, she said. They are from the Staroye Yamnoye Monastery that once stood here.

The coins were small and rusted. On one of them I could make out the date 1703, the year that Peter the Great founded St. Petersburg.

Two years later, in 1705, the first wooden church at Staroye Yamnoye was consecrated. By 1747, after the church had fallen into disrepair, a monk named Varsanofy gathered donations from the poor peasants in nearby villages to repair it, replace the roof, and build a wall around the cloister from pine logs and oak posts. A bell tower with six large bells, a bakery, two grain storage areas, and a barn completed the monks' compound. Just as today, the lands around the monastery were frequently flooded, cutting the monks off from the outside world. Without donations to maintain the church and support the monks, the monastery was moved in 1759 to Yamnoye, where a new stone church was begun but never finished. One man carried a 450-pound bell on his shoulders with his head inside it the four miles to the new site.

Soon after, a fire destroyed the wooden church, but an icon of John the Baptist survived and was taken to the new site. Legend says that the icon returned to the site of the old monastery that very night. The monks carried it back to the new site, but it returned three times, so the monks built a chapel for it at Staroye Yamnoye. In 1899 my friend Olga Ivanovna's mother stopped in the chapel to say a prayer and light a candle. When a monk came to pray, she left to collect berries in the woods. When she returned, the monk was still there and, not wanting to disturb him, she continued home. Almost to Chukhrai, she turned and saw smoke rising from where the chapel stood. Evidently, the monk had not put out the candles. The chapel burned down, but the icon again survived, and it was taken to Yamnoye. It was hidden in a private home during the Communists' religious repression and was later hung in another church. Now a solitary cross was all that remained to remind us of the church and monks who once occupied this hallowed ground.

I made *bliny* the next morning for Igor, in keeping with the Maslenitsa tradition. *Bliny* were easy to make and a staple of the Russian diet. I had discovered that they were very versatile; they could be served for breakfast, lunch, dinner, or dessert, and with all kinds of fillings, from jam and *smetana* to mushrooms or caviar. As no Russian woman would give me an exact recipe, saying, I just do it by eye, I worked out the proportions, more or less.

I cooked about a dozen *bliny* and opened a jar of strawberry jam from Lidya Mikhailovna. Someday I will make my own preserves, I thought.

Igor was outside digging a trench to lay a pipe from the well to the house. His little red short-haired dachshund named Kisa was digging with him. Igor received Kisa as a present from a friend in Moscow. I never particularly liked small dogs, considering them yappy and useless, but I had to admit that Kisa had a great personality. He wasn't much of a guard dog compared to Igor's small gray mutt, Poopah, but he was a dedicated friend and companion. He always wanted to be in the middle of the action, whether on my lap when I was reading a book, tagging along on a walk in the woods, or in the trenches with Igor. *Kisa* means "cat" in Russian. He got the name because when he was a puppy, whenever Igor would call the cat—*kisa, kisa, kisa*—the dog was always the first to arrive.

Igor came inside to eat breakfast, and Kisa trotted in behind him, his long red nose and short stout legs covered in dirt. Igor had Kisa demonstrate his repertoire of tricks, giving him miniscule pieces of *bliny* as reward. Kisa sat, lay down, begged, shook hands, and when Igor asked him if he was a boy or a girl, he rolled over and showed us that he was definitely a boy. Igor was so good with animals that I

BLINY

2 C. flour	2 extra-large eggs
¼ C. sugar	2½ –2²/₃ C. milk
½ t. salt	1 T. vegetable oil

Stir together all the ingredients except the milk and oil.
Add the milk, half a cup at a time, mixing well with a
whisk after each addition until all lumps dissolve. Stir
in the oil. The batter should be a little runny so it can
spread easily in the pan. Heat up a nonstick frying pan
to searing and add a little oil. Ladle ¼ cup of batter
onto the pan and turn it in a circular motion so the
batter spreads out thinly and evenly (or spread with the
bottom of the ladle). When bubbles begin to appear in
the center and the underside is lightly browned (1–2
minutes), flip the *blin*. When the other side is lightly
browned (1 minute), remove it with a spatula and put
it on a plate, quickly pouring a new dollop of batter in
the pan. Add oil to the pan as needed. Stack the *bliny*
one by one, spreading each with a dab of butter. Keep
them warm with a lid or overturned bowl.

wondered how he would be with children.

After breakfast, I went out to help Igor lay the pipe and
install a pump in the well to draw water. We had to keep pulling Kisa out of the trench to shovel the dirt back in, so then
we just shoveled over him and he got offended and lay down

next to Poopah on the front stoop warmed by the sun. From the well, we pumped water through the newly laid pipe to a tank in the attic over the *banya*, which then drained through two pipes, either to the *banya* itself or to the house.

When the work was done, we stoked up the *banya* to cleanse ourselves and try out the new system. After experiencing a Russian *banya*, I felt a shower just didn't get me clean (not that I had that option in the village). The hot steam from the *banya* penetrated my skin, opening my pores and letting the dirt out. After several contrasting sessions of hot steam and cold water—from a washbasin or from jumping into the lake—my skin grew taut. My cheeks turned red, and my head felt light and happy. Then we washed in the washroom, soaping up a sponge and rinsing off with clean water in a big tank warmed over the fire. Igor scrubbed my back and I scrubbed his. A Russian *banya* was a family affair, and even Kisa joined us. He lay sprawled on the floor with his tongue hanging out. When we came out to rest on the benches in the front room, he licked the salty sweat off our legs.

We were pleased not to have to fetch water in buckets from the well for the *banya* or the house. For the first time in the three-hundred-year history of the village, a house had running water.

The nature reserve had one horse, a dappled gray mare called Aza on which Igor explored the woods and patrolled for poachers. Aza had only just recovered from an injury. A disgruntled poacher had taken an axe to her in the middle of the night and left a gaping wound in her rear flank. Igor nursed her back to health, although the villagers told him she would have to be put down. He cleaned her wound and changed her bandages, bringing grain, hay, and water to her stall in the barn twice daily. After months of treatment, Aza's leg healed and we could ride her.

I brushed Aza and saddled her. She had a thousand ticks lodged in her mane, on her chest, and under her belly. The ticks came out in force in the spring, and no amount of bug spray could stop them. They crawled onto Aza's nose and climbed into unoccupied niches of her body while she grazed. There were even ticks on ticks. Their bites were painless, but I felt bad for the poor horse anyway. I plucked the swollen ticks off and crushed them under the heel of my boot. At the end of the day, I would take all my clothes off and make sure no ticks had crawled onto me.

Igor and I took turns riding Aza in the woods while one of us jogged along behind, trying to keep up. Sometimes we would ride double, with me sitting on Aza's wide rump, my arms around Igor's waist. I worried that Aza's leg would hurt from our weight, but Igor said that compared to the plow she was used to pulling, she couldn't even feel us. I was atop Aza and Igor was on foot when we spotted two small roe deer in a forest clearing. They lifted their heads as one to look at us and let out a warning bark that sounded like that of a dog. Then they began to run, leaping through the air with more spring than a jackrabbit, their white rumps standing out against their golden hides.

Go! Igor shouted to me. Run with them.

I gave Aza a kick and said, *Noh*, which is Russian for "giddyup." She ran after the deer, excited to play predator chasing prey. The roe deer turned at the end of the clearing and circled back toward us, looking for a clear path into the woods. Galloping across the field, I turned Aza and ran parallel with them for a moment. I could almost touch their bronze fur as they jumped over last year's grasses. Aza stayed with them, neck and neck, and I reined her to turn when they turned and jump when they jumped. It felt just like my old barrel racing days when, at thirteen, I rode my palomino quarter horse, Bree, to win the barrel racing competition at the county fair in Scottsbluff, Nebraska, where my dad and stepmom had moved two years earlier.

The roe deer turned into the woods, and I reined in Aza, saying, *Trrrr, trrrrr*, her signal to stop. Igor caught up to me and got on. As we rode home, he explained that roe deer lift their tails and flare the white fur on their rumps in reaction to danger. It is a mechanism to help them stay together while running to safety, even at night—a furry flashlight to guide the followers through the woods.

At home we saw a white stork pass over the house, then alight on the nest in the willow tree in the yard. The bird seemed tired after the long flight from Africa. The previous fall, Igor had placed an old wagon wheel in the crown of the tree, about thirty feet off the ground. He tied some branches to the wheel to attract the birds. Soon the stork's mate would join it. The pair would fill out the nest with their own branches, lay eggs, and then raise their chicks there in summer. Igor told me that white storks are generally unafraid of humans. In fact, they prefer to live in the open landscapes of villages and neighboring farmlands, where food is abundant and structures such as telephone poles and water towers are available to hold their massive nests. For the villagers, the arrival of the white storks signifies the start of the growing season, when they begin a new cycle of life. And because the white stork is considered a sign of happiness and good luck, we were delighted that the birds would be living with us for the warm season.

April arrived, and so did the bison. Two trucks with high, narrow boxes strapped to their open beds pulled up to the *zapovednik* office. We were there to meet them. Oksky Zapovednik, southeast of Moscow, had agreed to send five bison from its breeding center, but the staff could only catch three in the large enclosures where the bison roam. Ten more bison would be delivered later to complete our herd, which was then expected to grow naturally. The Bryansk Forest had ideal habitat for the bison, full of young saplings with succulent branches to nibble. Unlike the plains-grazing American buffalo, forest-dwelling European bison thrive on twigs and other forage. European bison were hunted to extinction in the wild by the early twentieth century and were preserved only in European zoos. Two breeding centers in Russia, in Oksky and Prioksky-Terassny *zapovedniki*, later bred bison taken from zoos over several decades to create viable herds of bison to release into the wild. Our *zapovednik* was the second in European Russia to receive bison for release, a result of Igor's lobbying for support for the project from WWF and the Russian State Committee on the Environment. Bison were released in a third reserve in the Caucasus Mountains, but poachers and ethnic strife in that region had destroyed most of those animals.

Igor and I got into the jeep with several journalists I had invited from local and regional newspapers to help publicize the event. Since most of the *zapovednik*'s neighbors knew nothing of the bison, it would be important for us to get the message across that this was an endangered species. Poaching an endangered species in Russia is a federal offense that is severely punished.

We led the caravan of trucks with the bison, the reserve staff, and the rest of the journalists to the release site. For two weeks Igor and his staff had been preparing a temporary enclosure in a forested area of the *zapovednik* about two miles from Chukhrai. The bison were to be held there for three weeks and fed daily so that they would know where to come if forage became scarce in winter. Igor had hired a young man named Andrei with a degree in game management to study and protect the bison.

One of the trucks got stuck in the mud on the road, so the men used logs to prop up the wheel and push the vehicle out. Soon we arrived at the release site and everyone gathered around. Since we didn't have a crane or forklift to hoist the heavy boxes off the bed of the large truck, eight men heaved each heavy box—a mature bison weighs about eight hundred pounds—onto the bed of a smaller truck, then pushed the boxes from that truck to the ground. They opened the crates, but the bison just stood there. They were weary from the ride, and their legs were unsteady. We all moved back behind the fence. Slowly, one by one, the wary animals ventured out. They gathered into a group and tottered to the far end of the enclosure, where they started to chew on twigs.

The journalists began to ask Igor questions. He told them about the bison and the reintroduction program and introduced me, his new head of the Environmental Education Department, an American. He told them how I had delivered a baby in a train. Suddenly, I was surrounded. Most of the journalists had never seen a westerner before, much less an American, except in the movies. One man asked me if the reason I was here was because there was nothing left to conserve in America.

America has plenty of wild places and national parks, I replied, as well as plenty of people working on their conservation, but I believe I can make more of an impact here.

55

THE STORKS' NEST

One woman said, Some readers might think that you are a recluse or outcast of American society, or maybe that you are ugly or deformed, and that is why you have escaped to this remote corner of the woods. But you are an attractive young woman. You are smart and energetic. Can you tell our readers why you would you choose to come here?

I explained to them how I had been searching for a way to be closer to nature, how I had become enamored with the *zapovednik* system, and that this seemed like the perfect opportunity. Then I added, In the end, it was Igor who convinced me to come here, winning me over with his commitment to nature conservation and his dynamic personality.

Another journalist was interested in the more mundane tasks in life and asked me if I had an indoor toilet. When I said no, he asked how I was adjusting to the lack of conveniences.

I don't mind, I said. I think the way Russians live in the countryside is a useful model for many of us, particularly Americans. There is absolutely no waste here. People know exactly where their food comes from. It is really as close as you can get to a sustainable livelihood, something most have moved away from in the United States.

After the release, we held a picnic in a clearing in the woods. Igor had bought Russian champagne, vodka, and snacks. I cut bread, cheese, and smoked sausages and handed them around. We made toasts to the bison, their health, and their future in the Bryansk Forest.

We walked back to the vehicles. Igor opened the door to the jeep for me, as always. Perhaps the journalists noticed the way he treated me, but they didn't question it. After all, most Russian men are courteous to women. On the way back to the reserve headquarters, we took a detour into Chukhrai to show the guests the remote village. We stopped to allow a buxom woman carrying water from a well to cross the road.

Well, at least the buckets are full, someone exclaimed. It is considered bad luck to see a woman crossing the road with empty buckets. A woman with any buckets is reason for worry. A man with full buckets is a much better sign.

Igor told the visitors that the woman was Tonka, short for Antonina. She was about fifty but looked more like sixty-five and had garnered one of only two jobs in the village, as the postlady. The other job belonged to a man named Vasily, who was the local forester, responsible for monitoring and taking inventory of an area of forest around Chukhrai. Tonka walked the six miles to Smelizh twice a week to collect the mail, which the postlady from that village brought by foot from the nearest post office, another two miles away. When Tonka returned to Chukhrai, she would give the mail to her drunken live-in boyfriend, Stepan, to deliver, as she was deathly afraid of the dogs all the villagers kept.

Stepan came to the area in 1991 from Ukraine, earning him the occasional nickname "Khokhol," meaning "a tuft of hair" (from the old Ukrainian custom of shaving the head except for a single tuft of hair on the top). Stepan spoke Russian and Ukrainian, but neither of them well. By the time he got around to delivering the mail, even the Suzemka newspaper was a week old. Soon I would begin receiving packages from my mom back home, and I learned that for delivery of a package, Stepan expected a shot of moonshine, since Tonka's job only required her to notify you that you had a package at the post office to pick up.

Stepan liked to dole out the mail leisurely, sitting on our porch stoop to dip into his torn and stained cloth bag. First he handed me the newspapers, then a letter, then a

57
THE STORKS' NEST

magazine, and finally a parcel notice. Perhaps he was trying to knock up the price of his services. Why I was pouring the moonshine for Stepan and not Tonka I couldn't understand. On the few occasions that Tonka entrusted Stepan with the task of going to Smelizh for the mail, he disappeared for several days. Often we would find him lying drunk on someone's porch in Smelizh. We'd load him into the jeep and take him home, the village's mail jutting from the cloth bag slung over his shoulder.

The journalists walked around the village. One of them stopped Tonka to ask her opinion of the bison.

Laura brought them from America, she said, using the local dialect, a mixture of Russian, Belarussian, and Ukrainian. I am not going in the woods with those beasts around, she said. I'm scared of them.

A week later Stepan brought the newspapers. Poopah marked his approach by barking fiercely and nipping at his heels. For just this reason, Stepan always donned thick *valenki* (felt boots) to deliver our mail. We read the articles about the release of the bison and my arrival. One of the newspapers, the *Communist Bryansk Worker*, wrote that I wore a *fufaika*, a coat of wadded cotton worn by the villagers, and carried water from the well on a *koromyslo*, a yoke to carry buckets. Actually, I had neither.

I quickly became a local celebrity. When I would go into Suzemka, children swarmed around me asking for my autograph. It bothered me that I was famous just because I was American and not for some good deed or accomplishment. People began to talk, and some said that I was a spy sent here to count trains crossing the Russian border.

Big fish in a small pond, my mom said when I told her of my newfound fame during one of our monthly phone conversations. She and my stepdad, Chas (short for Charles), would call me from Denver at a preappointed time at the reserve office, as there was no phone in Chukhrai. Three of my four parents were planning to come visit me this summer, first Mom and Chas, then my dad.

I can't wait for you to come visit, I said to Mom. Surely you'll understand why I love it here.

Don't count on it, Mom said.

I imagined Mom standing by the kitchen counter talking on the old rotary phone. Behind her, the old-fashioned wallpaper with big orange flowers was probably even yellower with age than I remembered. She and Chas had been meaning to remodel the kitchen for the twenty years they had lived there, but, as busy lawyers, they never got around to it. Now the wallpaper had become too familiar to change. Chas was listening in on the phone in the basement, where my brother, Mark, and I used to watch TV.

Have you changed that flowered wallpaper in the kitchen yet, Mom? I asked.

No. Still the same, she said.

Good.

The last Sunday in April was Russian Easter, which usually comes a week or two later than Easter in the West. The Thursday before is Clean Thursday. Everyone in the village cleans their houses and washes their clothes, and some take baths. On Good Friday, the Friday before Easter, one can't do anything fun or anything that makes one laugh, according to Orthodox tradition, since it marks the day that Christ was crucified.

Saturday I made Easter eggs, dying them deep red with

onion peels, which my friend Olga Ivanovna had suggested I set aside weeks before for this purpose. I also made a *kulich*, a tall, round loaf of sweetbread, and *paskha*, made of *tvorog* (a fine cottage cheese), nuts, and raisins. On Easter Sunday, all the villagers exchanged *kulich* and eggs, so I ended up with four different kinds of *kulich* plus my own and a half dozen different shades of hard-boiled eggs dyed in onion peels.

On Radonitsa, also called Rodichye (the Tuesday of St. Thomas week in the West), the population of our tiny village tripled as people flocked to the graveyard to honor their ancestors and tidy up the graves of loved ones who had passed away. An old picket fence, falling down in places, enclosed the graveyard. Within its confines, under the shade of tall pine trees, several dozen oak crosses and a handful of ornate iron crosses marked the graves of three centuries of villagers. On some of the crosses hung small oval black-and-white photographs of the deceased printed on ceramic plates. Most of the inscriptions on the crosses were illegible, having faded in the elements. Plastic wreaths of pink and purple violets, the edges of their amaranthine petals dirtied and tattered, adorned several of the crosses. For most of the year, the graves were overgrown with grasses. But for Radonitsa, loved ones descended upon Chukhrai to honor the dead, spruce up the graves, plant flowers, and drape swaths of white linen decorated with colorful embroidery around the large wooden crosses.

The celebration traditionally started at noon, when the men fired rifle shots into the air to wake the dead. The whole village walked around the graveyard three times chanting a prayer. Then they filed into the cemetery and sat at the graves of their families. Each grave had a wooden platform over it and narrow boards for benches on either side. This was where the villagers spread out their feasts, honoring their dead by sitting down next to them and having a toast in their midst. The families also honored the dead of the other families, walking from grave to grave and sitting for a time with the neighbors and their deceased. The family whose dead were being honored poured the liquor for the others. It was considered disrespectful not to drink with the dead villager's family, so people cajoled anyone skirting their graves into joining them. I drank with the villagers, honoring their heritage, sad for a moment to be so far from my own. People were joyous, telling stories and having a good time. Grief was an unwelcome guest on this day of remembrance.

My sixty-seven-year-old neighbor, Maria Balakhonova, sat by the grave of her mother. She was known as Glukhaya (deaf woman). She hadn't been able to hear since she banged her head on a train as she slid under it while crossing the tracks as a young girl. Now she was sitting quiet and alone, trapped in her silent world. All her loved ones were gone, and no one was left to revel in memories of them.

I walked over to her and sat down, smiling, saying the traditional phrase to honor her mother: May you rest in peace, may heaven be bright and the earth as soft as feathers.

She nodded, grateful that I had come, although she couldn't hear what I was saying. She offered me *bliny* and candies. We sat in silence for a time. Then I was called over to another grave, so I waved good-bye to her to go sit with Olga Ivanovna's family, her two grown daughters from Smelizh and Trubchevsk, and their families. On a tablecloth over a grave they had cut smoked sausages, bread, cheese, cucumbers, tomatoes, cookies, and cakes. They offered me a shot of homemade liqueur. It burned as it went down. Soon I was invited to another grave to honor the dead of a different family, and so it went for the rest of the day.

The two local drunks, known as Khovryach and Kiset—forty-year-old men who never left home—had a heyday, going from grave to grave and family to family to honor the dead of each, making sure not to miss a one. By evening they were sprawled out in the shadow of somebody's cross. As the villagers departed, they left glasses of vodka on the graves for the deceased. These would serve well to cure the two drunks' hangovers when they came to in the graveyard the next morning.

As I came to know Chukhrai and its inhabitants, I was amazed at how little the villagers needed from the outside world. Mostly they survived on what they reaped from the land and the forest. This was how they had always lived. The men used to make wooden barrels for storing flour, marinating cabbage, or salting *salo* to sell at the market in Trubchevsk. They fashioned containers out of birch bark for storing bread and grains. The women wove shoes called *lapti* from the inner bark of linden trees and baskets from willow boughs. They had to be discreet; chopping down a tree for bark, boards, and even firewood without paying the state had always been illegal, from the time of the tsars to the Soviets and even today.

But usually the government didn't notice if the villagers illegally chopped down a tree here or there. In fact, in the three centuries since the village was founded, the government hardly noticed Chukhrai at all, except to collect taxes, gather men for its army, or command votes in elections. The 1781 government land survey mentioned Chukhrai as belonging to the massive landholdings of Count Pyotr Borisovich Sheremetev—a senator and noted politician under tsarinas Elizabeth Petrovna (daughter of Peter the Great) and Catherine the Great. All peasants residing on the holdings of the Sheremetev family—one of the richest landowners in Russia—paid a collection tax of two rubles a year. By stealing a tree or two to make a barrel or weave some shoes, the poor villagers of Chukhrai earned money to pay taxes, which in turn paid for construction of Sheremetev's luxurious palaces outside Moscow.

Chukhrai was founded about three hundred years ago, when three fishermen landed their boat on high ground on the Nerussa floodplain and decided to stay. According to village legend, one man built a cabin on a hill he named Chiply-aevka. The second man built his house on another rise, where our house stood. The third man built his house on the banks of the Nerussa River, half a mile from the current village. One of the men was nicknamed "Chukhrai." *Chukhrai* meant "working man" in nearby Belarus. In that country the Communist slogan Worker's of the world, unite! was written *Chukhrai iz se kraiov gop do kuchki*. Because *kuchki* in Russian means "pile," to a Russian ear, *Gop do kuchki* (unite) sounded like "Hop in a pile."

Most of Chukhrai's residents were either Balakhonovs, descendants of the three fishermen, or Presnyakovs, descendants of another family that came here as refugees from the Polish invasions in the seventeenth century. Eventually others joined them, but Chukhrai's residents never had more than five different family names. Once there were three men named Ivan Mikhailovich Balakhonov and four women with the name Olga Ivanovna Balakhonova. To avoid confusion, each villager was given a nickname. Often it was insulting or one that stuck with a person from the taunting of playmates in childhood, for example, "Kudik" (stumpy) or "Khovryach" (swine). Nicknames good and bad stayed with families for generations, unless a particular representative of the family did something to earn an even more derisive moniker. Most of the villagers in Chukhrai didn't know why a family—even their own family—had been given a particular name. Some families had sobriquets such as "the Princes," "the Gents," or "the Merchants," which could only have been sarcastic in light of the villagers' general poverty.

Igor and I checked on the bison almost daily and made sure Andrei was giving the animals sufficient feed. They grew accustomed to our visits and waited eagerly for the treats we would bring—oats, apples, potatoes—although they didn't approach the food until we were at least twenty feet away. There were two females and one male. I enjoyed sitting on the fence rail observing their behavior and interaction. The male was not as big as the females; younger, I guessed. Clearly the larger of the females was in charge, because she was constantly nipping the flanks of the others when they got too close to the branches where she was foraging. Yet they remained together at all times.

Igor had me go inside the enclosure and chase the threesome around so he could photograph them in motion. I waved my arms and yelled, and they would run one way, then I waved and yelled again, and they would run the other. I kept on the lookout for a fat tree nearby in case one of them decided to charge me. Later Igor published the photos in newspapers, and, with his help, I wrote articles in Russian to let people know how the new arrivals were faring.

Three weeks after their arrival, Igor decided it was time to set the bison free. We invited the governor of the Bryansk Province, Evgeny Lodkin, to the event to publicize the bison reintroduction and to solicit his support for the reserve. Igor had known Lodkin before he was governor, when he was a journalist at the Communist newspaper the *Bryansk Worker*. Lodkin had worked diligently to expose the truth about the Chernobyl nuclear fallout, which affected western portions of the Bryansk Province bordering Ukraine. Lodkin also supported Igor's efforts to create the Bryansk Forest Zapovednik while Igor was still a schoolteacher.

Evgeny Lodkin was a Communist. Even though it was 1997 and the Communists had been out of power in the national government since their failed coup in 1991, they still controlled many regional governments, particularly in what was known as the Red Belt, a band of Communist-run provinces south of Moscow. I worried that Governor Lodkin would not want to associate with an American.

The governor arrived in a black Volga sedan with his bodyguard, a tall, thin fellow of about twenty-five. The governor, a small, attractive man of about sixty with a tawny complexion and dark hair, smiled and greeted us warmly. He shook my hand vigorously, allaying my fears about our meeting. His eyes were warm and animated, not like those of many of the Communist officials I had met while working in Moscow. We showed the governor the visitor's center, or what we could of it, as the electric company had chosen that day to turn off the power to save money against the district's debt to the national power company. Lodkin was very gracious, praising the reserve and Igor, and seemed genuinely interested in the *zapovednik* and getting to know us.

From the reserve office, we drove the UAZ jeep to the

bison release site. The governor's bodyguard got carsick from the rough road, and we stopped momentarily so he could throw up in the woods. At the enclosure, we watched the bison for a while and then asked Governor Lodkin to set them free. He pulled back the poles across the gate as Igor photographed the event. We had to chase the animals out of the corral. Like true Communists, they didn't want to leave, perhaps knowing the days of free treats were over.

Back at the reserve office, I took the governor aside as he was about to depart. I told him that his favorite newspaper, the *Bryansk Worker*, didn't tell the truth.

What do you mean? he asked.

I told him that in the article about the bison introduction, the correspondent wrote that I wore a *fufaika* and carried water on a *koromyslo*.

Actually, I said in all seriousness, worried about truth in reporting and the journalist's runaway imagination, that's not true. I don't have either a *fufaika* or a *koromyslo*.

Well, he said, I will have to do something about that.

In mid-April the Nerussa River swelled and began to flood its banks, fed by melting snow and spring rains. It engulfed the fields around Chukhrai and the road to Smelizh. The floodwaters merged the river with our lake. Igor took me in a motorboat from our house to the river, following the depressions and gullies between the meadows, moving over a half mile of what was dry land for most of the year. The buds on the trees were green and would soon open into verdant leaves.

Kisa loved to come with us in the boat, while Poopah always felt it was her duty to stay home and guard the house. Kisa would stand on the bow with his ears flapping in the wind until, cold and wet, he would climb under my coat and shiver until warm again. On one such outing, we saw a fox swimming in the water. His den had probably filled with water and he was looking for dry land. Beavers, which normally dig dens in the banks of the river, had built temporary huts of branches and twigs on spits of high ground to wait out the flood.

The Nerussa's floodwaters continued to rise each day, and soon they were nearly up to the outhouse, which was slightly downhill from our house. Igor's construction project stood on a spot that was slightly higher still. He assured me there wasn't much risk of the house ever being flooded, as it was on one of the highest rises in the village. Chukhrai hadn't seen water that high since 1931, when the Great Flood inundated the village completely.

My friend Olga Ivanovna was in the third grade at the time of the Great Flood. She went to class one day in April, but the teacher wasn't there. He was an avid drinker, so his absence was unremarkable. Until, that is, the older brother of one of the pupils came running into the school and yelled, The water's coming, the water's coming! Get out of here!

Water rolled over the snow in an enormous wave from the direction of Smelizh, making a sound like thunder. Everyone ran for higher ground, but the floodwaters surrounded them and submerged the entire village. Even on the highest point, people stood ankle deep in water.

The pupils couldn't go home because the water separating the three rises in the village was too deep. A man in a rowboat picked them up, but they didn't make it to Olga Ivanovna's house. The water had seeped into the snow, creating a slushy mixture the boat couldn't traverse. Olga Ivanovna waded through the slush to her house. All the houses in the village were flooded. One house was turned completely around so that its windows faced the road. (In olden times peasants were taxed extra if their windows faced the street. All the windows in the village faced the yards until after World War II, when the village was rebuilt.) The floodwaters rammed a big slab of ice into another house, turning it on its side so that the windows faced the ground and the door opened to the sky.

The Suzemka Communist Party Office sent a rescue committee with representatives from the Party, the hospital, and the police. They rowed the four miles to Chukhrai, but their boat hit a snag, turned over, and floated downstream. The committee climbed a tree to safety and called for help. The villagers heard them and rescued their rescuers.

The water submerged the village for nine days. The villagers laid boards from their beds to their stoves and put planks in the barns for the cows to stand on. Some moved in with neighbors or relatives until the water subsided. Only the man of the house stayed behind in a boat floating in the middle of the main room to guard the family's belongings. In low places, where most of the gardens were situated, water remained all summer. None of the gardens bore fruit that year or the year after, and many of the villagers starved to death in the Great Famine of 1933.

The floodplain was still submerged in water when we took two motorboats to Trubchevsk for the annual March for Parks event. Russia's *zapovednik* system borrowed the concept from a U.S. park system tradition, except in Russia nobody actually "marched" to earn money for parks, as in the United States. That wouldn't go over well in Russia, where *zapovednik* employees, with their steady albeit inadequate paychecks, were better off than most of the local population.

Igor and I were in one boat with a reserve ranger who would guard the boats when we docked below Trubchevsk. Nikolai, Igor's brother and the reserve's photographer and artist, skippered the other boat. It also held Natasha, Nikolai's wife, who worked part-time with me in the Environmental Education Department, and a young journalist from Bryansk. Loaded in the boats were framed photographs for an exhibit, posters and calendars to give away, toys and books for prizes, and a giant flag—our banner for the parade—attached to two eight-foot-high wooden poles. For the flag, Nikolai had painted the reserve's emblem and the words *March for Parks* on a white sheet.

We meandered downstream, at times not sure where the Nerussa River began and its floodplain ended. On patches of higher ground along the river, green bear garlic shoots were starting to sprout. We collected the piquant delicacy, munching it as we continued on our way. Later, at home, I would make tasty salads out of diced bear garlic, hard-boiled eggs, and mayonnaise.

As the crow flies, Trubchevsk is about twelve miles from Chukhrai. By the winding river, it is twenty-five miles. Yet to drive there, we would have had to circle most of the reserve, as the old logging road that leads north through the *zapovednik* to the Desna floodplain was submerged and temporary bridges to the north of Trubchevsk (located on the opposite bank of the Desna River) were disassembled during the spring floods. We would have had to drive twenty-five miles to Suzemka and from there another twenty-five miles to the permanent bridge across the Desna just south of Trubchevsk. So the boat was the more efficient form of transportation, but also a considerably colder way to travel. We dressed warmly to keep out the chill.

After about two hours we neared Trubchevsk, where the Nerussa joins the broad Desna River. Here the Nerussa abandoned its banks entirely and spread out in a broad sheet of water. The Desna had flooded its banks too, swallowing the mouth of the Nerussa and its shore for several miles upstream. We lost our course and ended up in the middle of a field with five feet of water under us. I could see last year's grasses through the clear, cold water. Fish swam this way and that, gladly feeding in areas not usually available to them. If we had been out in the open on the broad meadows that flanked the Desna, we would have been able to see Trubchevsk standing on the river's west bank about fifty feet higher than the east bank. We would have seen the white Trinity Cathedral, with its blue cupola, perched on the edge of the sandy cliffs. But we were lost in a maze of dense willow thickets. We couldn't see where we were going, and we couldn't find the river channel. I worried for a moment, then remembered that I was in Igor's capable hands.

We kept the two boats together, searching for the Nerussa or the Desna or Trubchevsk or anything that looked vaguely familiar. We came across a noisy colony of hundreds of gray and white herons, and we knew we had found the Nerussa. Igor said the herons nest in the same spot along the river every year. We were relieved to find this landmark, as we were cold and wet from the spray and late for our festival.

Finally, we came to the main channel of the Desna and saw Trinity Cathedral just half a mile upriver. We must have been quite a spectacle pulling into the docks below Trubchevsk with our banner flying in the wind above the boats. A jeep from the local administration was waiting for us to carry our paraphernalia up the steep slope that led to the town square. There, at the House of Culture, the Soviet name for the town's arts center, we quickly set up the photo exhibit and unfurled our banner. Then, on our cue, the festival began.

Three processions of marching students, representing the three schools in the town of sixteen thousand, merged in the central square waving banners and accompanied by a full brass band. The processions assembled in an orderly fashion before the podium.

Some children wore animal costumes. A big bear mascot danced around the square. The teachers organized their students in neat rows reminiscent of a tribute to Stalin. Instead of posters of Stalin, the students carried large-scale portraits of wild boars, bear, and bison. I was at once elated and shocked at the vehemence with which the town embraced the opportunity to line up in the square Communist-style.

What have we done? I thought, wondering if we had reincarnated a monster.

The mayor said a few words about how wonderful and important the Bryansk Forest Zapovednik was for Trubchevsk.

Igor whispered in my ear, This is the same man whose arm I had to twist ten years ago to sign the papers to create the reserve.

A few other officials spoke. Then Igor took the microphone and welcomed the crowd, thanking the people for their show of support. People applauded enthusiastically. Next was my turn, and I talked about the roots of March for Parks in the United States. The crowd cheered its approval, and I briefly considered a political career.

After the opening ceremony, I was invited to plant a tree in the square next to the tree the mayor was planting. The holes had already been dug. I put the spruce sapling in and covered the roots with dirt. We had not planned this, and I was honored. Igor looked on, visibly pleased and filled with pride.

We went inside the House of Culture, and the games began. We held contests to test the children's knowledge of the Bryansk Forest and invited them onstage to share their poems and songs about nature. We handed out dozens of prizes. Children asked me to autograph their calendars and posters, and I gladly obliged, again experiencing the guilty pleasure of unearned fame. We dimmed the lights and showed slides and a short video about the reserve's wildlife.

At the end of the day, our spirits lifted, we launched the boats and set a course upstream. Our boat left the other behind, as Igor was eager to get home; the next day we had to repeat the whole festival in Suzemka. We arrived home after dark. We listened for the second boat that held Nikolai, Natasha, and the journalist, but didn't hear the motor. We made the final preparations for the next day and then went to bed. I stepped outside several times in the night to listen for the second boat, but heard nothing. Poopah would bark if they came, I thought. But I was worried and told Igor I thought we should look for them. He took the jeep through the reserve, crossing nine rotten bridges in the dark to a downstream stretch of the Nerussa. He listened for the motor but heard nothing and returned in the middle of the night.

Nikolai is with them. He will take care of them, Igor said to comfort me. My brother knows what to do.

The next morning we left at 8 A.M. to reach Suzemka in time. Still there was no sign of the others. I was worried sick and also dreaded the thought of conducting the event in Suzemka without the help of my colleagues. We started the festival in the town square in front of the House of Culture. We had commissioned a local artist to paint large pictures of animals on the diamond-shaped billboards in the four corners of the square. The billboards once displayed Communist Party propaganda. Now, a moose, a bear, a kingfisher, and a stork adorned the square, facing the statue of Lenin in the center. Children and teachers from the two schools lined up, again in drill fashion, holding banners and signs with conservation slogans. One school, at the front of the line, displayed a banner in English reading Don't Disturb Bird Nesting Areas, evidently for my benefit. There was some commotion, and the banner moved to the back of the column. I was told the former head of the district's Communist Party Office didn't like children holding English-language banners in front of Lenin. The rest of the day was filled with events like those in Trubchevsk: tree planting, games, contests, slides, and a parade.

At the end of the day, the children took the banners and made an impromptu parade around Suzemka, passing the town market. The old women sitting at the market selling produce watched the procession. The children were moving too fast for them to read what was written on the signs. I overheard one woman say to another, Look! The government's not paying the kids their salaries either! She thought it was another demonstration like those to protest funding shortages and the government's chronic failure to pay teachers' salaries in the district on time.

When the festivities were over, Nikolai and Natasha turned up at the House of Culture to help us pack up our things. They looked tired yet pleased. Nikolai's curly hair was tousled and his angled jaw unshaven. Natasha had dark blotches of mascara smeared under her eyes.

What happened to you? we asked.

We got lost in the floodplain, and then the boat motor broke down, Nikolai explained.

They had spent the night in the floodplain. Because there was water all around, Natasha and the journalist had to stand up most of the night on the roots of willow trees while Nikolai fiddled with the boat motor. The journalist wore only a lightweight shirt, so Nikolai gave him his camouflage jacket. They lit a fire on a dry hummock in a clump of bushes to keep warm. By dawn Nikolai had fixed the motor, and they headed home after finding the Nerussa. Months later Nikolai saw the journalist in Bryansk wearing the camouflage jacket, but he didn't have the heart to ask for it back. To the journalist it was a hard-earned reminder of surviving a night in the floodplain.

In Russia, May ushers in one holiday after another. May 1 is May Day, or International Labor Day, a major holiday. May 9 brings Victory Day, marking the end of World War II. Offices and organizations around Russia virtually cease to function for the seven days in between. Chukhrai's two resident alcoholics find the May holidays a decent excuse to get drunk and stay that way for days, weeks even.

In May the ground warms and the villagers turn to the land. They mend the fences around their sizable garden plots to keep out cows and wild boars. They rotate helping plant each other's large plots, borrowing a horse to pull the plow. Two people walk in front with a pitchfork and spread manure. Behind them, a man leads the horse while another guides the heavy iron plow. A woman with a bucket following the plow tosses egg-sized potatoes saved from last year's harvest into the newly exposed furrow of black soil. Then the men replow the plot, covering the potatoes with topsoil. The person whose field is being plowed treats the rest of the villagers to *samogon*

and *salo* and bread when the work is done.

I began to tend our own small garden, dwarfed by that of my neighbor across the way, Trofimovna, who, at seventy-nine, was nearly three times my age. Our plot was all I could handle. The old woman spent every day from spring until fall and from dawn until dusk doubled over the earth planting seeds, picking weeds, removing potato beetles and cabbage worms. A spring day feeds you for a year, the saying goes. Her harvest would help her survive the winter until she could sow again. If she did not sow and reap, she would starve. Perhaps it was the struggle to survive that kept her fit, indeed alive, day to day, year to year.

Igor helped me till the soil and spread manure on our plot. Then I planted anything that wasn't afraid of a possible tardy frost. I carved neat rows with a shovel, overturning the earth, and trampled little paths between the rows. I sowed carrot, dill, radish, onion, parsley, and lettuce seeds in even lines, pulling out weeds as I went. Inside the house, on the windowsill, I had tomato and pepper plants waiting to be transplanted to the garden once the danger of frost had passed. I had never gardened before, so I asked the villagers for advice. I loved the prospect of growing our own food, particularly since we wouldn't be able to buy fresh vegetables in Suzemka until summer came.

Once the planting was done, everyone could rest until the weeds came up. Igor and I went to the woods with a bucket in hand and rubber boots on our feet. Although they say in Russia that there are only two seasons, winter and summer, I marveled at the delicate signs of spring. Little earringlike seeds of alder trees adorned the ground. Tiny green sprouts shot from under last year's rotting vegetation. Finding a large birch tree, Igor carved a small hole near the base of the

THE STORKS' NEST

trunk. He fashioned a spigot from a splinter of wood, and I set the bucket underneath. In a day's time we returned and collected birch juice fragrant with the sweet smell of spring and fresh blossoms.

Off in a meadow, a pair of common cranes, having arrived from some warmer place, heralded the arrival of the warm season with their trumpeting call. My spirits lifted knowing that summer could not be far behind. At home we drank some of the fresh birch juice. Igor poured the rest into plastic bottles with a little sugar, a couple of raisins, and a sliver of lemon peel. On hot summer days, we would drink the distilled brew, called *kvas*, and use it for the base of a cold summer soup.

After the May holidays, Igor and I returned to Trubchevsk to remove the photo exhibit in the House of Culture and confer with the schoolteachers about preparing information packets on the *zapovednik* for their curricula the following school year. We took the jeep north through the reserve and across the floodplain, using the most direct route since the floodwaters had subsided. The land gradually sloped down as we descended into the Desna's valley, which was carved by glaciers, the last of which receded about ten thousand years ago. When the glaciers retreated, they left enormous quantities of nutrient-poor sand in their wake. The only reason the Bryansk Forest remained intact is because the land is too poor to farm. A satellite image from space hanging in our visitor's center shows the dark green swath of forest surrounded by a sea of agricultural fields.

We passed through the tiny forest village of Solka, filled with timber yards and lumberjacks, all eating away at the

Bryansk Forest. Two miles beyond Solka, we reached the Desna River. We traveled south down a muddy road for several miles to a pontoon bridge that had recently been set up. The bridge was made of several sections assembled when the river retreated to its regular course in late spring. The bridge would remain through the summer, until it was disassembled in preparation for winter and stored on the shore.

In Trubchevsk, Igor gave me a historical tour of the town. We drove to Trinity Cathedral on the high western bank of the Desna and walked around the park and gardens, where we took in the spectacular view of the five-mile-wide Desna floodplain. In the distance a band of forest extended north and south along the river as far as the eye could see: the Bryansk Forest. It looked dark and foreboding. The name *Bryansk*, originally *debryansk*, came from the Old Russian *debri*—meaning "dense, impassable forests in a valley or canyon." I thought about how the Bryansk Forest had provided wood, furs, and other forest products for the residents of Trubchevsk for centuries.

A steep path led down the slope from the cathedral to the Desna. About halfway to the river, we turned into a small alcove sheltered by a wooden roof. A spring leaked from a crevasse in the hill. A holy monk named Nil the Miracle Worker was said to have built a hermitage on this spot around the turn of the sixteenth century. More than four centuries later, the spring where the monk quenched his thirst for spirituality still spilled cold, fresh water. People traveled from miles around to drink the holy water, which was said to have healing powers.

We drank from the holy spring and then climbed the acclivity to the church. We walked through the gardens to a bronze statue of the twelfth-century bard Bayan. Many believe that Bayan was from this region, though his exact place of origin was unknown. Bronze plates along the base of the statue told the story of Trubchevsk's past, from medieval knights wielding swords in battle to Soviet men and women plowing the land to the Red Army fighting the Nazis in World War II. The statue was erected for Trubchevsk's millennium celebration, in 1975.

Trubchevsk had long been an important trading center. Boats traveling on the Desna River from central Russia to the Black Sea used Trubchevsk as a stopping point. Once known as Trubetz, it was at various times ruled by Russians, Mongols, Lithuanians, and Poles. The name of the city comes from the word *truba* (pipe), an old term for a stream or river in a deep ravine. Such a ravine once ran through the heart of Trubchevsk, separating two large castles surrounded by walls and protected by the steep cliffs abutting the Desna. As the town prospered with trade in timber and furs from the Bryansk Forest as well as cattle and other goods, it outgrew itself and relocated six miles to the north.

Now I could see only low mounds, probably once foundations for the city's walls, giving away Trubchevsk's former location. Low earthen hills called *kurgany* (ancient burial mounds) from the ninth through the twelfth centuries dotted the surrounding plain high above the Desna.

Trubchevsk was ruled from the second half of the fourteenth century by the Gediminas dynasty of Lithuania, which then stretched from the Baltic to the Black Sea. In 1377 Trubchevsk was incorporated into Russia, and Russia's ruler, Dmitry Donskoy, confirmed Prince Dmitry Gediminas's sovereignty of the Trubchevsk princedom. After Gediminas's death, his son Michael adopted the name Troubetzkoy for himself, after the town, and became the first in a line of

Troubetzkoys who would leave their mark on Trubchevsk, and on Russia.

After exploring the historical landmarks of Trubchevsk, we drove down the steep embankment, crossing the Desna River on the pontoon bridge. We passed a herd of about a hundred horses grazing in the meadow flanking the river. A fog was settling into the valley, and the rays of the setting sun radiated off the horses' backs. We stopped to admire the beauty and serenity of the scene. Suddenly, a commotion to one side broke the calmness, and a big black stallion caught my eye. He circled the herd, kicking up his heels. His black mane flapped in the wind, and his tail lifted high. He galloped up to a large chestnut stallion and nipped at its neck. The two horses reared up and clashed hooves. They came down to the ground with a grunt and arched their necks, snorting on each other's flanks. The black stallion whinnied and tossed his head, striking his hoof out in front of him. His muscles bulged under his smooth hide, and his eyes were wide with rage. He backed away and galloped around the herd, then stood over to the side again, his skin quivering. I was taken by his beauty. We drove off, jerking and bumping along the muddy road, heading for home.

I turned twenty-eight on May 21. I spent the morning in the garden and then took a walk in the forest. Igor was chopping wood for the following winter and stacking it in the shed next to the outhouse. The ground in the woods was still damp, so I wore my rubber boots. The long green stalks of ferns had uncurled, and lovely purple gosling flowers lined the forest path. Yellow marsh marigolds bloomed on tall stalks emerging from a swamp. I walked by the bison enclosure and found that the animals had recently visited the feeding troughs, where the ranger still deposited oats occasionally. Then I headed toward home, first stopping by a badger den Igor had shown me in aptly named Badger Swamp to look for signs of life. Tracks in the mud outside two of the multiple entrances and fresh droppings in a pile nearby testified that the den was occupied. Badger families can use the same den for hundreds of years, constructing an intricate maze of underground tunnels and chambers. This one had probably been here for at least a century.

I returned to the village and noticed fresh horse prints. Aza was grazing in the fenced-in paddock behind our house, so they couldn't be hers. She would soon go into heat, and if we let her run free in the fields around the village, as Igor usually did in winter, she would take off to Smelizh in search of a stallion. There she would trample freshly planted gardens and run the risk of being shot. The tracks on the road must have been from the dirty white gelding that lived at the other end of the village from us, owned by the old man known as Kudinyonok.

I passed the barn and glanced into the corral to see if Aza was there. My jaw dropped and I nearly fell over backwards. There stood the great black stallion I had admired that evening on the Desna. I walked up to him and held out my hand. He sniffed it and tossed his head. The veins in his nose bulged, and his big brown eyes watched my every move. I ran into the yard to find Igor. He was stacking firewood in the shed. Seeing my excitement, he strode toward me.

Happy birthday, he said, glowing. The owner brought him half an hour ago. Led the horse here on a rope all the way from the Desna because he's never been ridden. He's yours now.

I threw my arms around Igor, thanking him profusely and kissing his face all over. I raced back to the corral with Igor following behind.

What's he called? I asked.

Orlik, he said. Little Eagle in English.

I spent the afternoon getting to know Orlik. In the evening, before the light dimmed, I tore myself away from the stallion to go with Igor for a walk in the woods. When we reached a clearing, Igor put his camera around my neck.

You wait here behind this willow shrub, he told me, and I'll skirt the clearing and scare up an animal for you to photograph. Don't move, and be very quiet.

I squatted near the ground, sitting very still, hearing only the sound of my heart beating.

Three minutes passed, and then a roe deer jumped out into the clearing, looking back, evidently to see if Igor was following. Igor hid behind a tree, and the roe deer stopped to sniff the air. The animal was not thirty feet in front of me, right in the middle of the clearing, its hide golden in the soft light of the evening sun. I centered the roe deer in my lens and twisted the ring to bring it into focus. As I was about to snap the picture, a fox trotted into the frame between the deer and me. It paused to look at the roe deer. I panicked. I knew I only had one chance to take this picture: the animals were so close they would bolt upon hearing the shutter snap. Yet I didn't know which animal to focus on. So I did something no good photographer would ever do: I focused on the space between them, hoping they would both come out sharp. Click. The fox spun around to face me, and the roe deer looked at the fox. They fled in opposite directions.

Weeks later when I saw the developed film, both animals were visible, though they were fuzzy and the grass in between was perfectly in focus. But I didn't care. With that picture, my new stallion, and Igor, it was the best birthday I'd ever had.

I spent several hours a day with Orlik for the next month, training him early in the morning before work and staying with him until late in the evening after I returned. Igor was only a little jealous. I explained to him that the stallion was still green and I had to start from the beginning. I had ridden horses since I was little, but I had never trained one. First I got Orlik used to my hands, my voice, and the oats I kept in my pocket. Within a week, he walked, trotted, and galloped around me on voice command at the end of a long rope. He pranced over poles, lifting his hooves high. By the end of the second week, I put a saddle on him, and Igor helped me strap heavy bags of sand to it to get him used to carrying weight. He protested at first, bucking and kicking, but finally accepted the burden.

One day I was walking him around the corral with the saddle when a few of the reserve rangers showed up in a truck. The head of the ranger service, Vladimir, had legs so bowed he was probably born on a horse. He laughed at me with my sandbag contraption and shouted, Let me at him!

I objected at first. Coercion by a Russian cowboy was not part of my training plan for Orlik. Igor, however, said he'd rather see Vladimir bucked off than me. So Vladimir grabbed the reins out of my hands, threw off the sandbags, and jumped onto the stallion while two others held Orlik at the head. Feet in stirrups, he yelled, Let him go!

Orlik's eyes widened with terror. As soon as Vladimir was

in the saddle, he reared up and bolted out of the gate, which the rangers had flung open, rodeo-style. Vladimir sawed on the reins, pulling at the stallion's mouth as hard as he could. But Orlik was unstoppable. He galloped around the lake to the fields on the other side, where finally the reins broke and the rider flew off. Vladimir walked back sheepishly with a length of leather in his hands, cursing that the damn bridle broke. The rangers piled into the truck and drove off. I went after Orlik, who stood where Vladimir fell, munching on green grasses as if nothing had happened. I led him home, all the while begging his forgiveness and promising that I would never let that happen again.

It took me a couple more days with the sandbags before Orlik got over his fright. His fear of men lasted for some time after that. When I was ready to mount, I led him to the middle of the paddock, away from anything hard or pointed. I rubbed his nose and gave him some oats, bribing him to be nice. Slowly, I lifted myself up into the saddle. I gave him the voice command to walk, afraid he might bolt again if I dug my heels into his side, but he just stood there. So I waited. After about five minutes, he started to get bored and took a few steps forward. I patted him on the neck, repeating the voice command, and he understood that this was good. I continued to use the commands that he had learned from the ground, and, within the hour, we were trotting and galloping around the paddock. I called Igor over to watch as Orlik and I executed a series of starts and stops.

Soon we began to explore the woods together and became the best of friends. Orlik would cock his ears back to listen for my commands, shooting them forward when he heard an animal ahead. Because his hearing was much better than mine, I watched his ears for signs of life in the woods.

I corralled Orlik away from the mare at first, as I was afraid he might hurt her. After a couple of weeks, I decided to get them acquainted. When I put them together, Aza was the one who kicked and bit the newcomer. Orlik just stood there and took it. I realized that, although he might fight other stallions, he would never harm a mare. Within a few days they got along nicely. In fact, when Orlik and I would come in from our rides, Aza would greet him with a prolonged whinny, having missed him dearly.

Aza went into heat. She hadn't mated for many years, since the old poacher Shamornoy sold his aging stallion to a sausage factory. Yet Aza knew exactly what to do to get Orlik's attention. She pranced around in front of him and occasionally squirted urine in his direction. Orlik became excited and curled his upper lip to draw in the full scent of her pheromones. I caught him with great difficulty and closed him in the corral.

One day Igor took Aza for a ride in the woods to see if black storks had occupied the nest in Badger Swamp. Black storks, unlike their white cousins, are fearful of humans and nest only in remote areas, far from disturbances. Igor was concerned that the place we released the bison was too close to the stork nest and might have frightened the birds away.

When Igor returned home about an hour later, Orlik noticed the horse and rider from a distance and began to whinny and run frantically around the corral. I walked out to meet Igor, and he told me the nest was empty. Orlik ran in circles and then galloped toward the fence at full speed and jumped right over it. He reached Aza and strutted around her, nearly knocking me over. Igor swatted at him with the reins, but he paid no attention. Orlik reared up behind Aza and put his forelegs on her rump. Igor turned in the saddle and batted him on the head with his arm. The stallion got down, then reared up again and grabbed Igor's jacket at the shoulder with his teeth and threw him to the ground. Then Orlik mated with Aza while Igor and I watched in disbelief.

Governor Lodkin visited the reserve again, bringing his ten-year-old grandson. His bodyguard drove them this time, in a Mitsubishi SUV, from Bryansk. When they arrived at the reserve office, Igor and I greeted them outside. The governor pulled a *fufaika* from the backseat and hung the coat over my shoulders, along with a colorful Russian shawl like all the *babushki* wear. Then he opened the trunk of the car and took out a long wooden yoke and two buckets and balanced them over my shoulder.

You see, he said, smiling, our newspaper never lies.

By the end of May, spring was in full tilt and summer was on the horizon. The leaves on the trees were bright green and soft. The seeds in the garden had sprouted. The mosquitoes emerged from the swamps and harassed us unmercifully. They came out in the morning and the evening, only avoiding the hot midday sun. They loved cloudy weather because they could search for blood all day without worrying about the desiccating heat. When the air was filled with the pests, I dressed in thick clothing from head to toe and pulled a mosquito net over my head. The other villagers appeared not to notice; with no bug spray or nets, they spent all day bent over their gardens. Trofimovna would come in from her vast plot each evening with her face all puffy and her eyes nearly swollen shut.

But worse than the mosquitoes were the hoards of tiny biting flies that swarmed around anything living at dusk and dawn. They were smaller than my smallest freckle and infinitely more plentiful. Usually I couldn't even see where they were biting. But I could feel it. They got into my mouth and nose when I breathed and flew into my eyes, causing swelling and painful stinging. They crawled under my clothing and into my shoes. Removing my jacket, I found red circles from the bites around my wrists. And, oh, did they itch. Even the horses hid in the barn from the tiny, outwardly innocuous flies. Only hunger drove them out to chew on grass in the middle of the night. Toward dawn they would gallop back to the cover of the barn, their necks and faces swollen from hundreds of bites. They rubbed their chests against the fence poles, nearly knocking down the fence.

One morning I went out to water the garden and feed the horses but found they were gone. They must have rubbed their necks on the rails that closed off the gate and inadvertently pushed them aside. I studied the tracks on the road. I found three sets leading out of the village. Orlik and Aza had taken Pyotr Nikitich's old chestnut mare, Anfisa, with them. Orlik had managed to mate with her the week before, escaping from the corral and swimming across the river to the ranger station. The horses' tracks turned left at the end of the village and led down the old logging road through the *zapovednik* toward the Desna River. Orlik had led the mares to his former home.

I ran to tell Igor and then got the saddle and bridles and put them in the jeep. We drove through the reserve toward the Desna. The horses' tracks showed clearly in the wet sand on the road. We followed them for about ten miles to where the road led out of the forest. Ahead of us, the floodplain of the Desna River extended for miles. We came to a channel that flowed into the river and blocked our way. We walked up and down the channel, trying to find a place to cross. The channel narrowed at one point and didn't seem very deep. Igor took off his clothes and began to wade across. The water was soon up to his chest. He made it across, and I took off my clothes and threw the bundle of clothes and the bridles over to his side. I crossed the channel and dressed. The water was cold, and goose bumps covered our skin.

We quickly lost the horse tracks in the grassy meadow on the other side of the channel. After about a mile we came to the old horse farm where we had first seen the large herd out to pasture. I could see two specks in the distance that looked like horses, so we walked toward them. We came closer and saw the two mares, but not Orlik. Igor caught Aza and put the bridle on. We walked to the bank of the Desna River and saw the large herd of horses grazing on the other side of the river. Orlik was running up and down the bank, looking from our two mares to the herd. Evidently he swam across the wide river but the two mares remained behind, afraid to cross in the swift current. Now Orlik seemed torn between coming after his two pregnant mares and staying with his scraggly company of former mares and yearlings. I rode up and down the bank on Aza, hoping to entice him to swim back across. But he wouldn't come, and the sun was nearing the horizon. We jumped on the horses' backs to ford the channel and returned to the jeep. The mares were eager to go home after their adventure.

I saddled Aza and rode home with Anfisa in tow. Igor took the jeep and drove ahead. I came to a fork in the road, and, not knowing which way to go, I dropped the reins and let Aza decide. She knew these parts much better than I did. After

THE STORKS' NEST

about a mile, we came to a marshy area. When I pressed Aza forward, her front feet sank to the knees in the boggy mire. She pulled herself out and backed up. I realized we couldn't get through. I turned her to the right in an attempt to skirt the swamp. Another mile on, the swamp was still to our left, with no end in sight. The sun dropped below the horizon. We were still miles from home. I backtracked to the fork and took the other road. We came to another intersection of overgrown logging roads. I hesitated, then turned right. Soon we came to another impassable swamp. We backtracked, and then I couldn't remember which road we had come down. Night was upon us. With no moon to see by, I could do nothing but let Aza find her way. I put the reins on her neck, and she brought Anfisa and me back to the first impassable swamp. Tears welled up in my eyes. I was dressed lightly, and the cool night air penetrated my skin. I cursed myself because I didn't even have a match. I turned the horses around. Just as I was sure I would have to spend the night in the forest, I saw two headlights shining through the trees half a mile ahead of us. Igor! I was relieved and so happy to see him.

How did you find me? I asked, my heart still racing.

I figured you got lost and that Aza would try to take you this way.

She kept leading me to the edge of a swamp, I told him.

Ah, Aza was right. She was trying to take you the shortest way, he said, but she's only gone that way in winter, when the swamp is frozen solid.

Igor told me to drive the jeep home following his tracks. He took the horses.

The *banya* is hot and waiting for you! he yelled after me.

The next day we took the motorboat down the Nerussa to fetch our stallion. After about an hour and a half, we arrived at the meadow with the herd of horses. I took the bridle and a bucket of oats and walked up to Orlik. He neighed softly in greeting and scooped up a mouthful of oats. I grabbed his mane. He didn't resist, and I saddled him up. The pontoon bridge over the Desna had come loose, floating along the bank of the river instead of across it, so I had to ride about three miles downriver, through the center of Trubchevsk, to the permanent cement bridge. Orlik whinnied loudly while running at a fast trot the whole way through town, drawing hundreds of stares. At one intersection, a traffic cop extended his black-and-white striped rod, waving me to a stop. I explained to him that my horse had escaped and I finally caught him and now I was taking him home.

This is a one-way street, he said. Then he chuckled and waved me on. But slow down! he called after me.

In Chukhrai, Orlik announced his arrival by neighing loudly through the village. Aza greeted him happily. I closed the horses in the corral, this time tying wires around the rails so they couldn't open them. Igor arrived in the boat half an hour after us. Orlik had been so eager to return, he had even beaten the motorboat home.

One morning the postlady's husband, Stepan, brought word that a baby moose had joined the herd of horses in nearby Krasnaya Sloboda. A man had taken him in and was looking for a home for the orphan. Igor and I hesitated a moment. As animal lovers, we knew that if we saw the baby, we would end up bringing it home. We took the jeep, with Stepan in the back.

89

THE STORKS' NEST

We arrived in Krasnaya Sloboda, eight miles from Chukh-rai and two miles beyond Smelizh, and asked directions to the house belonging to the son-in-law of the former town veterinarian, where the moose was being held. The man's nickname was "Zyat," which simply meant "son-in-law." He was an infamous poacher. We stopped at his house, and Zyat's wife greeted us. She called her husband, who was building a new cabin across the way.

He walked up and offered his wrist for Igor to shake, gesturing that his hands were soiled. I nodded my head in greeting, as is the custom. He explained that his horse had been tied in the pasture and a baby moose came up to it and wouldn't go away. We suspected that he actually shot the mother and had felt sorry for the baby and brought it home. His wife had been feeding the moose cow's milk for three days. It was living in the barn with their baby bull.

We walked into the yard, which was littered with boards and scraps of metal. Zyat opened the door to the barn to disclose a baby moose and a calf lying together on the hay. The moose was slimmer than the stocky calf, about the size of a newborn foal and covered with brown, fuzzy baby hair. He had disproportionately large ears, big brown eyes, and a tapered nose. He stood up on his long, lanky legs and slowly came out, unafraid. He walked around the yard and found a green plastic bottle, which he nudged delicately with his nose.

He drinks milk out of that bottle, Zyat's wife said from the porch.

If we were to leave him there, they would either have had to kill him or lead him to the forest and abandon him. There, without his mother's milk, he would have died. So we rounded him up, put him in the jeep, and took him home. Stepan and I could barely restrain the moose in the back of the jeep. He thrashed his legs and hit his head against the window, terrified of his first car ride. Igor drove slowly, but within half an hour we were home. It was already dark, so we put him in an abandoned barn across the way, which was dry and secure.

I asked my neighbor Trofimovna if her cow could supply enough milk for the baby. She agreed to give me a couple of quarts a day. She refused to take money but accepted the little gifts I would bring her: a box of baking soda, cookies, apples, and chocolates. Once I brought her a lemon.

What's this? she asked.

I told her to try it in her tea.

At about midnight that night, I checked on the baby moose. When he saw me, he began whimpering and stood up. He was shaky and his breathing uneven. The stress of the move had taken its toll on him. I offered him some warm milk from a bottle with a nipple that Stepan gave me, but he refused. He lay down again, and I scratched his neck and soothed him with my voice. Thinking that maybe he had a bellyache from the stress, I rubbed his stomach, which he seemed to like.

The next morning, we woke up with the sun at 6:30. I warmed some milk and checked on the moose. He stood up slowly and, after refusing to drink the milk, stepped out of the barn, eager to go outside. He followed me slowly to our front yard. As we crossed the road, we encountered a mare and her foal roaming freely around the village. They belonged to the old poacher Shamornoy. The baby moose and the baby horse were momentarily enchanted with one another. They strode toward each other, but the mare snorted warily, frightening both of them, and they jumped in opposite directions.

The moose followed me into the yard, where I coaxed

him into drinking some milk. He tilted his head up and curled his tongue and his upper lip in a tight seal around the nipple. He jerked his nose up and down violently, as if to massage an invisible udder. He sucked the quart down within twenty seconds and wanted more. But Trofimovna, who had experience raising calves, had warned me that I shouldn't give him more than a quart at a time.

I tried to hook him up with Aza, but she nipped at the stranger, so I was afraid to leave them alone. I led him over to the house, where I could keep an eye on him. On the way, our gray tom, Lorik, crossed his path and began to sniff the baby curiously. Instantly the moose thrashed out a front hoof, which came down mercilessly on the cat's back. The cat streaked away and bothered him no more.

The moose caught sight of the reeds near the lake and headed in that direction. He waded into the water, perhaps to rid himself of the swarm of mosquitoes that had gathered on his long legs, and then lay down in the tall grass on the shore to sleep. I went inside the house to take cover from the mosquitoes and in about half an hour, I heard whimpering outside the door. I led him back to the barn.

During the day he drank more milk, a quart at a time. I took him for a walk around the lake, and he nibbled on willow buds and marsh grass, lying down to rest periodically. Mosquitoes swarmed around him, but he quickly became accustomed to them, only occasionally shaking them off his long ears.

The old women in the village watched the moose walking around and asked what it was. One woman thought it was a goat; another thought it was a baby bison. I explained that he was a baby moose, an orphan. All were sympathetic. Those who had cows offered to donate fresh milk. Even the old poacher Shamornoy said he would provide milk. They asked his name.

Moosik, I said without thinking, adding the Russian diminutive to moose.

What's that mean? one woman asked.

It's English for moose, I told them. The name stuck.

The postlady's two grandchildren came to stay with her for their summer vacation, and the little girl and boy visited Moosik daily. They would pet him and scratch his neck, and he would move one back leg up and down like a dog. He enjoyed the attention and was gentle with them.

Igor let me take unpaid vacation time from work at the *zapovednik* to care for our moose. A week passed in the same routine. I would wake early, worrying about how Moosik had spent the night. I gave him warm cow's milk five times a day. I took him for walks in the mosquito-ridden swamp, where I stood knee-deep in the water. We swam together in the cool lake.

Moosik trailed me everywhere I went. One day he followed me inside the house, kicking the door open. He sniffed around the kitchen. Igor playfully gave him a banana, and he nosed it, knocking over the teapot. I gave him a bottle, and he settled down on the living room floor. The dogs and cats watched attentively but gave the moose wide clearance. My calico cat, Mysha (from the word for "mouse," for her skittishness), who had porcelain-white fur with splotches of red and black, climbed on top of the wardrobe and refused to come down until the moose left.

Igor and I had to leave one morning for the reserve office. I needed to submit a new issue of the *Zapovednik Scroll* to the district newspapers, so we drove to Suzemka and Trub-chevsk to drop off the draft I had prepared earlier. Everything took longer than we planned, and we arrived home late in the afternoon. We were worried that Moosik was hungry. I opened the shed and he sprang out, bleating and crying. He had missed two feedings.

Mommy's here, I said, and gave him a bottle.

THE STORKS' NEST

SUMMER

BY JUNE the days began to warm. From my perch in the outhouse, I saw that the leaves on the alder trees rimming the lake had turned dark green, hardened by the sun and wind. A breeze blew low over the water, forming small waves that rippled across the surface and lapped at the shore. Tall reeds now lined the entire perimeter of the lake, except the beach near the *banya* that Igor filled with new sand from the river each year. The grasses in the meadow grew green, and the first flowers blossomed.

The plants in our garden flourished in the sun and rain. I tossed large leaves of green lettuce with dill and sliced radishes to make fresh salads. Igor said that food tasted better when made with my loving hands. I thought it a poor excuse for him not to cook. The extensive plots flanking Chukhrai were verdant with the young foliage of potatoes, cabbages, and carrots. The villagers worked like oxen, hoeing, planting, watering, weeding. My neighbors Trofimovna and Glukhaya remained doubled over their vast fields like bows from dawn until dusk.

For me, tending a garden was not a matter of subsistence, as it was for the other villagers; it was a matter of convenience because we didn't have any nearby stores. And there was something profoundly therapeutic about kneading the earth with my hands, gently urging it to bear fruit. I felt satisfaction in growing my own vegetables without the aid of pesticides or chemicals. Yet I quickly realized that gardening didn't come easy. Mosquitoes and gnats pestered me and, with the sunshine, a new nuisance appeared: the great gadfly with its incredibly painful bite. The horses went wild from them and couldn't be ridden until the invasion subsided.

We waged an eternal battle with the black-and-yellow-striped Colorado beetle, which Russian farmers firmly believe the Americans sent over to devastate the all-important potato crop. Strangely, I'd never encountered them while growing up in Colorado. Oval in shape and about half the size of my thumbnail, the potato beetle was, until recently, only known in Russia to a few well-traveled entomologists. Today, however, even politicians aren't cursed as often as the little black-and-yellow-striped beetle, which has wreaked more havoc in rural Russia than economic crises and political reforms combined. The seemingly inoffensive creatures rob every Russian family of its main dietary staple: the potato. Armies of the invaders march out of the soil for the short growing season, occupying potato fields and summer plots from Ukraine to Siberia, destroying as much as 40 percent of the country's potato harvest.

I later read that the Colorado potato beetle originated in central Mexico, although it was first described in the Rocky Mountains by Thomas Nuttal in 1811. The native host for the insect was the buffalo bur, a relative of the potato. After settlers began introducing potatoes in the insect's original range in the western United States in the mid-1800s, the beetle developed a taste for the green leaves and tubers of the potato plant. The insect soon began its rapid spread eastward, advancing about eighty-five miles a year, reaching the Atlantic coast by 1874. There beetles hitched rides on potatoes crossing the Atlantic by ship and began an affront on Europe. By the end of the 1940s, the first insects crossed the western border of the Soviet Union to degust Ukrainian and Belarussian potatoes. The post-war famine that pervaded the country at the time did not help matters much: potatoes were transported to starving regions, and the beetles got a free ride into western Russia. Despite ensuing measures by the Soviet government to prohibit transport of potatoes to uninfected regions and to wipe out the beetle with pesticides, the devastation continued to spread. Even in the absence of potatoes, the hardy beetle can survive on a number of other plants in the nightshade family, including eggplant, tomatoes, peppers, tobacco, horse-nettle, and common nightshade.

Russia has felt the brunt of the beetle blight more severely than other nations, in large part due to the importance of the potato in the country's diet and culture. Peter the Great first introduced potatoes to Russia in 1867 as part of a campaign to modernize the country. The potato replaced the turnip as Russia's main staple, next to bread. By 1908, Russia was producing 29 million tons of potatoes a year. By the end of the twentieth century, Russia was the world's second largest producer of potatoes. Potatoes had infiltrated the lives of every Russian family.

My battle against the beetle began with meticulous inspection of the leaves and hand-plucking the adult beetles. After the insects laid their larvae, I squished the little orange jelly sacs or pruned the leaves. Some of the beetles avoided my inspection, and the larvae continued to develop. When the beetles covered the plants en masse, I swept them into a pail using a broom. While some villagers relied on pesticides, even the strongest chemicals had little impact: the next generation of the pests was resistant.

As if the Colorado potato beetle wasn't enough, an invasive plant the locals called *amerikanka* (American girl) would take over the garden if left unchecked. As an American from Colorado, I shouldered the blame for both banes. Soon I earned the local nickname "Amerikanka"—for my American roots, I hoped, and not the weed.

Igor went to the woods to photograph the black stork. In spring, before the birds arrived, he had built a wooden blind near a black storks' nest in a swamp surrounded by dense woods. He camouflaged it with branches and debris. After having made several visits to the nest since the birds' arrival, Igor was sure they were settled and wouldn't abandon their eggs if they happened to see him. One night he walked the five miles to the nest after dusk, crouching down and creeping the last hundred yards through the swamp and into the cover of his blind. He set his camera on a tripod and stuck the lens through a sack I had sewn out of green cloth that was nailed to a round opening in the frame of the blind. He put a long tube wrapped in camouflage fabric on the end of his camera so the storks wouldn't see the light reflected from the lens. He slept curled up in the cramped wooden box until the sun rose, then he photographed the birds in the soft morning light. He would wait to leave the blind until the birds flew from the nest to feed or until dark. Sometimes Igor stayed in the blind for several days at a time, photographing the birds whenever the light was right. I missed him dearly while he was gone and begged to join him, but he said that the box was too small and I would be uncomfortable, and that I would be consumed by mosquitoes. So I rode Orlik to within a mile of the swamp and took Igor sandwiches and hot soup in a thermos, leaving the food in a bag on a post marking the border of the nature reserve. Igor ventured out at night to collect the bag and leave me his empty thermos with a note inside expressing his love.

On the way back from one of my daytime deliveries, Orlik and I encountered the three bison near the northern border of the nature reserve's narrow buffer zone. At first they stood and looked at us, having grown accustomed to the horses approaching their enclosure with hay and grain. Then they bolted, scattering and running through the woods in all directions. I feared that they were heading away from the reserve, where poachers might shoot them, so I urged Orlik into a gallop and followed an old logging road that led me around them. I cut them off and herded them in the direction of the reserve. I zigzagged through the trees as they raced ahead. I ducked as branches loomed near my face. Finally the bison headed back toward the reserve, and I turned homeward.

Igor called me on the walkie-talkie the next morning, asking me to fetch him on Aza and Orlik. I saddled the horses and led Aza on a long rope into the woods toward the nest. While the black storks were out hunting, Igor quietly slipped out of the blind and walked to meet me. He straddled Aza and we rode home. On the way, we encountered two men in the *zapovednik* not far from where I had seen the bison the day before. They had rifles slung over their shoulders, although hunting is illegal in the reserve. Poachers. Realizing we were *zapovednik* staff, they dashed through the trees, trying to escape. They didn't have much of a chance as we were

THE STORKS' NEST

on horseback, but they ran in different directions, trying to outwit us. Igor chased after one and I went after the other.

My heart raced as I pursued my poacher, but I didn't feel scared. Instead, I was possessed with a vehement sense of duty, as though I had a God-given right to protect the reserve and its inhabitants from wrongdoing. The man ran through the trees, leaping over fallen logs and patches of bog. I galloped to cut him off. He threw his rifle over a log into some underbrush, disposing of the incriminating evidence. I caught up to him and stopped him with the horse. Orlik herded him like a calf, pushing his muscular shoulders into the man. The man was intimidated by the horse's might and my apparent will to stop him.

I held the poacher from the safety of my steed until Igor returned. Igor had taken the rifle from the other man and led him to where I stood. I showed Igor where my poacher had abandoned his gun. He retrieved it and handed it to me. Then he told me in English, so the poachers wouldn't understand, that I must ride back to the house as fast as I could and call the reserve headquarters for backup. The men looked at us strangely, perhaps realizing they were face-to-face with the American they had heard about.

Within an hour, four rangers arrived in a jeep to collect the men, but they were too late. While Igor was guarding them, one of the men bolted and, when Igor went after that one, the other one got away. We turned over their guns to the rangers, who would give them to the police. Igor knew the poachers' identities. They had escaped this time, but if they were caught in the reserve again, they would be apprehended and prosecuted.

In the summer of 1996, Igor was returning to Russia from a park exchange visit to Yellowstone National Park and was stuck between flights at JFK in New York. Seeing a phone book near a pay phone, he flipped through the pages. R, S, T, Tr, Troubetzkoy. He picked up the phone and dialed.

Is this Sergei Troubetzkoy? Igor asked in Russian.

Yes, an elderly man answered, also in Russian.

My name is Igor Shpilenok. I am from the Bryansk Province. I am the director of a nature reserve, half of which is in the Trubchevsk region. I saw your book in the Trubchevsk historical museum. I must admit I didn't read it, however, as it was in French.

The man on the other end of the phone laughed.

Igor told him that he was interested in the part the Troubetzkoys played in ruling Trubchevsk several centuries ago.

It is my dream, Sergei Troubetzkoy said softly, to visit Trubchevsk.

It would mean a lot to everybody, all the residents of Trubchevsk, Igor replied. I can help you with the arrangements.

There was a pause. Then the man continued, If I don't make it … I am almost ninety, you know. If I don't make it, my son will come.

A year later, we received a call from Moscow at the *zapovednik* office. It was Alexis Troubetzkoy, son of Sergei Troubetzkoy, twenty-first in line descending from the Grand Duke Gediminas, who ruled Lithuania in the fourteenth century, when the empire far exceeded its current boundaries. At that time it encompassed Trubchevsk and its environs, including our village of Chukhrai. He told Igor in immaculate Russian that he would like to accept the invitation to visit Trubchevsk on behalf of his father. He would be bringing his son, Andre, number twenty-two.

They arrived unruffled on the overnight train from Moscow, and we served them tea and cakes at the visitor's center. Alexis, about sixty-five, was tall and fit, with wavy gray hair. He listened to what we had to say about the Bryansk Forest and the nature reserve with genuine concern. When he smiled, it was with the grandeur of his noble heritage. He stood with straight back and broad shoulders, carrying himself with the air of a prince but without any hint of pomposity. His Russian, although faultless, was a bit archaic. Polite and learned, he made us feel comfortable in his presence. Alexis's son, Andre, a handsome young man of about twenty-five with dark undulating hair and an angled jaw, was less refined and more animated than his father, but affable and dignified all the same.

We took them in the jeep through the Bryansk Forest to Trubchevsk, where a gathering of local leaders awaited. No Troubetzkoy had been to the town for nearly two centuries, since the family moved to Moscow and from there to France, the United States, and Canada. We blew seemingly blind through thick underbrush, Alexis later recalled, through three-foot-deep pondlike puddles and rutted tracks of black mud soup. Alexis wrote:

> *The bucking, heaving vehicle is a marvel of Soviet*
> *engineering and Igor is no less a marvelous driver.*
> *None of nature's obstacles is too great and we are*
> *unstoppable ... that is, until our undercarriage*
> *becomes well and truly pinioned on an ugly stump,*
> *both rear tires spinning mud in angry protest. Andre*
> *and I exchange a knowing glance—curtains; better*

forget Trubchevsk (where we are supposed to be in an hour's time). Laura remains quite unfazed as the unflappable Igor dons thigh-high rubber boots and exits the shoaled vehicle to work his magic. Heavy-duty winch is attached to sturdy tree and, with Laura at the wheel, the vehicle is determinedly jacked off its perch. Equipment gathered, mud scraped off, and we buck our way once more. Eventually we exit the forest and come onto the open floodplain of the Desna River, across which in the far distance are visible the spires of Trubchevsk's Trinity Cathedral. Peasant women tell us that most of the bridges were washed away by the spring floods ... one remains, some five kilometers downstream. We find it, cross it, and mount the steep hill leading into Trubchevsk's outskirts.

We parked in front of the town hall. We were an hour late. Our guests were distraught. Princes are not tardy.

They'll wait, I told them. They've been waiting for two hundred years.

We walked into the town hall and were greeted by nearly three dozen people, all crammed into the mayor's office. Present were the town mayor and his functionaries, the director of the historical museum, the editor from the newspaper with a journalist and photographer, Father Alexander of Trinity Cathedral, and two dozen others. Many were dressed in their quasi-official uniforms: plain gray polyester suits with the lapels bearing Soviet pins and medals. Father Alexander, who was draped in a plain black robe from head to foot topped by a red velvet hat resembling a tea cozy, stood out from the crowd. We sat in chairs around the perimeter of the room.

Each person gave a short speech to welcome the visitors.

The mayor began, saying how the town owed so much of its history to the Troubetzkoys. An elderly man with a Communist war veteran's red star pinned to his lapel wished the princely family long life and happiness. Another said he hoped the Troubetzkoys would return to where they belong, Trubchevsk. The meeting was emotionally charged yet tediously drawn-out. Communist bureaucrats, historians, and religious leaders joined together in a hearty welcome to the descendents of princes who once ruled their humble town and the nearby Bryansk Forest.

We were led to the town restaurant, called Vityaz, meaning "a medieval knight or hero"—appropriate given our princely entourage. A banquet six tables long awaited us in a large rectangular room with parquet floors and windows darkly hung with thick velvet drapes. As we feasted on herring, caviar, and a host of salads and meats, we raised our glasses countless times to the Troubetzkoys. Much of what had been said earlier was repeated in a more jovial milieu as Alexis and Andre, not wanting to offend their hosts, graciously swallowed successive tumblers of vodka.

After lunch we walked to the town park and Trinity Cathedral, with a diminished gathering of townspeople in tow. We stopped at the bronze statue of the bard Bayan. Alexis pointed to the medieval knights depicted on the plates at the base of the statue.

Troubetzkoys, no doubt, he said quietly to his son.

Father Alexander, absent from the banquet, greeted us at the church. He explained that the fourteenth-century crypt under the cathedral had been unsealed for their arrival. It had been closed since the 1960s, when vandals were discovered trying to break into the tombs. Within it are buried several generations of feudal Troubetzkoys, Father Alexander said.

THE STORKS' NEST

We filed down a short staircase at the back of the church into the outer room of the crypt. The cramped, cold chamber was lit with candles. Sunlight barely penetrated through bars on the small windows. The earthen floor had been swept clean and the cement walls whitewashed. Father Alexander directed Alexis and Andre to a rug laid in front of two tombstones. Alexis stood next to the grave of Prince Simeon Ivanovich Troubetzkoy, seventh generation in the Gediminas lineage, who died in 1553. Governing Kaluga and Kostroma, he was infamous as the head of Ivan the Terrible's secret police. Andre stood next to a stone slab with intricately carved designs, although the inscription was illegible.

Andre, you're standing at the side of a probable great-grandfather, Alexis said softly to his son.

Through a small door was another chamber containing thirteen graves of Troubetzkoys, one in a large ambry. All dated from the same period, 1492 to 1602. Looking at the tombs, I thought that these forefathers must surely have explored and hunted in the Bryansk Forest. Perhaps even among them were its first guardians. Behind me I found the grave of Prince Andrei Troubetzkoy (died 1557), who governed Bryansk, Pochep, and Novgorod. He was the last autonomous governor of Trubchevsk. Without a son to inherit his holdings, Prince Andrei willed his lands to his thirteen-year-old godson, Tsar Ivan III. So ended the Troubetzkoys' nearly two-hundred-year reign over Trubchevsk and the Bryansk Forest, though the family continued to play an important role in the Russian government and, later, in academic and philosophical circles through the nineteenth century.

Father Alexander held a small urn with burning incense at the end of a long chain. As he chanted a prayer, he swung the urn, spreading the scented smoke around the small, cold chamber. Several women sang softly while Father Alexander recited a repose for the dead: Grant rest eternal in blessed repose, O Lord, to thy servants who have fallen in sleep … and make their memory everlasting.

The small, damp room resonated with warmth and life for the first time in centuries.

Moosik loved to gallop around the yard, kicking out his heels and forelegs, attacking an imaginary wolf. Sometimes he practiced on the dogs, and they learned to steer clear of his dangerous hooves, one blow of which could crack their skulls. When Kosha sat on my lap, he sniffed her and then licked her velvety black fur and the crooked white blaze on her nose. She didn't appreciate it one bit and complained whiningly, trying to free her claws from my protective grip.

Trofimovna bent low over the lake's edge in our yard, washing the winter's dirt from her clothes in the sun-warmed water. She sprinkled some gray powder on the gray clothes and rinsed them in the lake. Then she wrung them out and put them in her washbasin to carry home, where she hung them over the fence. She stopped for a moment to look at the low brick walls and foundation of Igor's house-in-progress. She seemed to be trying to make sense of the strange structure, contemplating what use it could possibly have and what motivated us to build it when we had a perfectly good wooden cabin next door.

I watched her go as I gathered radishes and cucumbers from the garden to make *okroshka*, a refreshing cold soup of chopped vegetables in a base of the birch *kvas* we had collected in spring.

OKROSHKA

4 medium potatoes,
    boiled in their
    skins
4 hard-boiled eggs
1 chicken breast or
    similar quantity
    of pork or beef,
    cooked

5–6 radishes
2 medium cucumbers
1 small onion
1 C. loosely packed, chopped
    fresh dill, parsley, and
    chives, combined
Salt and pepper

Peel the boiled potatoes and eggs once cooled. Finely
chop the vegetables (except for the radishes) and the eggs
and meat. Slice the radishes into rounds. Mix together.
Add salt and pepper to taste. Spoon into soup bowls and
pour enough *kvas* over it to nearly cover the mixture.
Top with a dollop of sour cream or mayonnaise. You can
buy *kvas* in specialty stores or make it from birch juice or
water with fermented bread.

I sat drinking tea with Olga Ivanovna in her two-room log
cabin. I had brought a bouquet of flowers from the meadow to
learn their uses. She had been one of several medicine women
in the village, although some believed she was a witch.

Are any of these flowers good? I asked.

All flowers are good, she said. You just have to know
how to use them. This one is a tansy, she said, pulling a stem
with bead-size yellow flowers from the bouquet. It is used
for expelling worms from dogs and children. This one with
the purple blossoms is wild thyme. It calms the nerves. This
one is milfoil, with the tiny white flowers. It is for women's

problems. St. John's wort is an overall immune builder. I also collect birch and pine buds to make an infusion for an antiseptic and cure-all. And I use flowers of the linden tree to help cure bronchitis and other ailments of the lungs.

I was trying to file the uses of the plants away in my brain when we heard the gate to the yard open. A man walked by the front windows to the door.

His grandfather is the one who stirred up trouble for my father, she whispered to me, back in the time when the *kulaki* (rich peasants) were persecuted by the Soviets and the poor.

The short, stout man walked in the door without knocking, as is the custom, and said hello to Olga Ivanovna.

Zdravstvyui, Vasily, she answered, using the informal version of hello.

He nodded in my direction in greeting, surprised to find the old lady had company. He said he had just come from the graveyard, where he had been tidying up his father's grave. Beads of sweat stood out on his forehead. His clothes were dirty and old. He remarked that there was hardly a trace of the house next door where he grew up. It had disintegrated from age.

Olga Ivanovna nodded and inquired where he was living now. He said that he was planning to move from Smelizh to an apartment he obtained in Suzemka.

How do you obtain an apartment these days? she asked, surprised at his good fortune and choice of words.

Previously, one could "obtain" an apartment through connections to the Party or one's place of employment. But those days were over.

People, he said, people make things happen, and he shifted his eyes to the floor.

Money, I thought. He means money.

During the Communist campaign to collectivize agriculture, a Party Commission first came to Olga Ivanovna's house in 1930 to seize her family's money and belongings. She was nine years old at the time. Throughout Russia, Stalin was confiscating the possessions of rich and even not-so-rich peasants and forcing them to join *kolkhozy* (collective farms), a process called *raskulachivanie* (a term meaning the demise of a class of rich peasants called *kulaki*). A *kolkhoz* was being organized in Chukhrai, but, suspicious of its intentions, none of the villagers chose to join. The Communists persecuted the better-off peasants—*kulaki*—for refusing to work on *kolkhozy*. The poorest peasants—the *bednyaki*—were encouraged to make allegations, often false, against their more prosperous neighbors so that the state could label them *kulaki*, with horrendous consequences.

Olga Ivanovna's father, Ivan, was a storekeeper as well as a farmer and was reasonably well off, with three horses and six cows. A poor peasant named Aleksei (the grandfather of the man I had just met), who held a grudge against Ivan, falsely accused him of charging rent to his suppliers for selling products in the store.

Shortly thereafter, three men from the Communist Party Office in Suzemka marched into Ivan's house, kicking open the door. One man tore down the icons hanging in the corner of the main room and smashed them under his heel. They said they were confiscating the family's belongings to pay the fine being levied against Ivan. The men took one of his horses and four cows.

Three days later, the Party Commission was back with new allegations and penalties. They took the remaining horses and cows. They packed up the family's pots and pans and stuffed clothing and coats into burlap bags. They took everything and gave the family twenty-four hours to pay the fine and buy their belongings back. Otherwise their things would be sold or given to the *bednyaki*—the poor, or the idle and lazy, as Olga Ivanovna called them.

The *bednyaki* met secretly in the village to decide who to punish next. After one such meeting, a woman came to warn Olga Ivanovna's family that they would be targeted again. Olga Ivanovna's mother gave the woman some of their remaining clothes, asking her to hold them.

Soon the house was completely empty, with nothing but the four walls, Olga Ivanovna told me with tears in her eyes. They took everything. All we had was what we had managed to hide with sympathetic neighbors.

Bogus accusations and fines were levied against other families in the village, and people were stripped of their belongings and livestock. If a family stood out from the other villagers in any way—with a bigger house, more cattle, or nicer clothes—they were targeted. Some villagers escaped the plundering by abandoning their land and fleeing. Once the Party Commission took your belongings and you had nothing more with which to pay, they would take apart your fence, your barn, or your house.

The villagers could do nothing but start anew. Olga Ivanovna's family wove *lapti* for shoes and fashioned barrels and sleighs from wood to sell at the market in Trubchevsk. They saved enough money to buy a cow in 1931, the year the Great Flood submerged Chukhrai. The flood swamped the fields, and the villagers could not plant their crops. The year 1932 brought more bad weather. It was cold and rainy all summer, and come fall there was no harvest to reap. Most of the villagers had no livestock, money, or food reserves as a result of the Communists' plunder.

THE STORKS' NEST

So they starved. Nearly half the people in Chukhrai died of starvation in the winter of 1932–33. Some exchanged their clothing and shoes for bread in town, going barefoot and wearing rags rather than starve. Others combed the meager town markets for leftovers: a discarded leaf of cabbage here, a rotten potato there. Those who still had cows or horses ate them. People were bloated and swollen. They ate whatever they could find in the forest and in the fields and walked miles to find the last reserves of edible plants. Olga Ivanovna remembers helping her mother collect the beadlike seeds of the sugarberry plant. They would dry them, crush them, and use the powder in place of flour to bake tiny loaves of bread. They collected cattails, splitting the leaves to extract the white phloem, then cut it up like pasta and boiled it.

In 1933, Party officials renewed efforts to organize the villagers of Chukhrai into a *kolkhoz*. Olga Ivanovna's father was reinstated and, ironically, named chairman of the collective farm. Five households in Chukhrai joined that year. The next year the *kolkhoz* brought in a good potato harvest and the carrots were as fat as beets. All the families in Chukhrai but four joined the *kolkhoz*. The famine was over, but the land now belonged to the state.

The villagers of Chukhrai never knew that their suffering was part of what would be known as the Artificial Famine, organized by Stalin to force the peasants into the collective farms. Even in the Ukraine, where the harvests were bountiful those years, Stalin took the food for export or distribution in the cities, and more than 2 million people in the countryside starved to death.

The white stork pair on the willow in our yard welcomed four downy chicks into the world. After more than thirty long days of incubating the eggs while waiting unflinchingly under the hot sun and pelting rain, the storks' efforts had finally paid off. The parents traded off hunting in the shallow waters along the lakeshore for fish, frogs, and other delicacies to feed their hungry clutch. They dribbled water collected in their throats into the gaping beaks of the chicks. When it was hot, they showered the water on the chicks' backs and spread their wings to create shade. I was fascinated by the storks and closely observed their behavior. I sat for hours on the narrow deck skirting our *banya* taking notes in a little field book: how long each parent was away, what they brought the chicks to eat. Moosik dozed at my feet, occasionally plunging into the lake to cool off. Every now and then, one of the storks would fly over my head, carrying a branch in its long beak. It affixed the branch at an awkward angle on the edge of the nest, forming a kind of toddler rail to keep the callow chicks from falling.

While the storks fortified their abode, we began to fortify our own. Igor renewed construction on the house and welcomed my input. I didn't think beyond the part that we were building a house together. Someone once told me that if a couple can get through building a house together, they can get through anything. I was happy that we had few conflicts in this infant stage of our relationship.

Taking advantage of the fact that the road from Smelizh to Chukhrai had dried, Igor brought in a truckload of bricks. We unloaded the bricks one by one and stacked them near the foundation. He hired a bricklayer named Misha from Trubchevsk to help lay the walls of the house. The brick-layer came for two weeks, living in the small room off our entryway until the bricks ran out, as it was too far to return home each day. I fed Misha three meals a day. Misha would give half his food to Kisa, as he loved animals. He had three dogs and fourteen cats at home, all strays he had picked up on the street.

At first I resented being tied to the kitchen during bouts of construction and vented my frustration on Igor, who would return to the house exhausted at the end of the day. He was patient and understanding, explaining that my job was perhaps the most important contribution toward building the house. This pacified me somewhat, but I was relieved when he offered to help peel potatoes or wash the dishes. I offered to carry bricks in return. We hugged each other tightly, glad that one of our first arguments was easily diffused.

Igor hired Vasily the Forester from the other end of the village to mix cement for $2 a day, good pay in the village, where no other employment was available. The work was hard and tiring, and the only rest came during lunch.

After lunch, sometimes Igor would stay with me for a spell. We would crawl into the eagle's nest to talk or cuddle, then nap. I often woke to find Igor staring at me.

What? I asked.

I love to watch you sleep.

Do you want to have more children? I asked him one day. I mean, you already have two sons.

I want to have your children, he replied.

Why?

I want a little girl, he said. So she'll look just like you.

In the afternoons, I would take Orlik for a ride to the river or to look for the bison. Sometimes I cleaned the house or did laundry in a basin in the *banya*, hanging the clothes out to dry in the sun. When the bricks ran out, Misha went home, and I was glad for the break. The walls of the house now stood nearly four feet above the cement-and-stone foundation.

Vsevolod Stepanitsky, the head of the *zapovednik* system in the State Committee on the Environment, whom I had come to know through my work at WWF in Moscow, invited Igor and me to go to South Africa as part of a group of Russian reserve managers. The group would tour the country's national park system, looking for ideas to improve Russian *zapovedniki*. I was to be the translator. Igor and I shared a desire to explore parks and wilderness areas in different parts of the world. He had been on two national park exchanges, to Yellowstone in Wyoming and Denali in Alaska, before we met, and I had visited many of Russia's *zapovedniki* as part of my WWF duties. This was our first trip together, and our excitement was building as the departure date drew near. But leaving was difficult with the large number of animals to tend to, all of which had to be trusted to someone else's care. We had the moose, the three cats, two dogs, two horses, the owl, and the chickens—about a dozen last time I counted, although their numbers gradually diminished as chicks fell prey to the occasional swooping hawk.

Moosik had grown noticeably stronger and bigger in the short time he had lived with us. He was five inches taller and his legs were more muscular. His head now reached up to my chest. He needed to forage for food ten hours a day to get enough nutrients. He mainly ate the tall reeds along the lake, willow twigs and leaves, and dried alder leaves from branches Igor pruned in spring, but he would sample just about anything. Once a day he trotted up to his favorite muddy spot near the lake and stuck his nose in up to his nostrils. Making a loud slurping sound, he came up chewing a mouthful of mud. He must have needed minerals or salt from the soil. His staple, however, was still cow's milk, which he would need to drink until he was about four or five months old.

We asked Igor's younger brother, Dima, then twenty-four, who lived in Bryansk with his wife, Vita, and three-year-old son, Nikita, to care for Moosik and the rest of the animals while we were in Africa. Dima was launching a film studio to produce nature documentaries, so he was happy to spend time with his camera near the reserve. I cut Moosik's feedings down to three times a day to make caring for him easier.

I explained everything to Dima, and I had him feed Moosik and the other animals the two days before we left to make sure he knew what to do. I showed him the bag of treats hanging on the kitchen door to give to Trofimovna in exchange for milk.

We departed for South Africa, first taking the train to Moscow and then flying to Amsterdam, where we transferred to a plane to Johannesburg. I was sad to leave Moosik behind. I worried less about Orlik and the other animals. We spent two weeks in South Africa traveling to six national parks. We had a wonderful time observing and photographing elephants, giraffes, rhinos, and learning about that country's park system. At one park, the rangers reenacted a raid for us while decked out in uniforms and guns. A wild ostrich nearly mauled Igor in the parking lot at another reserve, annoyed that Igor wouldn't stop trailing it with his camera. I often thought of getting back to Moosik. I imagined how we would drive up to the house and I would jump out of the jeep and run over to his barn calling his name, hoping that he hadn't forgotten me.

Finally, we arrived home and found Dima in the yard. Moosik was nowhere to be seen.

Dima, hi! Is everyone alive and well? Igor asked.

No, Dima replied glumly.

I felt my heart jump into my throat.

Who died? Igor asked, his voice cracking.

Moosik.

Tears welled up in my eyes. Igor remained calm, but I could see he was trying to control his emotions. I collapsed on the grass in a heap.

No, it can't be, I wailed.

Then I cried while Igor held me. It's not fair, I said. He was so young.

Igor tried to soothe me, telling me that these are the laws of nature. Some make it and some don't. Moosik wasn't supposed to live after his mother was shot.

Remember all those impalas we saw in Africa? he reminded me. Thousands of them are killed each year by lions and leopards. You don't feel sorry for them, right? And what about the mice that your cat kills and brings home for us to feed the owl. What about them?

He was right, but my heart was heavy. This was Moosik. Not some field mouse or African impala. I was devastated.

I looked up and saw the shed where he had slept, the lake where he loved to swim, and the reeds he loved to nibble. I covered my face with my hands.

Igor asked Dima what happened.

He said that about halfway through our absence, Trofimovna had refused to give him milk for the baby moose. She said that she had mated her cow with a bull, and tradition calls for abstinence from milking the cow for three days afterwards. But even five days later, she would not give Dima milk. I realized that Dima hadn't given her the treats I usually offered. I felt sick to my stomach when I closed the kitchen door and saw the bag of cookies I had left for her, still bulging with the treats.

After Trofimovna had refused to give Dima milk, he rounded up milk from four different cows in the village. The concoction had been fatal for Moosik. His stomach had bloated and crushed him from the inside. If there had been a vet, or even a phone, the problem could have been resolved. Maybe some spiteful local resident had poisoned him, as Dima had even taken milk from the old poacher Shamornoy. In any case, Moosik had suffered for two days and then died. The worst part for me was that Moosik was already eating grass and twigs. In theory, he could have survived without milk. Dima buried him just beyond the paddock fence. The postlady's granddaughter brought flowers to the grave. I had traded Moosik for Africa. I regretted we had ever left.

In July it was almost unbearable to be outside at midday due to the heat. Our only relief was the rain, which occasionally poured from thundering black clouds, accompanied by flashes of lightning.

The villagers mark the Orthodox holiday Ivan Kupala (John the Baptist Day) on July 7, the day the prophet was born. In the Russian countryside, it is considered a sin to work on religious holidays and Sundays. No laundry or cleaning for the women. No hitting anything with a hammer or chopping wood for the men. Most of the men in the village find these holidays, which seem to come several a month, a good excuse to get drunk.

Within a week, the villagers celebrate Petrov Den (St. Peter and Paul Day), although not like they used to. Before the war, the entire village reveled on this day, dancing and singing. The men rigged up a revolving wooden wheel, called a *reili* from the Old Russian verb meaning "to soar." It had four wooden seats, each holding two people, hung at opposite ends of two sets of long beams affixed at right angles. The whole contraption rotated around a crossbar resting on high wooden posts. Two men stood below and pushed the seats up and over the crossbar with long poles. For only two eggs to compensate the men for their troubles, one could take a ride on Chukhrai's own Ferris wheel.

I was surprised to learn how devoted the villagers of Chukhrai were to the Russian Orthodox faith, considering their many pagan beliefs. Igor said they had kasha (porridge) in their heads. They mark church holidays and, at the same time, revere shamans and good and evil spirits in the forest. They believe that nymphs lived in trees and mermaids in the river. Over time, pagan rites have even worked their way into celebrations of Orthodox holidays.

On the eve of Ivan Kupala, for example, it is local tradition for the brave to venture into the woods after midnight in search of the flowering fern. This special kind of fern supposedly blooms once a year and very briefly, only for a few seconds. The person who finds the tiny flower immediately becomes omniscient by virtue of a divine imparting of knowledge.

Olga Ivanovna told me how a man from Chukhrai went into the woods on his horse the day before Ivan Kupala. He lost his way and even his horse in the forest. He fell asleep, and that night a fern flower bloomed and fell into his shoe. When he woke up, he knew where his horse was and the way home. He could hear what his family was talking about at home. Upon his return, he took off his shoe and the minute flower fell out. Suddenly his afflatus vanished and he turned into the simpleton he had been before.

The villagers would attempt to collect the elusive oil of ants on the same night the fern blooms. Before the sun rose on Ivan Kupala, ants are said to roll a ball of oil to the top of their anthill. Once the sun is up, the oil melts and is impossible to gather. The villagers believed that whoever succeeded in gathering the ant oil would be blessed with eternal health.

Despite the Soviets' efforts to stamp out religion and pagan beliefs in the countryside, centuries-old traditions held fast in Chukhrai. Considering religion a tool of the exploiting class, the Soviets tore down churches, burned Bibles, and persecuted worshipers. Religious repression was particularly great during the purges of the 1930s. Yet many villagers feared God's retribution more than the Soviets', believing that those who helped destroy churches would suffer terrible fates as God's punishment.

Following the demise of the monastery at Staroye Yamnoye, where the ranger station stood today, the nearest church was in Krasnaya Sloboda, eight miles from Chukhrai. The villagers went to that church to mark important religious holidays. In the early 1930s, Party officials ordered the church destroyed. The building was taken down, icons smashed, and Bibles burned. Soon after, the man from Krasnaya Sloboda who toppled the bell from the bell tower started barking involuntarily like a dog. He couldn't say more than three or four words without barking. The townsfolk nicknamed him "Gafkula" (barker). One day Gafkula slit his own throat. Sixty-five years later, his family was still suffering. His daughter died at the age of fifty of alcohol poisoning. Her husband drowned drunk, with his head in the river and the rest of him in a boat. Their son died that summer in a car accident, and his brother was nearly killed along with him. The local people believed it was God's will.

Centuries-old churches were destroyed in Trubchevsk as well, but two were left standing: Trinity and Srechensky cathedrals. The villagers of Chukhrai used to hear the bells of the Church of Egor ringing all the way from Trubchevsk, about twelve miles as the crow flies, before it was taken down and a public *banya* built in its place. In Chukhrai the villagers clandestinely celebrated religious holidays. On Easter they gathered in the house of the woman known as Stepanovna, who used to live next door to Igor. There they would pray and sing. But if the head of the village council caught them, he sent them home, threatening to report them to the Communist Party Office in Suzemka.

July 14, 1997, marked the ten-year anniversary of the Bryansk Forest Zapovednik. We organized a celebration, inviting the reserve staff and supporters from Suzemka, Trubchevsk, and Bryansk. I had a carpenter build two picnic tables by the pond near the *zapovednik* office for the event. The women from the accounting department and the secretaries laid out a huge spread of food on the tables. We made *shashlyki* (shish kebabs) of mutton over a fire pit. Stepan, the postlady's husband from our village, played the accordion while people danced.

Igor beamed. He proposed a toast to the black stork. We all wouldn't be here, he said, if it weren't for the black stork.

He was being modest. We all knew we wouldn't be here if it weren't for Igor.

Igor discovered his first black storks in 1975. That summer, as a teen, he stumbled across a pair of large black birds feeding in a remote swamp during one of his frequent explorations of the woods around his home. The birds' long legs and beaks were bright red. They resembled the white storks he had seen nesting on telephone poles in villages and towns but were slightly smaller and all black except for their white bellies. Igor told townspeople about the strange bird, hoping they might help him identify it, but they only accused him of seeing things. In the school library, Igor found the bird in a field guide. Black storks, he read. The black stork was yet unknown to the Bryansk Province. He learned that the rare bird lived only in mature, isolated forests surrounded by impenetrable swamps and that it wintered in equatorial Africa.

Igor collected everything he could find on the subject, filing papers and handwritten notes into a special folder. Sadly, most of his notes were about black stork nests toppling from trees that had been logged or about birds that had been shot. One man bragged about making a delicious soup out of a black stork he had killed. Igor was determined to find more of the rare birds. He sketched a map of the forests and swamps within walking, boating, and hitchhiking distance from his hometown of Belaya Beriozka, dividing the southern tip of the Bryansk Forest into quadrants. Spending all his free time, and sometimes truant from school, he combed the forest for black stork nests, walking through each quadrant noted on his map. During the next four years, he found nothing that resembled the massive nests of the black stork he had seen in books. He feared that the black stork had disappeared from the Bryansk Forest forever.

In the summer of 1980, Igor—then twenty—bought a rubber boat, sewed a tent, stocked up on film and supplies, and hitched a ride to a corner of the woods that remained blank on his map. The Nerussa River, surrounded by impassable swamps and old-growth oaks, meandered through this part of the forest. He made his way slowly downstream, camping out on the banks and exploring inland woods and swamps. One evening, as he was looking for a place to camp, he came across a deserted cabin on the bank of the river. An unkempt apple orchard stood in front of the house and an abandoned garden stretched out back. The windows, doors, and anything else of use had been carried away. As it grew dark, he climbed up into the attic and unrolled his sleeping bag. Later Igor would learn that, two centuries earlier, the Staroye Yamnoye Monastery had stood on this secluded spit of land.

Igor camped in the attic for the rest of the summer, exploring the surrounding woods and swamps. He lived mostly on apples from the orchard, fish he caught in the river, and mushrooms and berries from the forest. On one of his forays, he wandered for the first time into Chukhrai, less than two miles from the cabin and on the other side of the river. The villagers gave him milk from their cows and vegetables from their gardens. They told him they had seen the black bird he described planing in the sky high above the village. One day at the end of August, as he packed his boat to return for his last year at a teaching college in Bryansk, he spotted three black storks flying overhead. Buoyed by the sighting, Igor returned the next year to the small forest village of Novenkoye, only six miles from the cabin, to teach Russian language and literature to elementary students in the small village school and continue his search for the black stork.

Black stork populations were declining worldwide, and the species had disappeared altogether in much of Western Europe. Extremely cautious birds, black storks only nest in isolated areas far from humans. They require old forests with large trees to support their massive nests, which they reuse from year to year. Their nests can stretch five feet across and weigh more than four hundred pounds. Throughout Europe and Russia, logging was leaving few such trees. The birds feed on fish, frogs, and aquatic invertebrates found in shallow wetland areas such as those along the Nerussa River. Many of these wetlands were being drained for farming.

Igor moved into the forest cabin, even though it meant he had to walk six miles to and from the school to teach every day. He organized a photo club at the school and took his pupils with him into the woods to photograph wildlife. After work and on weekends, he explored the area around the cabin. One day in 1982, he investigated a swamp only half a mile from his home. Half swimming, half crawling, he worked his way across the mucky bog onto a small island of alder trees. There he spotted a large nest high in the crook of one of the alders. He recognized it as a stork nest because no other birds in the Bryansk Forest build nests so large. Overwhelmed with joy, Igor hopped a victory dance right there in the bog with mosquitoes swarming around his head. That very day, he found a second black stork's nest in a giant pine tree.

Igor began to write about his findings in what was then the only newspaper in the Bryansk Province: the *Communist Bryansk Worker*. Under the title "Letters from the Cabin," Igor wrote of the endangered black stork and the significance of the Bryansk Forest for saving it. He described threats to the forest and its inhabitants, illustrating the effects of logging, hunting, and wetland drainage with his photographs.

I fear the Bryansk Forest is turning into a factory for peat and timber production right before my eyes, he wrote.

Igor called for the creation of a nature reserve to protect the Bryansk Forest and save the black stork. In 1983, Igor's "Letters from the Cabin" won first place in a national nature journalism contest, and the *Bryansk Worker* received an award for supporting environmental issues. At the newspaper Igor befriended a journalist, Alexander Nestik, who later became its chief editor. Nestik fought alongside Igor for creation of a protected area, writing articles to complement Igor's and joining him in meetings with Party officials. The newspaper's editorial office received hundreds of letters from its readers in support of their proposal. They called on the regional Communist Party leaders to stop the destruction of the Bryansk Forest and create a protected area.

One morning in the spring of 1984, a shiny black Volga sedan pulled up to the tiny school where Igor taught and whisked him to the local Communist Party Office in Suzemka. Igor was ushered into a room where the local Communist chief ordered him to prepare for an upcoming visit from First Secretary Anatoly Voystrochenko, the top Party boss in the Bryansk Province.

A week later, Voystrochenko arrived at Igor's cabin.

I read your articles in the newspaper, Voystrochenko said, and I wanted to see what all the fuss was about.

Igor led Voystrochenko through the woods around the cabin and explained the impacts logging, hunting, and wetland drainage were having on the Bryansk Forest and, particularly, on the endangered black stork. Impressed with what he saw and heard, the first secretary invited Igor to make a presentation to other Party decision makers the next day in Bryansk. At the meeting, Igor, standing before an army of burly medal-laden generals and war heroes, nearly lost his voice. Relying on his stash of slides and love for the Bryansk Forest, Igor presented his case. That very day, the administration signed a decree creating a three-thousand-acre regional-level sanctuary.

Igor was put in charge of the newly created sanctuary—with his cabin smack in the middle of it. He invited his father, Pyotr Nikitich, to join him. The two of them fixed up the cabin and each day surveyed the protected lands and talked to people about the new protection regime.

But Igor wasn't satisfied with the small size of the sanctuary. Many of the stork nests he subsequently found were outside its boundaries. He campaigned to create a larger, federal, strictly protected nature reserve, which would earn the Bryansk Forest a place among the country's elite system of national *zapovedniki*. He drew new borders for the proposed reserve, published articles in the regional press, and attended meetings with Party bureaucrats to push the issue forward. He knew that the federal status of *zapovednik* would not only guarantee greater protection of the Bryansk Forest but would also provide better funding opportunities for conservation measures.

In 1987 the federal government in Moscow approved Igor's plan for creating the Bryansk Forest Zapovednik, nearly ten times bigger than the original sanctuary. Igor became the reserve's first director. At twenty-seven, he was the youngest director of the then more than seventy *zapovedniki* in Russia. He was also the only non-Communist director in the country, unheard of at the time, but a reflection of political changes taking place in Russia under Gorbachev's campaign for economic restructuring (perestroika) and openness (glasnost). Nevertheless, Party officials constantly pressured him to become a member of the Communist Party.

Gorbachev is promoting pluralism these days, he told them. I am a pluralist.

The Communists had killed Igor's great-grandfather, along with millions of others. He would not become a Communist.

At first, local decision makers and industries were not prepared to support the new reserve. Just days before the *zapovednik*'s charter was brought into force, in July of 1987, the Trubchevsk state logging enterprise catapulted its six logging brigades and all of its heavy machinery to the very heart of the planned protected territory to log old-growth trees that would soon be off limits. Ten years later, I could still see the bands of birches and other secondary growth trees that had begun to cover the wounds left by these clear-cuts.

People living in neighboring villages also resented the new *zapovednik* and its strictly protected regime. They continued to hunt on the protected lands. They fished in spawning areas and disrupted reproduction. They refused to change their ways to honor the newly protected status of lands they had used for centuries. Now this eager young man and his father roamed the forests in camouflage uniforms telling intruders that they were violating the protected regime, taking down their names, and talking to them about saving storks and swamps.

Igor hired and trained some of the local residents as rangers to combat poaching and logging for firewood in the reserve. However, he appreciated the needs of the local people and looked the other way if they cut down a few trees for firewood in the buffer zone, a narrow belt with a lower level of protection encircling the strictly protected core. To build public support, Igor wrote articles in regional newspapers and appeared on television. Soon he was well known in the Bryansk Province, gradually earning the respect of decision makers and the public.

Obstinate poachers tried to outsmart Igor, going out at night or on days when they knew he was away. But Igor persisted, carrying out night raids, lying in ambush next to traps set by the poachers for wild boars. Occasionally, the more aggressive poachers confronted him, pointing their rifles at him or threatening to burn down his house. Igor remained calm and explained that he was hired by the state to protect the wildlife here.

You can hunt a lot of places, he told them, but this is the only place the animals can find respite from your rifles.

Igor had the right to apprehend violators and take their weapons, but, if they promised to abide by the rules thereafter, often he let them off with a warning. Some poachers he would catch over and over, and then he would fine them, turn their rifles over to the police, and take them to court. All too often, corrupt judges dismissed their cases, claiming a lack of evidence.

With money provided by Moscow, Igor hired scientists from other parts of Russia and Ukraine to inventory the nature in the Bryansk Forest and to develop plans for its further conservation. The government paid for construction of an office and housing for reserve staff and helped erect a new ranger station at Staroye Yamnoye on the Nerussa River. But with the fall of the Soviet Union in 1990 and the ensuing economic crisis, state funding for Igor's reserve and other *zapovedniki* began to disappear.

Igor looked further, seeking support from international conservation organizations, a number of which were expanding their activities to the new Russia. Igor found out about WWF's interest in the *zapovednik* system and wrote a proposal to build a visitor's center in the Bryansk Forest. That's how I came to meet Igor in 1993 at our WWF office in Moscow.

A week after we celebrated the tenth anniversary of our *zapovednik*'s creation, two of my four parents arrived in Russia. My mother and father divorced when I was two and my brother, Mark, was one. Mom packed us in the station wagon and drove off the Rosebud Indian Reservation in South Dakota, where we lived for Dad's two-year alternate military service during Vietnam. She headed for Denver to look for a job as a lawyer. She found one, leaving my brother and me during the day with a kindly African American woman named Betty who lived across the street. Betty sewed me my first dress, although later I turned tomboy and refused to wear dresses until I was well into my teens. Mom eventually became the first woman partner in her large firm. After Dad's two-year stint delivering babies in South Dakota, where he developed an interest in cowboy hats, boots, and rodeo, he moved to Denver to be close to my brother and me and became a radiologist at a Denver hospital. He met a radiation therapy technologist named Pat, who treated cancer patients. She became my stepmom when I was eight. Two years later they had a son, my half-brother, Eric. About the same time, my mom met a real-estate lawyer, Chas, who became my stepdad. So I have had four parents for about as long as I can remember. Only in retrospect did I realize how lucky I was. Growing up, there were eight eyes watching my every move and four mouths to reprimand me every time I did something wrong. Then again, my brother and I always had two Christmases and two birthday parties to look forward to each year.

I met Mom and Chas at the Moscow airport in my beat-up Lada car. I had told them casually over the phone how enamored I was of Igor, but when Mom asked if I was seeing him, I had said no, not wanting to alarm her, as I knew she feared that I was becoming too entrenched in Russia.

We stopped at a traditional Russian restaurant for lunch, and I broke the news.

I didn't tell you the truth about something, I said. I'm seeing the reserve director, Igor. We're in love.

My mom's jaw dropped. She hardly said a word for the rest of the day. I took them around Moscow, to the Kremlin and the Pushkin Museum. She was silent, introspective, so unlike her usually cheerful and positive personality.

The next day we drove eight hours to the Bryansk Forest in my Lada because my parents wanted to see the countryside. As the old white car vaulted over potholes and bumps on the highway, I had to reassure Mom that the ten-inch hole in the floorboard under her feet wouldn't suddenly yawn open and dump her onto the road.

Mom smoothed her short red curls and Chas dragged a comb across his windswept gray hair as we drove up to the *zapovednik* headquarters. Igor met us outside, smiling. Mom and Chas were polite but reserved. After getting settled at my old house in Beriozovka, we took an evening stroll in the woods with Igor and collected mushrooms. Igor showed them animal tracks and identified some of the trees.

That evening Mom and Chas were wary when I served them a plateful of the savory fresh mushrooms we had collected, on a bed of rice. But they ate the meal graciously and were notably pleased to discover that they were still alive the next day.

Igor and I took them by boat to Trubchevsk via the Nerussa River, inviting Igor's son Petya to come along. At one point Petya, wanting to test his developing muscles, offered to demonstrate a new wrestling move he had learned on his father. Igor complied. But when Petya painfully twisted Igor's left arm, Igor sharply turned the steering lever on the boat motor with his right. The boat abruptly scooted in a tight circle, nearly throwing my mother overboard. Her sunglasses sank slowly to the bottom, reflecting the light as they went.

At the end of their stay, I accompanied my parents to Moscow to see them off at the airport. As we stood in line for customs, I tried to crack Mom's firm exterior to learn what she was thinking.

Isn't Igor great? I asked.

He appears to care for you a great deal, Mom said. But I'm concerned that he's so well established here. Clearly, his roots are in Russia and he can't just pick up and move with you to America.

I suppose I will have to stay then, I replied, if I want to be with him.

That's what worries me, Mom said.

I began to understand her reservations. My parents had always eagerly supported my desire to explore other countries and immerse myself in their cultures, first with language-exchange programs as a teen in France and then in my career in Russia. I knew they were proud of my accomplishments and respected that I had created a niche for myself. Yet somehow they had always assumed that my Russia phase would come to an end and I would base myself in the United States, close to them, and not thousands of miles and ten time zones away in the Russian countryside. I supposed every parent must harbor such fears. On the one hand, my parents had always pushed me to find my flying wings, but never did they realize I would soar so far from their nest to build my own.

We exchanged hugs, and they proceeded through customs and on to passport control. I felt a tightening in my chest as I waved to them over the shoulder-high barrier. Then

I found comfort in the thought that we would see each other in half a year's time, when I planned to visit them in the United States.

I wished my parents were still in Russia to enjoy the succulent wild strawberries that came to fruit in the fields around Chukhrai the following week. I scoured the meadow for the berries, their bright red hue disclosing them under dense green foliage. Young trees now flourished in the fields where the *kolkhoz* crops once grew and cattle grazed. Soon the meadows wouldn't be recognizable as fields at all, but would blend in with the surrounding floodplain forest, changing slowly in succession from birch and alder to oak and linden.

I continued on to the river, winding through the fields and woods, wading through puddles, and sinking deep into the mud in my rubber boots. Along the way, I glimpsed roe deer bounding away and a wild boar crashing through the undergrowth. I took delight in every encounter, every brush with wild nature. The boars made walking through the fields difficult. Under the cover of night, they dug for roots, upturning clumps of grass and clods of dirt for hundreds of yards. Recently the boars had become bolder, encroaching on the village while we slept to dig for roots along the dirt road. Because Chukhrai is situated in the *zapovednik*'s buffer zone, where hunting is prohibited, the animals had nearly lost their fear of humans in the ten years since the reserve's creation.

I sat down on a log on the riverbank and watched the water flow by. A layer of cottony willow fluff clung lightly to the surface, buoyant seeds drifting downstream to find a place to take root. While I was at the river with my mind on fluff, Igor received a call over the radio at home. Andrei, the ranger responsible for the bison, was calling: Forest Five answer Forest Six. Forest Five answer Forest Six.

Igor's call name was Forest Five. Andrei reported that he heard a gunshot in the reserve and, when he went to check it out, from a distance he saw Shamornoy, the notorious old poacher, with one of his sons skinning what appeared to be a young moose. Their black mare stood nearby. They were on the dirt road that ran along the northern border of the reserve. Andrei was hiding in the bushes some distance away, waiting for help to arrive.

Igor was hastily saddling the gray mare, Aza, when I walked in the gate from the river. I asked him what was going on.

Stay on the radio in case I need you to call headquarters for reinforcements, he called to me.

I yelled to him to be careful as they scampered away.

Igor reached the place from which Andrei had radioed him in twenty minutes at a steady gallop. Andrei walked out of the woods to meet him. Shamornoy and his son were rolling up the hide of the skinned animal with the bloody side facing out. Igor jumped off the horse to seize the evidence.

Wait! It's not what you think, the poacher's son pleaded.

Igor grabbed the hide and unrolled it. The skin was not from a moose at all, but the remains of the little black filly that their mare had given birth to early that spring. They had butchered the baby right in front of its mother. They said they were going to sell the meat to a sausage factory.

When Igor came home and relayed the story to me, I thought back to how the filly had made friends with our Aza. She roamed free with her mother around the village and would come to our barn to visit Aza every day. I tried to pet the mother, but she was old and had clearly been abused, and she shied away. I coaxed her with oats and eventually she gobbled them up, probably tasting the treat for the first time in her life.

The old poacher's real name was Mikhail Presnyakov, but the villagers called him Shamornoy, a name he inherited from his father. Shamornoy was tall and extremely thin. The wrinkles on his aged face formed deep crevices, and his eyes were a colorless gray, washed out from time. He was eighty-seven years old, but strong and healthy as a bull.

His house was old and run-down, despite the ornamental wooden casings his sons had recently hung on the windows facing the road. It was the first house we passed on the right as we drove into the village from Smelizh, while our house was the last. We were as far apart in the village as we could be, which suited both him and us. His was the third house he had built in Chukhrai. Log cabins were not as resistant to the weather and to the years as the old man.

His wife had passed away only recently. She had been sick and immobile for more than five years. He always accused her of faking illness, and he remained unsympathetic to the end. He wouldn't let her go to the hospital for treatment. Let her die at home, he said.

Shamornoy and his wife raised five sons and three daughters. Some had moved to Bryansk, others to Trubchevsk or Suzemka. Often his sons visited him to poach game in the woods around Chukhrai. Shamornoy was too old to hunt or fish much himself nowadays, but when he was younger, he poached to supplement his diet and his income whenever he could.

Shamornoy was seventy-seven when the Bryansk Forest Zapovednik was established and Igor made director.

The reserve border passed less than a mile from Chukhrai, encompassing his favorite hunting grounds. Shamornoy submitted petitions with false signatures demanding closure of the protected area. He sent them to the regional authorities and to Gorbachev's administration. Ultimately, Igor was asked to respond.

Igor explained to the old poacher and his sons why the forest and its inhabitants needed to be protected. He said that people had access to hunting grounds in 99 percent of the extensive Bryansk Forest, but the animals could find refuge only in the 1 percent protected in the *zapovednik*. He told them about the rare black stork that nested only in isolated areas, many of which were protected in the reserve. He spoke of the wolves, the lynx, the moose, and the deer that would come to the reserve to breed and find sanctuary each year, their progeny eventually spilling over into areas where hunting was permitted. Finally, Igor told the old poacher about his efforts to work with children in the region, including Shamornoy's own grandchildren in Trubchevsk.

Shamornoy didn't want to hear any of it. He was certain that government officials had created the protected area to serve as their private hunting grounds. The old poacher wrote to Mrs. Gorbachev, thinking that she wasn't interested in hunting in the reserve and would listen to his plea. Dear Raisa Maksimovna, he wrote, I've written to Ryzhkov, Vorotnikov [naming all the government officials he had appealed to]. I've even written to your husband. But none of them has paid any attention to my request to close the Bryansk Forest Zapovednik. You are my last hope. Please, Raisa Maksimovna, find the right moment. Wait until your husband is in a good mood, and then go to him. Please explain to him that the reserve must be closed. As a postscript he added, If for some reason it is not possible to close the reserve, please ask him to move the boundaries from the Hunchback Bridge to Nikita's Willow Grove where it meets the Sandy Trail. Signed, Mikhail Presnyakov, resident of Chukhrai.

Two weeks later, Igor received a copy of the letter from the government with a request to prepare an answer. He drafted a response and sent it back up the line. In another two weeks, the old poacher received a letter with Igor's text signed by Mrs. Gorbachev herself.

When Shamornoy realized that his efforts to close the reserve had no effect, he came to Igor and offered to make a deal. He would be Igor's covert informer. If Igor let him hunt in the reserve, he would provide information about what other poachers were doing. Igor knew that Shamornoy simply wanted to eliminate his competition. Igor told him that he would not be allowed to hunt in the reserve under any circumstances, and neither would anyone else.

Shamornoy was an experienced informer. In 1937 the political police had approached him just before his discharge from the army. They said that when he returned to Chukhrai, if he heard anyone say anything bad about Stalin or the Soviet regime, he should let them know. They gave him a stack of preaddressed envelopes in which to send his correspondence. To this day, Shamornoy recounts with pride how he used every last envelope. When he had an affair with a woman in the village, he sent a letter informing that her husband had criticized Stalin. The man was taken away to prison and never returned. After Shamornoy argued with his next-door neighbor while they were cutting hay, he sent an envelope with his neighbor's name. The man was summoned to Suzemka and was never heard from again.

Throughout the 1930s and even during the war, all over

the Soviet Union people like Shamornoy were informing on their countrymen. Friends and neighbors wrote denunciations of each other to the secret police, first called the GPU, then later the NKVD, and finally the KGB. Black vans, known as *chornye vorony* (black ravens), swooped down in the night and took people away. The fortunate ones were taken to camps in Siberia, where at least they had a chance of survival. Others were shot on the spot.

Igor's great-grandfather Pyotr lived in the sizeable village of Vitemlya on the Desna River near the border of Ukraine. He was one of the few there who refused to join the *kolkhoz*. Instead, he worked on the railroad. As a result, the state only allotted him one-tenth of the land allotted to the other villagers. But on his meager plot, he grew bigger and better tomatoes than the entire *kolkhoz* could produce. People were envious. His neighbor, Ivan Khonenko, was in charge of the storehouses for the *kolkhoz*, where all the grain and vegetables were kept after harvesting. Pyotr noticed that his neighbor was stealing goods from the storehouse he was supposed to be guarding. When Khonenko berated Pyotr for not joining the *kolkhoz*, Pyotr, in a moment of anger, said to the man, I won't join because you will steal it all anyway.

Still the man harassed Pyotr. Fed up, one day Pyotr said to the man, Watch it or I will inform the police about your stealing.

You won't have time, answered Khonenko.

That night a black raven swooped down and took Igor's great-grandfather away. They never saw him again.

Some time later, when Khonenko was on his deathbed, he called for Igor's father, who is named Pyotr in honor of his grandfather.

I will soon be meeting with God, he said, weeping. Pyotr,

The Storks' Nest

I would like to ask you to absolve me of the sin I committed against your grandfather. I confess. I wrote the indictment against him. I said that he was criticizing the Bolsheviks and the Soviets. That is why the secret police took him away.

Pyotr, Igor's father, grandson of Pyotr, forgave him.

One day Shamornoy came to our end of the village and walked in the door. Knocking was considered rude in the village because it meant that you were a stranger. Even if Igor was his enemy, Shamornoy didn't consider himself a stranger. His face was pale, and he was holding his hands to his head. Igor asked him what was wrong. He said he felt sick and his head was splitting.

He asked if we had any pills to cure him. Igor inquired as to whether he had a fever, and he answered that he didn't know. Igor pulled out a thermometer and told him to put it under his arm. Shamornoy walked out the door.

The next day the old poacher came back with the thermometer wrapped in a white handkerchief.

This thing works wonders, he exclaimed as he walked in the door.

Igor asked what he meant. He said that he went home and put it under his arm and held it there all night. By morning he was cured.

When the grasses grow long and the sun shines, the villagers make hay. All day they swing their scythes, making nearly full arcs around their bodies. The grass falls in neat rows, and soon the open fields around the village are laid flat. The villagers stop only to sip *kvas* and eat *salo* and bread. The women wear white scarves tied tightly around their heads to divert the heat. One cow needs approximately three tons of hay to last the winter. One fit person could make this much hay in approximately twelve days. Hay is usually cut twice: first in July and again in August. About three days after the hay is down, if there is no rain, the villagers help each other stack the dry grasses and compress them into dense piles. The men toss the hay up on the stacks with their pitchforks, and the women trample it with their feet.

With two horses to feed, Igor and I were out in the fields too. We grew tired within a day while men and women twice our age kept at it for two weeks. Their muscles had been trained for this for years. We would buy hay instead.

After haymaking, the villagers washed off the grime in the river. With no running water, most washed infrequently, sometimes in barrels of water warmed on a woodstove. While *banya*s were traditional in northern Russia, they were generally uncommon in our more southerly region. Our sixty-one-year-old neighbor, Kalkan, had probably been clean only a dozen times in his life. The last time he bathed in a barrel, he came down with a bad cold and vowed never to do it again. We invited him to wash in our *banya*, but he refused.

Old Kalinyonok, who lived at the opposite end of the village, wobbled over to our house one day. He was the only one left in the village who still knew how to make a wooden sleigh, and even he said he was getting too old for it. He paused outside the window, calling Igor's name.

Can I take Aza? he asked. I need to bring the hay in from the fields.

His hands trembled and his eyes were bloodshot. I went with him to get the bridle and catch the horse. As we approached the barn, he gently touched my arm to stop me.

Laura, pour me a hundred grams.

I lifted my eyebrows. Doesn't look like you need any more, I said.

Laura, if you don't pour it, I may die.

I was stunned. I wondered whether it was possible to become so addicted to alcohol that if you didn't have a drink, you would die.

I walked back to the house and told Igor that Kalinyonok wanted a drink.

Give it to him, he replied, or he will die.

Igor fetched the plastic bottle of *samogon* we kept in the corner of the kitchen and filled half a glass. I offered it to Kalinyonok with a slice of rye bread. He swallowed the strong drink in one gulp and sniffed the bread deeply, then handed it back to me. He walked out the door and took the horse to get his hay.

On midsummer afternoons, low, dark clouds often rolled across the sky casting a shadow over the land. Lightning bolts flashed from sky to ground, illuminating the dark backdrop. We counted the seconds between the flashes and the roaring thunder. With a drumlike roll, the clouds ripped open and poured sheets of rain on the village, drenching the land, the people, and the storks. Strong surges of wind drove the pelting rain against the windows.

Kalkan is probably under the table in his house across

the way, Igor commented, looking out the window. His roof had been leaking for years, but instead of fixing it, Kalkan crouched under the table when it rained.

We watched as a sudden burst of wind blew the mother stork out of the nest that stood in a tree above our yard. She hovered above the nest, her wings outstretched, as her young crouched low, scarcely holding on. The wind died down as suddenly as it began, and the stork settled back down onto her clutch.

Dozens of baby storks were just blown from their nests all over the region, Igor said somberly, most to their deaths.

The lights flashed, and suddenly the room went dark. The electricity was out, and could stay out. Probably a tree fell onto the power line, which ran along a single row of wooden poles the six miles from Smelizh to Chukhrai. We would have to wait for the electric company to come, which could take days. Or we could try to fix the problem ourselves.

When the rain passed and the dark clouds moved elsewhere, we saddled the horses and rode along the power line. After about two miles, we saw a tall, thin pine leaning on the two wires, pushing them together and short-circuiting the system. Igor untied an axe from the saddle and began to chop the tree at its base. I worried that he would be electrocuted, but I remained silent, knowing that he understood these things better than I. Eventually the tree fell, though a small branch remained hooked on one wire. Then we had to go to Smelizh and turn the circuit breaker back on. We rode down the line to Smelizh, checking to make sure that no other trees had fallen. In Smelizh Igor opened the large metal box holding the breaker and flipped the switch. It held. The line was clear. The extent of Igor's talents never ceased to amaze me.

In the first week of August, I received a call on the radio from the reserve's ornithologist. A black stork chick had been blown from its nest during a storm. He asked if we could please take it in.

We drove to the reserve office to collect the baby stork, which was just over a month old. Returning after dark, we put the bird in a small wire enclosure near the barn. The stork rested on a bed of hay in a large wicker basket. The chick was two feet tall when standing, but mostly it sat on its flexed knees. It had white, downy baby feathers, which were gradually being replaced by thick black feathers with an iridescent hue. In this in-between stage it looked gangly and incomplete. The chick's left wing was broken at the last joint. One leg was fractured below the knee, and the middle toe on the other leg was askew. This chick would likely never fly. It was meant to die, but we would help it live.

The next morning, I went out to feed the animals. The horses whinnied and trotted to the barn, waiting for their oats. The chickens scratched at the ground near the gate, and the rooster crowed. I went around the corner of the house to the owl. He was bathing in the tub of water on the floor of his cage, flapping his wings and splashing. Seeing me, he jumped up on a bar propped across the cage and gingerly took the piece of meat from my hand.

I walked over to the stork with the cats and dogs trailing me. They must have thought I had forgotten to feed them, but I was anxious to see how the newcomer was faring. The chick stood up and let out a frantic, raucous cry, blowing air in and out of its nose and throat, tossing its head up and down all the while. The sound was like the muted honking of geese and was accentuated with each toss of the stork's head. From a bucket I took a small fish that Igor had brought from the

143

river. The chick responded by making quick, recurrent chirping sounds—*deedeedeedeedee*—which seemed to indicate that it was pleased. I held out the fish, and the chick quickly took it from my hand, swallowing it in one gulp. The fish bulged in the curve of its neck before finally sliding down to its gut.

Kisa sniffed at the stork through the wire fence. The chick ruffled its feathers, making it appear larger. Then the chick stabbed its hard, sharp beak into the soft flesh of Kisa's nose, made a shrill growling sound, and clicked its beak. Kisa squealed and gave the bird its space. Not even two months old and this baby could already defend itself. I was amazed at the range of noises the chick could make, considering that adult storks lose their vocal chords and make sound only by clicking their beaks. We had no way of knowing the chick's sex, but we referred to it as a male, if only because the word for stork in Russian is masculine.

After a few minutes, the chick began to honk and toss his head again. For the rest of the day, whenever he saw me walk by he honked and tossed, honked and tossed, every once in a while chiming in with a click or two of his beak. Stork parents must go mad with the racket caused by three or four chicks in the nest, I thought. No wonder they spend most of the day away from the nest when the chicks are this age.

In one short summer I had gone from moose mother to stork mother.

One night Poopah's barking woke me. Kisa joined her from inside the house, and the windowpanes rattled from the racket. I went outside to see what the matter was since I had to pee anyway. Poopah never barked unless it was important. Outside I didn't see anyone, but after a while I heard wolves howling a long, sad melody. Poopah barked in response, the black and gray hair on her back standing on end. I shivered at the howling, though I was glad for the sound since it helped break the silence. Often when I would come out at night, I would stop and stare at the millions of stars in the dark sky and just listen. At first I would hear nothing. Then the silence would start to surround me and fill my ears with a low buzz. The silence was so intense and so complete that I thought I could hear it. As I listened harder, the buzzing would get louder. Maybe it's the engine of a car off in the distance, I would think, or maybe a flying insect. But the silence would keep getting louder and louder, finally buzzing so hard that it was deafening, and my head would begin to spin. My deaf neighbor, Glukhaya, had told me that if it weren't for the loud buzzing inside her head, she might be able to hear.

Do I hear anything at all? I would think to myself. Would Igor hear it too?

I would shake my head and try to hear nothing again. But the buzzing would come back, softly at first, then louder and louder. I wondered where it was coming from. The air? My eardrums? Inside my head? And before I went mad, I would quickly pee, glad for the tinkling sound, and then go back inside to sleep.

That night Poopah's bark broke the silence. I went inside, calling to Poopah to come, but she refused. I put the wolves out of my head and climbed back under the warm covers next to Igor, holding him closely, his back to my belly, like two spoons nested in a drawer.

The next morning when we got up, Poopah was gone. We walked around the lake to look for her. We found her tracks along the sandy shore. Her prints were dwarfed by the giant paw prints of a wolf. One, two, then three more wolves joined the tracks of the first. A few feet away, we found her head. The wolves had killed her while we slept not a hundred yards away. Instead of running and hiding, she challenged them, defending our home and us.

With tears in our eyes, we buried Poopah's head under a small pine next to the house. Igor positioned a large boulder, which he had been saving to adorn the new house, to serve as her gravestone. Kisa sniffed around and helped us shovel the dirt back into the hole.

That day Olga Ivanovna taught me a chant to ward off wolves.

My Grandfather Lazar was good at fending off wolves, she explained. When he was on his deathbed, my mother asked him to teach this chant to her:

> *Saint Egory, take your hounds.*
> *On the sea-ocean,*
> *On a steep mound stands an oak.*
> *Lock this oak with your keys.*
> *Oh wolf Okanye, she-wolf Malaniya,*
> *Wolf Khrom, she-wolf Khovra,*
> *Bind their teeth, lips, claws, nails.*
> *Knock against something with an axe*
> *And the wolves won't kill the cattle*
> *Won't even leave a scratch.*

To round out our days and our diets, Igor and I would collect succulent blue bilberries, which are smaller and tangier than blueberries, and meaty mushrooms in the woods. More accurately, I collected berries and we both collected mushrooms. Igor, like many Russian men, didn't like to collect berries. I admit that berry collecting is a tedious endeavor, one that requires the innate patience we women posses.

I wrapped myself from head to toe and sprayed my hands to ward off the mosquitoes, which were thickest in the cover of the woods. Kisa followed me into the forest, but once he realized I was going nowhere quickly, he abandoned the journey, heading for home with his tail tucked and rubbing his flanks against heather thickets to rid himself of the swarm.

I was on my own. Bucket in hand, I squatted over a berry patch. Virtually the entire floor of the coniferous forest flanking the floodplain was covered with berries, one continuous berry patch. I began the monotonous chore of picking berries one by one and dropping them into my bucket. When I had plucked all I could within arm's reach, I moved a few yards and squatted and plucked. Move, squat, pluck. Once I started picking berries it was hard to stop. I couldn't look at the woods the same way any more. All I saw were berries: big ones, small ones, juicy ones. Berries that needed to be picked and eaten or made into jam. A few berries made it into my mouth, but most went in the bucket, for to eat them I had to push the mosquito netting covering my face aside. As I collected the berries, I advanced slowly across the forest, forgetting to look up to see where I was.

With practice, I became agile and learned to gather the berries quickly. Yet it still took me nearly three hours to fill a five-quart bucket. During these dull hours of dreary berry picking, my mind wandered. I thought back to events that had happened when I was a child. The time I jumped off a fence in the alley behind our house on Locust Street in Denver and landed on a glass bottle with my bare feet. The first time I rode my Pink Panther bicycle without training wheels and begged Dad not to let go. He let go. I rammed into a parked

147
THE STORKS' NEST

car, banging my pelvis on the crossbar. My earliest drinking experience: wine coolers in ninth grade behind a Woolworth's on Colfax Avenue with my best friend, also named Laura. And how a strange but concerned woman drove us home in her Volkswagen bus. The summer in college I volunteered for the Sierra Club in Boulder and paid the rent by working as a carhop on roller skates at the Last American Diner. A string of random events linked only because they happened to me.

I imagined what I would do if I encountered a bear feasting in the same berry patch or a wolf passing on its daily route. I tried to recall the wolf chant Olga Ivanovna taught me. I pictured how I would stand up and wave my arms, shouting in my bravest, most guttural voice, Go Away, Wolf! Go Away, Bear! This is my berry patch! Or what if a viper lurked beneath a fallen log and bit me? Would I have the strength to make it home? If I collapsed right here in this berry patch, would Igor ever find me?

The mosquitoes swarmed around my head and hands. I ceased to notice them. I only focused on the berries and my thoughts. My imagination continued to wander as my bucket filled. I cherished this time of tedious berry picking as much as I loathed it. It was a time for philosophy, for absurdity. After a while, whether my bucket was nearly full or not, I would stand. My back ached. My head spun. My hands and face were swollen where the mosquitoes had penetrated my defenses. I looked around to orient myself. I had wandered far from the path. I found the ball of the sun shining through a thin layer of clouds. I walked toward it. Chukhrai is south. I was sure. Well, not exactly sure. Eventually I emerged from the woods onto the old logging road through the nature reserve. Okay, not Chukhrai, but at least I knew where I was. I followed the road south to the ruins of the collective farm and turned right to Chukhrai. My bucket was full of berries, and my mind full of reflections.

Mushroom hunting is different. Igor and Kisa love mushroom hunting. So do I. We could walk for miles combing forest paths and abandoned logging roads in the pine stands beyond the village. We kept our minds on the task at hand; if our thoughts strayed too far, we would miss our prey. The mushrooms usually sprouted a day or two after it rained, butting their phallic heads through the moss-covered earth.

When mushroom hunting, I don't see berries at all. I see right through them. All I can see are mushrooms, and my heart races when I spot a juicy, young edible bolete with its dark-brown viscous cap perched on a thick white-speckled stump. The bolete is the king of mushrooms, the most sought after in the Russian forest. Cooked, it has a consistency close to meat, with a sweet, nutty flavor.

In my mind, there are three types of mushrooms. The ones I know are edible, the ones I know are poisonous, and the ones I don't know. When collecting mushrooms on my own, I stick to the first kind. Igor knows infinitely more about mushrooms than I do, so with him, we take a wider variety of mushrooms. Still, our favorites are the meaty edible boletes, red-capped boletes, and shaggy boletes. Igor taught me to squeeze the stem to see if it is soft. If it gives under the pressure of my fingers, it has been eaten away from the inside by tiny white worms. If the stem is solid, I cut it close to the ground, checking once again to make sure there are no worm holes. Sometimes the cap will still be okay even if the stem is infested. The small, young mushrooms are the best, as generally the worms have yet to devour them. But they are

THE STORKS' NEST

also the most elusive. Just a curved rim might stick out from under a pile of leaves or a spongy patch of moss.

One day as we were out hunting mushrooms, I noticed a rise in the soil and scraped the old leaves and pine needles aside, revealing a day-old baby bolete. Carefully I cut its stem and saw it was worm-free. I used the edge of the knife to scrape off the sand and tossed it in our basket.

Up ahead, Igor found a colony of chanterelles, yellow funnel-shaped mushrooms with an undulating edge and gill-like folds underneath. I like to collect chanterelles because they grow in large clusters and are rarely infested by worms. We cut the stems, eliminated pine needles and sand, and filled the basket. A moor frog hopped across the moss. I caught it and put it in my pocket for the stork chick. A few minutes later, I checked my pocket and the frog was gone. It had wiggled its way to freedom, not inclined to be stork food that day.

Down the path I found a couple of blue mushrooms. They are easily identifiable because when you cut them or touch them, they turn a beautiful royal blue. Mushrooms sprout mainly where people cut them. Many of the villagers frequented these paths. Some collected mushrooms to marinate for the winter. The village drunks took them to Smelizh to sell by the pound. Sometimes we intercepted them and traded a bottle of *samogon* for their take. In any case, there were always new mushrooms along the trodden paths. When we wandered off the trail to places where people didn't collect them, we would find none, so we stuck to the beaten trails and soon our baskets were full.

At home Igor cleaned the mushrooms, scraping off the remaining debris with a knife and cutting out any parts with worms that we had missed. I took a bowlful and sautéed them.

Once all the liquid dried up, I added some chopped onions. When the mushrooms were cooked through and browned, I turned off the heat and added creamy *smetana*, crushed garlic, and grated cheese. They were delicious. We boiled the rest of the mushrooms in salted water, drained them, and put them in plastic bags to freeze for the winter.

Dad arrived with his knee-high Wellingtons and a suitcase full of fishing gear and instant macaroni. As soon as he could, he organized his tackle, pulled on his boots, and made for the river. He took out his rubber worms and pinned them on the fishing line of his fancy pole. He cast as Igor and I watched. Nothing. Cast. Nothing. Two men from another village were fishing a few yards down the river. They pulled in pike after pike.

Laura, Dad said, go ask them what they're using.

So I walked over to them and told them my dad was visiting from America and he had a suitcase full of rubber worms but the fish weren't biting.

Intrigued, the men asked to take a look. We walked over, and Dad displayed his tackle.

I guess you've never seen such an array of flies, worms, and hooks, I said to them.

Yeah, the fish have never seen them either, replied one. That's why they're not biting. Russian fish need good, simple Russian food. Like Russian men.

The man walked over to a bucket by the shore and pulled out a long, slimy mud loach. Try this, he said, handing it to my dad.

Where do you get them? Dad asked.

The man laughed. From the bottom of my well, he said.

THE STORKS' NEST

Dad took the slimy fish and tried to stick the hook in its back. It squealed so loudly that he jumped and dropped it on the ground. I never knew fish could make such piercing noises. I picked up the fish, and we tried again. This time Dad got it hooked. He tossed it into the river, but in a moment the water was still. The loach had wiggled off the line. The men kindly gave us another. Squeal, toss, wait. Still nothing. We waited for a half hour, then tired. We set the loach free, though it probably wouldn't live with the hole in its back.

That evening, Tonka, the postlady, walked in the door. She had a scarf wrapped from the top of her head to her jaw and under her chin. She broke into tears.

I heard you were a doctor, no? she said to Dad.

I translated. He nodded.

My tooth, she cried. It's really hurting. You have to do something. Can you pull it out, please?

Whoa, whoa, Dad said to me. Tell her I'm a radiologist, not a dentist.

I translated.

So, she retorted. Just pull it out. She opened her mouth and pointed to her aching tooth, the only one in the top half of her mouth.

Laura, get me a flashlight.

I brought one over, and he shone it into her mouth.

Holy smokes, Dad gasped.

Her tooth was so rotted it was hanging by only a skinny sliver. The gum was swollen and probably infected.

I tell you what, he said, here's what I'll do. He disappeared into the small room off the entryway, where he was sleeping, and came back with two bottles of medication.

Laura, I was going to give these pills to you, he said to me. They're general-purpose antibiotics. They're expensive—$90 a pop. But I get them free as samples. Maybe I should give them to her?

Yeah, sure, I said. Of course.

So he explained to Tonka how to take the medication, and I translated.

Take two of these once a day for ten days with food, he said, handing her the antibiotics. And take two of these little orange ones every four to six hours to relieve the pain, he added, giving her a handful of ibuprofen. And call me in the morning, he said, laughing.

She didn't get it and was puzzled by his laugh.

Thanks, thank you so much, she said. God bless you. God bless. I will repay you. I will bring you some *salo* when I butcher my swine, she said to me, if God lets him live that long.

Her Russian was so dialectical, much of it sounded like gibberish to me, but I got the gist.

No, it's okay, I said. Really.

The next morning I tried to get Dad up on a horse. He was the one who taught me to ride, after all. He declined. It had been a while since he rode, since we had our palomino quarter horse, Bree.

After Dad met my stepmom, Pat, while working at the hospital in Denver, they moved to Parker, twenty miles to the southeast. There they had three acres of dry Colorado prairie and a spectacular view of the Rocky Mountains from Pikes Peak to Longs Peak. Dad would pick my brother and me up at Mom and Chas's for weekends and summer vacations. He would coast along the road to Parker telling us we had run out of gas. He said that he wasn't sure we would make it. I

THE STORKS' NEST

believed him every time. I was worried sick that we would be stuck out on the empty road with no gas. But we always made it to the gas station at the bottom of a hill—on gas fumes, he said. Sometimes Dad was called in to the hospital in the middle of the night and he would pack us, still sleeping, in the back of the car and take us back to Mom's.

I loved the big house in Parker, which was essentially a large wooden box with a flat roof. Inside there were multiple levels and railings through which you could look down to other levels. Big windows two stories high in the living room overlooked the rolling prairie and the dramatic mountains in the distance.

The summer I turned nine, Dad built a fence around the pasture out back. He constructed a lean-to and a small corral.

What for? I asked.

Rabbits, he said. We are going to have lots and lots of rabbits. Don't you like rabbits?

I did. But I was concerned that the rabbits could easily get out under the lowest rail of the fence. He assured me he would put chicken wire around the corral later.

My brother, Mark, and I were playing in the yard one day when a truck pulled up with the back enclosed in black plastic sheeting.

What is it, Dad? I asked.

It's the rabbits, he said.

The truck backed up to a low hill, and Pat's grandparents, the Pages, stepped out and opened the tailgate. Out jumped two beautiful ponies.

Surprise! Dad said.

It was probably one of the most thrilling moments of my young life. I immediately claimed the smaller one, the mare, named Mandy. She was dark brown with white patches.

THE STORKS' NEST

My brother got the other one, named Patches, who was light brown with white patches.

Mandy taught me to ride. I taught her a thing or two, too. She could be ornery at times, as ponies are, but mostly we got along. Once I tied her to the boardwalk that led from the garage to the house. She spooked and tore six feet of railing off, dragging it behind her for half a mile. Mandy and I rode all through those hills around Parker, exploring every gully and galloping down every dirt road.

Soon I outgrew my pony. Mark never rode Patches much anyway. We sold the ponies. Dad bought me a quarter horse named Bree from one of Pat's uncles. I started riding in shows. I liked the rodeo events best. I raced Bree around barrels, and we zigzagged through poles. We competed in "reining," where we rode in a set pattern around the ring and performed sliding stops. I won some blue ribbons. When Dad transferred to Scottsbluff in the Nebraska panhandle, he boarded Bree there at a ranch owned by a nice old couple named the Berggrens. They had two grown daughters who were champion barrel racers on the rodeo circuit. I looked up to them as if they were royalty.

I spent every summer vacation riding Bree. I entered shows and joined the 4-H club. I learned a lot about horses. Most of the other kids had cows and other livestock to show, but I stuck with horses. I remember how Dad would hook the pickup to the horse trailer and take me to shows. He disconnected the trailer and left for the hospital. I was the only one there with just a trailer. Everyone else had pickups and parents. Sometimes, if there were no emergencies, Dad made it back from the hospital in time for my events. I won more blue ribbons, and some reds and yellows, too. When I went to boarding school at fifteen, I was sad to sell Bree, but we found him a good home with a cowboy who wanted to keep barrel racing. And I was lucky; the boarding school had a riding program, so I could continue to ride and show.

Come on, Dad. Get up in the saddle, I urged him. Aza's about the nicest horse on earth. She wouldn't hurt a baby.

No, that's okay. Lost the knack.

So I hooked Aza up to the wooden wagon and we went for a ride around the village with Dad proudly holding the reins.

We skirted the fields around Chukhrai and swung around to the other end of the village. There we ran into Tonka, who was helping Stepan bring in the hay from the fields.

How's your tooth? Dad inquired.

I translated.

Still hurts, she said.

Are you taking the pain reliever pills? he asked.

What pills? I don't got any more pills, she cried. I took them all last night!

All? What do you mean "all"? Dad was horrified.

Dad, leave it, I said.

Later we learned she drank *samogon* through the night and took all the antibiotics and ibuprofen pills at once, thinking it might help the moonshine relieve her agony.

And you're not supposed to drink alcohol with those pills, Dad said, shaking his head.

Dad decided to learn some Russian while he was here. He pulled out a little spiral notebook and jotted down some words.

Okay, tell me how to say "hello," he said.

Zdravstvuitye, I answered.

Zrda—what? he cried.

Privyet, I said. That's easier. It just means "hi."

P-r-i-v-y-e-t, he wrote in his notebook.

Okay, how about "thank you"?

Spasibo.

He wrote it down. Now, what about "sorry"?

Izvinite, I said.

And, how about "stupid"?

Glupo, I said. But it's pronounced "glup-a."

G-l-u-p-o, he wrote. I like that one, he said, rolling it off his tongue a couple times. Glooopaa. Glooopaa.

We lunched on instant macaroni from his suitcase stash. Igor said it tasted like the rubber worms.

I think I'll take a walk, Dad said after lunch. He pulled on his rubber boots, because that was what everybody wore in the village, and stuck his spiral notebook in his pants pocket.

Halfway through the village, he ran into Khovryach and Kiset, the village drunks. *Khovryach* is Old Russian for "swine," whereas *kiset* means "a tobacco pouch." They had inherited the names from their forefathers.

Most of the men in the village were occasional drunks, but for these two, drinking was a way of life. Other men would go on binges, but they still had sizeable gardens to hoe, livestock to feed, and wood to chop. These two did nothing but drink and had nothing but the leaky roofs over their heads and dirty clothes on their backs. Everything except drinking was secondary or entirely irrelevant. They once had wives and children, but their families kicked them out and they came back to Chukhrai to drink and live off their old mothers' meager pensions. They were both about forty, going on fifty-five. Kiset had a plastic plate in his head, which had been installed after a metal part flew out of a lathe he was operating and smashed the front part of his skull. With only half a brain remaining, he received official invalid status, which paid him nearly enough each month to buy booze and bread. The rest he took from his mother. Khovryach had also lived with his mother, until she died two years earlier, then he lived alone in her house with a skinny black dog that always came around begging for food.

I often saw the two men on my way to the woods, when they were out walking to clear their heads. Or I would find them lying nearly unconscious in the middle of the rutted road. Once Igor was riding Aza in the dark, and she stopped dead in her tracks, refusing to go forward. When Igor dismounted to find out what was wrong, he found Kiset lying sprawled across the road. We had encountered them many a time walking the road between Chukhrai and Smelizh. Since there were no longer any bootleggers in Chukhrai, the locals went to Smelizh to refuel. When I saw them on their way to Smelizh, they were always walking quickly, one of them holding a cloth bag stuffed with empty plastic soda bottles. If they were on the way back, we nearly ran over them lying in the road or saw them stumbling more or less in the direction of Chukhrai, each holding a half-empty soda bottle of *samogon*. One such time, Khovryach lifted his hand to wave to us and his pants fell around his ankles. Evidently, he had forgotten that his hand was occupied holding up his pants. Another time we found the grubby cloth bag abandoned in the middle of the road with three full bottles of booze in it. In their drunken stupor, they had lost their stash of moonshine. We took the bag home and gave it to them a couple of days later, after they had time to sober up a bit.

Seeing Khovryach and Kiset ahead on the road, Dad pulled out his notebook and quickly flipped to the page with his words.

Privyet. He called out to them.

Zdravstvuitye. They replied under their breath in unison without looking up.

Dad looked to see if he had any other words he could use. At that moment, he stumbled over a hummock of grass and fell face-first into a muddy puddle. Looking up from the puddle, he said, *Glupo.*

The two men didn't even flinch, but just kept walking.

Dad returned soaking wet and related the encounter. We laughed so hard, tears streamed down our cheeks. Dad couldn't understand why they hadn't reacted to his falling into the puddle.

Dad, for them, lying facedown in a puddle is a normal state of affairs, I told him. Seeing you there just seemed natural to them.

By mid-August the flies were gone and the wind swept the mosquitoes out of the village into the cover of the trees. The sun came up early, and the days were warm and long.

Early one Saturday morning, I was lying lazily in bed reading when a call came over the radio.

Beep. Beep. Forest Five. It was the night guard from the reserve office. The Pazhetnovs are here, he said. What should I tell them?

Valentin Pazhetnov and his wife, Svetlana, are to bears what the Horse Whisperer is to horses. They live in the Central Forest Zapovednik in the Tver Province, halfway between Moscow and St. Petersburg. They have been taking in bear cubs orphaned by hunters since they opened their biological station in 1974.

Send them to Chukhrai, I answered the guard.

I went outside to find Igor. He had been up since dawn cutting the grass around the house with the scythe. Our one major difference was that he liked to get up early and I liked to sleep late. To resolve this conflict, I made an effort to get up and get out with him early some days, and some days he kindly let me sleep in.

I was eager to meet the Pazhetnovs, as I had heard so much about them from Igor. We drove down the road from Chukhrai to meet Valentin and his grown son, Sergei. We all got out of our cars. Igor shook their hands warmly and introduced me. Valentin was about sixty-five but looked younger. His expression was jovial, and his eyes glistened. I immediately warmed to him. Sergei was a handsome man of about forty who shared his father's cheerful outlook and passion for bears. We peeked into the back of their truck and saw three low cages, each holding a six-month-old bear cub.

The Pazhetnov family takes in an average of eight to ten orphaned bear cubs a year. When they are strong enough, the bear cubs are returned to the woods. Although releasing ten bears per year in the Tver region where they live probably does not significantly boost the bear population, which fluctuates around two thousand, rescued bear cubs can be released into other regions from which bears have nearly disappeared.

The bear population in the Bryansk Forest had nearly been wiped out by hunting. Probably no more than a dozen bears remained in the region. The previous year, the Pazhetnovs had released two seven-month-old bear cubs in our nature reserve. Now they were bringing three more, in all helping increase the local population by nearly half.

Back at our house over breakfast, Valentin told us the story of one of the bears to be released. Early one morning last winter, Valentin stepped outside and found a tattered burlap bag on his porch step. He picked up the bundle, calling to his wife, Svetlana, and son, Sergei. They opened the bag to find four bear cubs, each smaller than a grapefruit. Only one of the infants showed signs of life. Three had frozen to death during the night, when the temperature dropped to -15°F. Over the next few weeks, the couple nursed the cub back to health. They fed him warm cow's milk from a bottle and gave him medication for his pneumonia.

We took the bear cubs to a pine stand in the middle of the nature reserve. Looking around, Valentin and Sergei decided that the place was suitable for release. We unloaded the cages from the bed of the truck. Sergei opened one cage and grabbed the bear by the scruff of its neck. He lifted it out. It must have weighed twenty-five pounds and was squirming and scratching its handler. Sergei took a yellow tag from his pocket and used a special hole puncher to put the tag through the cub's ear. The cub squealed, then was set free. He scampered a few feet away, then turned around to look at Sergei and Valentin, the only parents it ever knew.

Shoo, Sergei shouted, waving his arms.

The cub bolted into the woods. Soon the two others followed. They were free to roam around their new home in the protection of the nature reserve. The Pazhetnovs departed as unexpectedly as they arrived. Still bears to care for back home, they explained.

A few days later, I was scouring the woods near the release site, hoping to find signs the cubs were adapting. Within a half mile of the spot, I heard the cracking of branches and shuffling of leaves. I quickened my pace and caught a glimpse of a bear cub with a yellow ear tag scooting away. I followed. I could see by the tracks that the three cubs were still together. I caught up to them within a hundred yards, just in time to see them scaling a tall pine. They shuffled up the trunk with amazing speed and hung their bodies over the crooks of branches near the top. I waited, but soon realized that the cubs wouldn't come down until I left. The Pazhetnovs had trained them well. I headed for home with the picture in my mind of three baby bears hanging like decorations in a tree. Christmas in August.

The white storks departed from the willow in our yard. I had watched the chicks as they learned to fly. First they practiced flapping their wings gently in the nest. Then they jumped out one by one, soaring on a maiden flight across the field, landing a few hundred yards away, free of the cramped nest for the first time. They returned to the nest at night, but spent the days with their parents hunting for food and training for their long flight south to Africa. The entire family would fly in a broad circle high up in the air, higher than the highest clouds. I could barely pick them out as tiny dots circling in the sky. Then they glided lower and lower and landed in the nest to rest before trying again. They must have been training their muscles and their lungs for the long migration south.

Then, one day in the third week of August, they were gone. They left no note, no forwarding address. Just flew away and never looked back. Their parents led them to warmer climates in sub-Saharan Africa, where they would bathe in sunshine and have plenty to eat all winter long. The adults would return the next year, but the chicks would stay in Africa until they were two or three years old and ready to mate. Then they would revisit Chukhrai and nearby villages, seeking an empty nest in which to raise another generation of white storks.

Only our recuperating black stork chick remained. He had molted, shedding his baby fluff for a glistening topcoat of black feathers with snow-white feathers on his underside. He had gained strength and his bones had healed, though not properly. He was not meant to spend the winter in Russia. But he would, in the henhouse with our chickens. I pitied the poor bird. He followed me around the garden as I harvested, piercing the soil with his beak looking for worms or slugs.

My tomatoes were sweet and juicy, the potatoes were plump, and the cabbages formed tight heads. I collected basil and tied the stalks in bunches, then I climbed the ladder to hang them in the attic over the *banya* to dry. On the way out, I noticed a wasps' nest. Three angry wasps bit my leg and, in my haste to get out of there, I fell down the ladder to the ground, catching myself in a clump of prickly nettle.

For the first time in my five years in Russia, I decided to can vegetables for winter. I longed to be like resourceful Russian women who pull jars of vegetables and fruit preserves from endless supplies in their cellars in the middle of winter when it seemed that there was nothing more to be had. I thought of how proud Igor would be to have an American girlfriend who could make pickles. Cucumbers and pickles are as much a staple of the Russian diet as potatoes. I asked Igor why cucumbers were so popular.

Because we never had bananas, he joked.

I laughed. While the relation to cucumbers may have been in jest, Igor explained that he really didn't have bananas growing up. The first time he ever tried a banana was when he was thirty. Now he could eat a dozen without pausing.

Making up for lost time, I supposed.

So why is there such a fascination with cucumbers and marinated vegetables in Russian cuisine? I wondered. Perhaps the reason is that cucumbers are one of the few vegetables that grow without hassle in the short Russian summer. And like *bliny*, they are very versatile. They can be eaten fresh, chopped into salads, marinated, or pickled. They are an irreplaceable accompaniment to vodka. The cupboards may be nearly empty, but as long as there are pickles, *salo*, and *samogon*, guests will be happy. A good homemaker will have endless stores of each.

I collected a pail of cucumbers and a dozen red chili peppers. Igor's mother had given me a pickling recipe. After soaking the cucumbers for an hour or so and cutting off the ends, I boiled water and sterilized the jars. I added the cucumbers, peppers, spices, and herbs to the jars and poured boiling water mixed with vinegar, salt, and sugar into them. I sealed the jars with a canning tool that swivels around the tops and pinches the lids closed. I was finished. I was triumphant.

Kisa barked as Olga Ivanovna walked in the door.

Come in, come in, I said. I just finished canning some cucumbers. I swelled with pride. I was one of them. I had heroically pickled my own cucumbers.

But Laura, she said, today is Spas (Feast of the Transfiguration). It's a sin to do any housework today or cut anything with a knife or sew with a needle.

Homemaker I may have been, but good Christian I was not. I sighed.

It's okay, she said. You didn't know.

We sat down to have tea. Olga Ivanovna said she had collected her cucumbers from the garden but was waiting until after the holiday to can them. She related how once, many years ago, she was out in the garden collecting cucumbers when she heard a moaning cry beyond the fence. She grabbed the scythe standing by the gate and walked out. Thinking it was an injured young moose or boar, she called, Well, well, go ahead and cry. Now I will do you in with my scythe and we will have meat for dinner. She swung her scythe in the direction of the sound, slicing through the tall grasses as she went. When she reached a rotten stump from where the sound had come, she found only a small snail slithering out of a hole. Soon she heard the cry again from a nearby bush. She realized the sound wasn't made by an animal, but by a person, perhaps a woman, groaning. She swung her scythe in the direction of the bush, but again she found nothing. The sky was as black as night in the direction of the sound. In the other direction, it was light as day. Frightened, Olga Ivanovna ran home. Back at the house, a forester and his mother came visiting. Olga Ivanovna told them what she had heard.

The forester laughed and said, A bird probably scared you off.

But his mother said, No, not a bird. That must have been the wood nymph giving birth. You probably frightened her, the woman exclaimed. Once, old man Martin went to the woods and saw a baby lying on a log, mosquitoes piercing its naked skin. He tore the sleeve off his jacket and wrapped it around the baby. Before he reached the road he met a woman, who took the baby from him. She asked how she could thank him, whether he wanted riches or health. Well, old man Martin lived 104 years. He had met the wood nymph and saved her child. She had rewarded him with a long, healthy life.

By the end of August, tart cranberries ripened on mossy hummocks in the swamps. I put on my hip boots and headed to the nearest swamp to collect the berries to make cranberry juice and to freeze. As I walked down the now familiar logging road, I listened to the sounds of the forest: the creaking of tall pines as they swayed softly, the wind whistling in their crowns. Fearing the wood nymph might be near, my senses were acute. I crept silently though the trees. I jumped when a louse fly landed on my nose. The louse fly was a new pest in the woods, appearing only at the end of summer. The little fly landed on me and stuck with the force of superglue. Once it landed, it shed its wings, a mechanism evolved to ease its movement through animal fur. In my hair, the bugs crawled around, hugging my scalp. Usually I could feel them, but I couldn't catch them in the thick of my locks. When I pinned one down, I got my fingers around it, then slowly worked it out. Sometimes only parts would come out, and I would have to wash the rest out at home. Igor's father would shave his beard and head each August just to make it easier to remove the flies after patrolling the reserve.

I walked along the border of the nature reserve until I came to a swamp. I looked only to the right, not wanting to be lured by the forbidden fruit on the left, in the reserve. I thought back to the first time I saw Igor in Moscow, when he showed me the picture of the women with buckets of cranberries stolen from the capercaillie. I looked around for signs of the birds and, finding none, I kneeled on the soft pillow of moss. Water seeped up from the bog, but my knees were protected from the moisture by my thigh-high rubber boots. I plucked the tart berries from a hummock and tossed them into my bucket, and my mind began to wander. I walked a few feet to the next hummock, and my leg sank into the soft

THE STORKS' NEST

bed of moss up to my knee. I took another step, and my other leg sank to the top of my boot. I panicked, recalling a story by Prishvin called *The Sun's Pantry* about two orphans who were nearly swallowed by a bottomless swamp. I quickly lay down, soaking my elbows and shirt in the damp moss.

Like the bog in the story by Prishvin, the swamp where I lay had been slated for peat extraction. In the 1980s, bulldozers carved canals to straighten meandering streams through the bog and allow drainage. Tractors slashed gaping wounds to exhume the peat. Careless workers threw cigarette butts into the peat, which burned for days, months even. Peat takes hundreds of years to form: vegetation, after soaking up the warmth and energy of the sun, dies and rots, compressing into thick layers of black humus, called peat. Rich in nutrients, peat makes excellent fertilizer. But it is also the foundation on which a bog exists; the rich, firm mats of peat support plants, shrubs, and trees in an otherwise nutrient-poor habitat. The vegetation then flowers and fruits, which in turn supports insects, birds, and other wildlife, all the way up the food chain. Swamps are also an important natural filter, sieving water as it drains from the fields and forests into the rivers and eventually to the seas.

A bulldozer's sharp blade can undo centuries of Mother Nature's handiwork in a matter of hours. Such was the case in Horse Swamp just before the Bryansk Forest Zapovednik was created. Tractors gutted a canal right down the center of the swamp for drainage. A road was built along what now formed the northern border of the reserve atop a long dam, which directed the water toward the river. Igor and his father worked surreptitiously to try to counteract the destructive processes. They would hire the same tractor driver charged with carving the canal during the day to plow the earth back into place at night.

Fortunately, with the creation of the reserve and the economic crisis following the collapse of the Soviet regime, plans to extract peat in the area were thwarted, though parts of the canal and road were constructed nonetheless. In the decade since, beavers had plugged the canal in places, reconstructing the natural flow of the meandering stream through the swamp. Igor had also taken a shovel to the dams in several places, carving gullies for the water to roll along its ancient path across the floodplain.

With my face firmly planted in a carpet of sun-warmed peat that had averted extraction, I considered my predicament. If I stood up, I would surely sink. Maybe not entirely, but enough that I might not be able to work my way out. Slowly, I crawled over to the nearest hummock and pulled myself up out of the moss. A dead birch jutted from the grasses on the mound. I knocked it down to form a bridge across the swamp to the next hummock. I gradually made my way across the slippery narrow log, placing one foot gingerly in front of the other. I hopped onto the next hummock and from there jumped to dry land near the path down which I had come. I jogged home to Igor as quickly as I could, with only half a dozen cranberries rolling around the bottom of my bucket and my heart still thumping from nearly being made into peat fodder.

Having gathered all we could from the land for the cold months ahead, we were afforded a short rest. The villagers sat outside on benches in the evening watching the sun set.

I walked over to Trofimovna and asked, What's your favorite time of the year?

Ahk, they're all bad, she said, shaking her head. The work is never done.

Alas, summer was over shortly after it had begun, with barely enough time from frost to frost to reap a meager living from the land. Soon, the only reminder of summer's warm days and green grass would be the jars of cucumbers and tomatoes I'd pull from the root cellar hidden under our kitchen floor in the dead of winter.

FALL

IN SEPTEMBER the nights turned chilly, while the days still clung to summer's warmth. Early in the morning, a thick fog blanketed the fields around the village, and only the treetops pierced its downy white veil. The grasses were still green, but patches of dry vegetation capped low hills. Only the cabbages, beets, and a sprinkling of herbs persevered in my garden, impervious to frost and the icy-cold mist. Soon they too would be turned into marinated cabbage and borsch.

School began for the only child in the village, a ten-year-old boy named Dima, son of our resident forester, Vasily, and his wife, Tatiana. The Forester walked his son to the school in Krasnaya Sloboda—eight miles away—two or three times a week. Sometimes they skipped a day. A week even. The tiny school had more teachers than pupils, yet even their combined effort left the children with only a smattering of knowledge.

One day I was riding Aza back to Chukhrai with a sack of bread from the small store in Smelizh when I saw Dima perched in the crook of a tall pine.

What are you doing up there? Where's your dad? I called to him from below.

Bursting into tears, he said, He's still in Smelizh, drunk.

Come on, I'll take you home, I said.

He shimmied down the tree. I helped him climb behind the saddle onto Aza's broad rump.

As we rode home, I recalled a story Olga Ivanovna had told me about another forester's son who once lived in Krasnaya Sloboda and walked with his father to school every day. This forester, Phillip, fell ill one day and couldn't take the boy. The boy walked alone, but, after several days, his mother offered to accompany him to school. Don't worry, Mother, the boy said, the other boys walk me to school.

What boys? his mother asked.

I don't know, he said, but as soon as I leave the house, there they are.

The mother sought advice from the elder women in the village. They told her to have her son give the boys some treats next time he went to school and to ask them about his father. How long would he be sick? Would he die or recover?

The boys took the cakes and boiled eggs she made. The son asked the boys about his father. There is a spring near your house, they answered. Have your father clean it out, fetch water, and tell your mother to wash him in the water three times.

The boy came home and told his parents. The father rose from his bed, finding the energy to clean out the spring and fashion a wooden frame for a well. The mother washed her husband three times in the water, and soon he recovered.

The spring became renowned. The women from the village hung an icon on a nearby tree and went there to pray. Then the chairman of the *kolkhoz* and the school principal plugged the spring with a tractorload of manure, trying to quell the unproductive ritual. The village women cleaned it out. Two days later the principal got sick and wandered into the woods, disappearing for a month. She finally turned up miles away, her mind befuddled. After that she took to drink and was never the same. The chairman of the *kolkhoz* also became ill, and the doctors couldn't heal him. His family took him to medicine women until finally one healed him in the very same spring he had tried to stop. Olga Ivanovna swore the story was true.

Our black stork chick learned to wade in the shallow waters along the lakeshore, poking his long beak into the silt, finding snails, small fish, and aquatic insects. He shivered in the chilly night air, not suspecting that the blazing African sun was meant to warm his feathers. We walled off a section of the barn for him, hanging an infrared heat lamp low over a stump for a perch, and he settled in for the cold months ahead.

Our stallion, Orlik, however, was less docile. He jumped the fence in the paddock and was gone. We knew we would find him with the herd on the Desna and decided to fix the paddock fence before going after him. Igor put wooden rails between the posts above the top wire, making the fence five feet tall. I wound bailing wire around the posts and between the rows of wire to keep them from sagging.

I went inside to make lunch, putting on a big pot of water to make borsch. Since Russians say borsch is best on the third day, I figured we could finish it the next day or the day after, after we'd ventured out to catch Orlik. Borsch, Igor's favorite soup, is hearty and meaty, and slightly sweet from the beets.

BORSCH

1½ lb. soup bones or ribs with ample meat
        (pork, beef, or lamb—I like pork best)
14 C. water
1 heaping T. salt
2 beef or chicken bouillon cubes
2 medium onions
2 medium beets
2 large carrots
3 strips salo or bacon
2 T. vegetable oil
¼ C. tomato paste or ⅓ C. tomato sauce or
        2 very ripe tomatoes
4–5 medium potatoes
1 wedge of cabbage
1 C. loosely packed, chopped fresh herbs such as
        parsley, dill, basil, oregano, and/or chives
        in any combination, or 3 T. dried herbs
2 garlic cloves
Salt and fresh-ground pepper

Wash the meat thoroughly and trim the fat. Place in a large soup pot with the water. Heat on high. Before the water boils (after about 15–20 minutes), skim the scum off the surface with a spoon. When the water boils, add the salt and bouillon cubes. Turn heat to medium-low and simmer for 1½ to 2 hours, until a third of the water has boiled off.

While the broth is cooking, chop the onions, shred the beets on a medium shredder or chop finely, and slice the carrots. Chop the *salo* or bacon (or you can omit this and just use vegetable oil instead). In a frying pan, melt the *salo* in 2 tablespoons vegetable oil. Add the onions and brown them. Add the carrots and beets. Sauté until lightly browned, then cover and simmer on low for 15 minutes. Turn off the heat. Add the tomato paste, sauce, or finely chopped or shredded fresh tomatoes (this is important to keep the beets red). Cover the frying pan to keep warm and set aside. Peel and cube the potatoes. Cut or shred the cabbage into thin strips.

Remove the meat and bones when done from the soup pot and set aside. Turn heat on medium-high and bring the broth to a boil. Add the potatoes and cabbage and cook for 10 minutes. Meanwhile, when cool to the touch, remove the meat from the bones and cut or tear it into large chunks, returning to the pot. Add the beet mixture and cook for another 5 minutes. Remove from heat. Toss in herbs and minced garlic (if using dried herbs, add to pot with beet mixture). Add fresh pepper to taste. Cover and allow flavors to steep for at least an hour. Reseason as needed. Ladle into bowls, garnishing with a dollop of mayonnaise or sour cream and a sprinkling of fresh herbs. Serve with pumpernickel or rye bread.

We each ate two bowls of borsch in the evening and went to bed. The following day was Sunday. We went after Orlik, leaving in the boat after breakfast. The ride through the *zapovednik* down the Nerussa River went smoothly, as Igor wove through the snags. We left the reserve and entered the buffer zone, where we encountered dozens of people fishing along the river, taking advantage of one of the last warm weekends of the year. Fishing is allowed in the buffer zone and other parts of the river not protected in the *zapovednik*, but only with fishing poles and not with electric fishing rods or nets. We came around a bend when Igor noticed an illegal net anchored in a cove.

We checked the licenses of two fishermen downstream who claimed they knew nothing of the net. We returned one hundred feet upriver to another campsite with a car parked next to it. Two dozen empty beer bottles were scattered around the site. Three young servicemen from Bryansk said they were fishing with poles. Igor showed them his badge and asked them to open the trunk of their car. We found nothing.

Igor disappeared into the willow thickets lining the riverbank. Five minutes later he came back holding a net bag containing about thirty medium-sized fish. He dumped the fish out on the grass. Some still flopped around. He found scrape marks on their sides and missing fins, signs that they had been caught with a net. The men admitted that the bag was theirs, heaving sighs of despair. We checked their identification and took down their names. Igor explained that he had the right to levy a fine of one to twenty minimum monthly wages ($15 to $300). He assessed each a fine of two minimum wages, but agreed not to write their names in the citation, as the men would have been dismissed from the army for breaking the law. Igor then went out in the boat to take up their net and found two more. We burned the nets on their campfire.

While sympathetic to the fact that people enjoy fishing and many may even need to fish to supplement their meager incomes, Igor and I knew that those who break the law by using environmentally destructive methods must be punished. Fishing nets trap large numbers of fish and can cause muskrats and other animals to suffocate. Some poachers place nets in fish spawning areas or wintering grounds, important for sustaining and regenerating fish populations. Fishing with electric rods is devastating not only to fish, but to river crabs, insects, and anything else the shock waves reach.

We continued downriver and found another campsite whose occupants had recently fled upon hearing our motor. An illegal net was anchored nearby. I untwined half a dozen fish from the net. Perhaps some would live. Then we cut down the net and burned it.

Half the day was gone by the time we arrived at the pasture where the horses were grazing. We docked the boat at the pontoon bridge. We asked the stable hands from the collective farm to help us round up the herd of horses and run them a mile downstream to a large corral with six-foot-high fences that had been erected only the day before. In the corral, Orlik grew tense, running in circles around the pen, sensing something was amiss. A crowd of Sunday-strolling onlookers gathered.

Two young men wearing only grubby blue jeans entered the corral with a long rope, unafraid that their bare feet might be trampled by the more than one hundred horses. Sensing the crowd rooting for them, they marched bravely through the mud around the corral, shouting at the horses and tossing the rope. A smaller enclosure in one corner fenced off

THE STORKS' NEST

a ten-foot-square section on three sides. They herded Orlik into the smaller pen. He jumped the six-foot fence from a standing position into the open field. The men easily herded him into the corral again, since he was drawn to the other horses that were still there, but they couldn't get him back into the corner he knew was a trap.

The horses and men darted around the corral for half an hour. At times we only glimpsed the men's bare feet among the horses' legs or their muscular chests through arched equine necks. The men made a large loop with the rope, extending it across an area of about five feet. When they forced Orlik to pass between them, he ran into the loop. The first time he leapt right through it. The second time one hind hoof got caught in the snare and, although he bucked and kicked several times, he couldn't free his leg. Finally he calmed down and grew still. I walked up with the bridle, and he let me put it on. We led him out of the corral and put on the saddle. People stared in disbelief.

You aren't actually going to ride that crazy animal, are you? a man asked me.

I thanked one of the young men from the corral for his efforts.

Thank you isn't enough, he replied. You'll have to pour us a drink.

Having foreseen this, Igor had brought a two-quart bottle of *samogon* and cans of smoked fish. He handed them to the two men. They were pleased, and they swigged the *samogon* straight from the plastic bottle.

I mounted Orlik and rode toward the forest. I looked back to see the crowd watching me. I pressed Orlik into a gallop so as not to disappoint them. Later I learned from Igor that the men had a fistfight over who would take the remaining quart of *samogon* home.

On the ride back, I scared up a young moose and two roe deer. I locked Orlik in the barn with Aza, who pummeled him with her rear hooves, apparently angry that he was gone for so long. Later that evening, I let the horses out and secured Orlik with a thick, heavy chain to a stake in the pasture.

My face and arms were bright red from being in the sun all day. Igor's back hurt from the twisted position in which he sat to maneuver the boats. A jump in the lake temporarily relieved our aches and pains, but only a trip to the *banya* and a good night's sleep made us right.

Indian summer, known in Russia as *babye leto* (Old Wives' summer or Indian summer), was upon us at the end of September. The long leaves of the sorrel plants bordering our lake turned crimson. The grasses in the fields beyond formed a backdrop of mild earth tones: yellow, orange, brown. The warm days of *babye leto* beguiled us into thinking summer would remain.

One balmy afternoon, I watched spiders fly. Loosening the strands of their webs from branches and grasses, the spiders waited for a strong wind to seize their web and lift it skyward, like a kite. Dozens of spiderwebs, glistening in the sun, floated leisurely over the house, sailing on uncharted courses to destinations unknown. The autumn flight disperses the young spiders. They float on currents of air and are blown tens and even hundreds of miles away. Alighting in a distant tree or bush, a young spider disembarks from its arachnid dirigible and spins a web to start life anew.

At work I launched the Adopt a *Zakaznik* program to involve regional schools in our conservation efforts. A *zakaznik* is a sanctuary with a lower level of protection than a strictly protected nature reserve, but where destructive forms of resource use, such as logging, wetland drainage, and use of pesticides, are still prohibited. *Zakazniki*, however, unlike *zapovedniki*, are accessible to the public for fishing and hunting during appropriate seasons, and berry and mushroom collecting. In Igor's ten years as director of the *zapovednik*, he and his staff had created eleven *zakazniki*, which, together with the strictly protected reserve, protected a fifth of the Bryansk Forest. Since the *zakazniki* were scattered, the reserve's ranger service could not ensure their protection. I saw a potential role here for the schools, and Igor encouraged me to push ahead.

I met with the biology teachers at School No. 1 in Suzemka and proposed that the school be responsible for research and conservation activities in the nearby Nerussa Zakaznik, on the banks of the Nerussa River, fifteen miles upstream from Chukhrai. The *zakaznik* was accessible by commuter train, just one stop from Suzemka. The teachers embraced the idea.

I produced a color booklet describing the nature and terrain of the *zakaznik*. The booklet also outlined activities the students could undertake, such as watching birds and wildlife, identifying plants, testing water, sampling soil, and cleaning up trash. I explored the area, mapping out a route to introduce the students to the sanctuary.

I arranged our first meeting during the warm days of *babye leto*. The students arrived by train carrying large signs they had painted at school. Two of the signs read Nerussa Zakaznik, Adopted by Suzemka School No. 1. Another read

Picnic Area. Still another described the protected regime of the reserve and asked visitors not to litter.

My assistant, Natasha, and I led the children on a walk around the sanctuary, talking about the forest as we went. Spiderwebs were adrift, and we explained the phenomenon to the group. We passed a doddered oak with holes drilled in its trunk.

Woodpeckers, I said. The Bryansk Forest is the only place where all ten species of European woodpeckers have been found—a woodpecker crossroads, one might say.

Massive oaks surrounded us. The children joined hands and formed a chain, wrapping around one tree. It took six of them to complete the chain. The oaks were several centuries old.

These oaks have been preserved because, until recently, there were no roads into this area, I explained. One of the reasons for the urgency of creating this sanctuary was to protect these trees from logging when the road was built not far from here two years ago.

We passed a fallen oak. I explained to them how the dead tree supported as much life as a live oak. Russian forestry practices traditionally call for ridding the forest of these rotting trees. I told the children how field mice nested in the fallen tree's rotted cavity. Pine martens, polecats, raccoon dogs, and otters could find shelter here, along with countless species of insects. Woodpeckers and other birds feed on the insects in rotting trees. In time, the oak would disintegrate and release nutrients into the soil to be used by future generations of trees.

We came to a lovely meadow with a scattering of old oaks on the bank of the Nerussa River.

This should be our picnic spot, a student exclaimed.

They hammered the post for the picnic sign into the soft earth. Then they sat under an oak tree and ate the sandwiches and apples they had brought in their backpacks.

After lunch we played environmental learning games I had adapted from American textbooks and literature. We pretended to be predators and prey in a game of tag. We fell out of line one by one while pretending to be trees being logged in a forest. We conducted an orientation and mapping exercise. I taught the children that if they were lost in the forest, there were many ways to determine direction even if the sun wasn't out. Moss usually grows on the northern side of tree trunks. Ants construct their hills on the southern side of trees. We showed them how to decode the numbers on posts marking every quadrant of the state forest.

As we led them back to catch the train, Natasha and I explained some of the activities outlined in our instructional booklet to the teachers and students. They vowed to return regularly to inventory birds and plants and to pick up trash. The commuter train paused to collect them from the platform, and we went back to the reserve office.

The next day, Natasha and I wrote an article for the local newspaper on the Adopt a *Zakaznik* program. After the piece was published with pictures we took of the students, Suzemka's other school, imaginatively named School No. 2, expressed interest in adopting a different sanctuary. Soon after, we learned from the students of School No. 1 that the signs they had placed had been knocked down and riddled with bullet holes. Two students then wrote an article in the local newspaper about their role in caring for the *zakaznik* and asking people for their cooperation. I was glad the children had taken their responsibility seriously and hoped others would respect their efforts.

Igor brought Misha the bricklayer to Chukhrai to continue working on the house before the weather turned sour and the road to Smelizh became impassable. It rained the whole week, but Misha didn't mind.

It's better than mosquitoes, he said. Besides, I'm not made of sugar. I won't melt.

The walls now stood seven feet above the decorative waist-high stone border covering the cement foundation. Igor had gathered stones and boulders from far and wide to assemble the attractive hem around the house's perimeter.

Did you know stones sprout from the earth? Igor asked.

Don't hang a noodle on my ear! I replied, using the Russian expression equivalent to Stop pulling my leg.

No, really! You don't see any rocks lying around these parts, do you? That's because the receding glacier left a thick surface layer of sand, he explained. Each year I scour the land and find new stones coming up. Growing, so to speak. As a result of freezing and thawing processes, the stones left as part of the glacial till gradually work their way up from deeper layers, emerging from the earth in the spring when the snow melts.

Rock collecting had become a hobby for Igor. If he saw a large rock jutting from the ground, he made a mental note of its location, then later returned to dig it out and bring it home. If Igor had lived in an area where the ground was covered with rocks, I wondered if he would search for sand or some other rare resource.

By the time the bricks ran out, Misha had completed the walls for the first story of the house. We took him home by motorboat, since Igor wanted to test the new twenty-horsepower Suzuki outboard motor he had purchased the week before in Moscow. He said he needed the powerful

THE STORKS' NEST

but quiet imported motor to sneak up on and catch poachers, who used noisy and slower Russian "Vikhr" motors. We dressed warmly and set course down the Nerussa. Kisa took his place at the bow of the boat, ears flapping in the wind. The waters of the Nerussa had risen slightly as a result of the rain, swallowing many of the snags in the river.

In just over an hour, we deposited Misha on the shore of the Desna below Trubchevsk and waved good-bye.

On the way back, we were motoring smoothly along, navigating the bends in the river to the soft purring of the motor, when suddenly silence surrounded us. We looked at the motor, thinking it had stalled. But it was gone. Instead of a $3,000 Suzuki motor, there was now empty space, in its place only the frayed end of a metal cord: the safety line that was supposed to tie the motor to the boat.

Igor used an oar to turn the boat around and steer us downstream back toward Trubchevsk.

There must be a snag underwater, he said calmly. It caught the motor and snapped it right off.

Igor stabbed the oar into the murky water, feeling for the motor. After a few minutes, he located a V-shaped snag just under the surface. The motor evidently got caught in the snag and popped off, sinking to the river bottom. The oar was too short to reach the bottom, so Igor noted the location and we took turns rowing the boat home against the strong current.

Igor found a large metal hook in the barn and fastened it to the end of a twenty-foot pole. He attached our old motor to the boat and returned to the spot where we had lost the Suzuki, radioing his father at the ranger station for help.

Igor thrust the long pole into the water just below the snag, searching for the motor. After several attempts, he hooked onto something and pulled. By its weight, Igor guessed it was the motor, although it was nearly buried in sand. The motor slowly surfaced. Igor dropped the pole to grab the motor with both hands, but he couldn't lift the 150-pound waterlogged motor out of the river and over the side of the boat. He held onto it, leaning out over the water, while his boat slowly floated downstream. He drifted into an eddy and was carried toward shore. Wild boars descended to the water for a drink. They looked at him curiously, not understanding that the immobile figure in the river was a person. Igor's arms went limp in the cold water, and he dropped the motor into the shallow water near the bank just as he heard his father's boat coming around the bend. The two of them lifted the motor into the boat.

At home Igor found the owner's manual for the outboard motor and flipped to the troubleshooting section. If the motor is submerged under water for any length of time, he read, immediately take it to your nearest Suzuki dealer. That would be Moscow.

Igor took the cap off the motor and drained the water from the carburetor. He fired up the *banya* and stood the motor against the wall near the stove. The new casing was scratched and dented from being stabbed with the hook-topped pole. Two hours passed, and Igor anxiously pulled the cord. Brrrrrrr. It worked. The *banya* healed again.

As the sun was setting one evening, I saw Ivan Mikhailovich, the old man from the other end of the village, walking past our house. He was known as Kudinyonok (small or runtlike), a nickname he had inherited from his stumpy stepfather, Kudik, who came to the village from Smelizh. While not blood kin, Kudinyonok also happened to be small in stature.

185

THE STORKS' NEST

He always wore a dirty wadded-cotton jacket over a button-down shirt so grease-stained that I could only guess at its color. He donned a blackened cap and carried a long stick in one hand. He walked at a fast clip for his more than sixty years, vigorously swinging the stick out ahead, catching up to it in one stride, and then swinging it out again.

At the same time each evening, Kudinyonok came to collect the cows, which usually grazed in the pasture beyond the lake. All the cows from the village remained together, unattended, during the day. In the evening, when milking time came, Kudinyonok shooed them home, lifting his stick high in the air and cursing them: Get on, you lazy old bitches. As he walked through the village, each cow stopped before its own house, waiting for its respective owner to open the gate. By the time Kudinyonok got to his house at the far end of the village, only his two cows remained. He escorted them into the barnyard, where his wife waited with a pail to milk them while his dirty white gelding looked on.

Kudinyonok's house was one of the better-kept houses in the village. There was a flower bed in front with tall red hollyhocks in summer. The windows were decorated with ornate wooden frames, and the roof appeared to be solid, in contrast with the other ramshackle houses. Five large haystacks stood to the right of the house. A three years' supply at least. Next to the haystacks, neat rows of firewood were piled chest high.

I was surprised to learn from Olga Ivanovna that the seemingly harmless and capable old man many years ago had raped a sixteen-year-old retarded girl named Olga. Drunk, he lured the girl into a root cellar, promising her candy. Some-one saw him leading her and called her brothers. They were too late, and he ran away before they arrived. They found him and meant to kill him, but he said that he would turn himself in to the police if they didn't touch him. The brothers sent word for the police, and when the police jeep drove into the village, Kudinyonok lay down in the road, apparently hoping it would run over and kill him. The jeep stopped in time, and the police took him to jail. He received a sentence of fifteen years, which was then reduced to eight because his family brought gifts to the judge. Kudinyonok's wife waited for his release. She said that if the girl was pregnant she would take her in with the child. But she wasn't. Kudinyonok and his wife never had any children of their own.

When I saw Kudinyonok in the village, I would look for contempt or remorse in his eyes, but I saw nothing except the tranquility that came with age. I was certain he had no idea I knew of his crime. Even if he did, would it matter? It was so long ago, and he had served time. The rest of the villagers had accepted his past as part of life, another tale in the history of Chukhrai. They had forgiven him for his moment of weakness, because he was their kin.

Igor and I took the horses for a ride one morning. Autumn leaves wafted from tree to ground, only to be lifted treeward again as we galloped through them. We reached the rickety Hunchback Bridge, its rotten logs arching over a small creek that marked the southern boundary of the *zapovednik*, and slowed the horses to a walk. I patted Orlik on the neck and leaned down to adjust my stirrup. Suddenly, Orlik leapt four feet off the ground. Off balance and unprepared, I flew out of the saddle, first up, then down. I hit the ground hard. I lay there for a moment in a daze, the breath knocked out of me. Orlik stood nearby in disbelief, not wanting to leave my side. Igor, riding thirty yards ahead, turned around and galloped toward us, scaring Orlik, who fled toward home, reins dangling close to the ground.

Can you get up? Igor asked with mounting concern in his voice. He jumped off Aza to lend me a hand.

No. My hip, I gasped. I think I broke my hip.

The last time I hit the ground that hard I was sixteen, riding in a spring gymkhana at my boarding school, outside of Colorado Springs. It was Mother's Day and all my parents were watching. I was on a substitute horse since Tip, the feisty little roan I usually rode in rodeo events, was lame. The mare belonged to Fletcher, the riding master, and had been known to barrel through closed gates and jump over high fences, rider and all. Fletcher was confident I could handle her. In one event, two riders galloped to a barrel one hundred yards away, turned a tight circle, and galloped back to the finish, the fastest horse winning.

For the event, I was placed against Joy, the other redhead on the riding team. The starting gun went off, and each of us raced toward our own barrel, digging our heels into the horses' sides and whipping their rumps with the long reins. As we neared the barrels head-to-head, we pulled up on the reins to slow for the turn. Being left-handed, I kept the barrel to my left and started to rein the mare around it, toward Joy. She reined her horse to the right, toward me. Then my mare took the bit in her teeth and bolted past the barrel, failing to make a tight turn. I looked over and saw that Joy's horse wasn't turning either. In a second, my horse rammed into the side of Joy's also out-of-control horse at top speed.

I was told that horses and riders flew in all directions.

Joy's horse rolled over her. I flew a few yards to one side and hit the ground, landing on my back. I didn't come to for about five minutes, when I heard Dad asking if I was all right. Mom was yelling at him, You're a doctor. Do something! I slowly sat up. Fortunately, both Joy and I walked away from that accident.

This time I couldn't get up.

Igor put his hands under my shoulders to lift me, saying, Try to walk; you can do it.

I couldn't. My left leg didn't work. Pain shot into my hip when I tried to stand on it. I sank back to the ground. Igor's face grew tight with worry. Tears streaked down my cheeks.

Wait here, Igor said. I'll catch Orlik.

I lay on the ground looking up through the crowns of the trees to the sky. Mosquitoes, still numerous in the forest though they had disappeared from the village, swarmed around me. Water gurgled in the creek. Everything was blurry. At first I thought it was from my tears. Or maybe I had a concussion. Then I realized that I had lost my glasses. They must have flown off when I hit the ground. I tried to stand to look for them in the grass. Pain tore up my leg like lightning. I sat back down to wait for what seemed like an eternity.

Igor finally rode up with Orlik behind him.

Do you think you can get on? he asked.

I'll try, I said.

I told Igor I had lost my glasses and asked him to look for them. Igor searched up and down the road and in the grass on both sides. He picked up what looked like a silver piece of rope and brought it over.

Here's the culprit! he cried.

Igor held the limp body of a foot-long, silver-colored blindworm, a species of legless lizard that resembles a snake. Orlik spooked when the creature slithered across our path, jumping up then landing on it and crushing it with his hooves. I patted my horse on the neck and managed to get on him while Igor cradled my leg.

Without pressure on it, my leg didn't hurt in the saddle. I rode slowly home. Igor continued to search for my glasses. I rode up to the door of the house and climbed down on my good leg, tying Orlik to the front stoop. I hopped inside and lay down on the couch. I probed my hip and thigh, trying to figure out what hurt. It didn't feel like anything was broken.

How would I know? I thought to myself. I've never had a broken bone in my body.

Quickly, I pretended to spit over my left shoulder three times, *Tfu, tfu, tfu*, warding off the devil lurking behind who might be listening and turn my thoughts into reality. The Russian custom had become as second nature to me as knocking on wood.

Igor came home without my glasses. I had a spare pair. I told him I didn't think my hip was broken. He asked what I wanted to do.

Don't you think I should go to the hospital? I said.

What's the point? he asked. Do you really think it will help? Although he was sympathetic, he knew that the quality of medical care in the local hospital left much to be desired.

I conjured up an image of Mom's face if she learned I was injured and didn't even see a doctor. I described it to Igor.

Let's go, he said.

We drove down the muddy road to Smelizh, every jolt jarring my hip and making me cringe with pain. At the Suzemka hospital, a long two-story building of gray bricks that were crumbling in places, we were directed to a small room near the entrance.

We sat on a three-legged bench propped against a wall. Half of the lime-green tiles on the wall were missing. The brown tiles on the floor were chipped, and the cracks were black with grime. A bathtub with a rusty hue occupied the center of the room, also balancing on three legs. Beyond the bathtub, a pile of buckets, jugs, and a mop teetered haphazardly in the corner. The room was cold and dim, smelling of bleach.

A tall, somber man walked in wearing a white robe and a high white hat resembling that of a pizza chef. I assumed he was a doctor, though there were no introductions. He asked me what happened, then directed us into another sparse room, telling me to lie on a narrow cot. I slowly slid my jeans down over my hip. He prodded my hip bone and the surrounding flesh. I winced at his forceful touch.

You probably bruised the bone, he said, but it could be a fracture. Let's do an X-ray to make sure. Go up to the second floor and down to the end of the hall.

I limped out the door, leaning heavily on Igor. We walked over to the elevator and pushed the button.

Doesn't work, a woman sitting behind a desk in the entryway informed us coolly.

So I hopped up the stairs with Igor, gritting my teeth as I swallowed the cries I wanted to scream with every step. On the second floor, I skipped for what seemed like a mile down a long, dark corridor. Lightbulbs hung from every third socket, dangling gloomily from the low ceiling. We entered a

THE STORKS' NEST

dark room with only a large, antique X-ray machine in the middle. The doctor was waiting for us.

We should have gotten you a wheelchair, he said.

I lay down on a table, and everyone disappeared when the machine lit up, detonating a blast of radiation over my hip. A woman took something out of the machine and went into the next room, sectioned off by windows. Within a few minutes, the X-ray was ready, and she brought it out to the doctor.

No fracture, he confirmed. Try to stay off that leg for at least ten days, he added. That means bed rest. You can take pain medication.

No money or pieces of paper exchanged hands. I might have said thank you. We left the hospital without wheelchair or elevator. Igor lifted me into the jeep. Knowing I wouldn't lie in bed for ten days, we stopped by the drugstore and bought the only pair of crutches in town, for two dollars.

In a few days' time, I was out and about, having a blast on my crutches. I swung my legs through the aluminum props, nearly sprinting around the yard. I casually leaned into them as I stood and proudly laid them beside me when I sat. When my underarms got sore, Igor wrapped cotton around the hard plastic handles. Igor cooked all our meals and cleaned the house, and I luxuriated in my incapacitation.

One day I was leaning on my crutches in the garden, collecting the last of the herbs to dry for the winter. Trofimovna came through the gate and proceeded to the well to fetch water, as she did twice daily. We had the only functioning well on our side of the village and were happy to share it with our neighbors. She slid the long pole down the shaft with our bucket securely fastened to the end. The wooden pole had been burnished from years of scraping against the side of the well. Trofimovna unhurriedly drew up the full bucket, leaning back slightly, adroitly placing hand under hand on the pole as she lifted while bracing one foot against the side of the well. She poured the water into her own bucket then sent the pole down a second time. She filled the other bucket and, seeing me, walked over to the garden. The skin around her eyes was so wrinkled from squinting in the sun that I could hardly tell if her eyes were open. A white kerchief was tied around her head. She leaned over the waist-high fence bordering my garden, straining her eyes to see what was growing.

What's that? she asked.

Cilantro, I said.

She shook her head, indicating that she'd never heard of it.

Here, try some. I snipped off a leaf and handed it to her.

I don't have any teeth, Lorochka, she said, calling me by the diminutive. But it smells mighty fine, she cooed. That's a mighty fine smell.

Then she looked at me and scrunched her mouth into a worried grimace.

What happened to your leg? she finally asked.

I understood that this was the point of her visit. I told her that I had fallen off a horse, but that I was feeling much better already.

Oiy, oiy, oiy, she said, shaking her head. You had better watch out. Those horses are dangerous. A horse killed my nephew Vasya. He used to live here, in your house, before Petrovich, she added, calling Igor by his patronymic, as all the villagers did as a sign of respect.

His horse hated the smell of alcohol, she continued. One day Vasya was hauling manure to his garden on the horse and cart. He had been drinking. I was milking the cow when my sister ran into the barn, calling me to help. I dashed across the road so fast I didn't even finishing milking. I saw Vasya just lying there. He couldn't move. The horse had kicked him twice in the back. We sent word for the doctor, and he came and took Vasya away. The horse had broken two of his vertebrae. Vasya never got up again. On the seventeenth day, he died in the hospital.

Oiy, oiy, oiy, she said again, still shaking her head. Dumb things never happen to smart people. She paused and let out a deep sigh. You be mighty careful, Lorochka. Those horses will get you every time. My nephew was buried ten years ago today. Wouldn't you know it?

She walked over to the well, picked up her buckets, and carried them away. Slowly, so the water wouldn't slosh over the sides.

I hopped down the road to Olga Ivanovna's. She had just finished eating and paused to cross herself and say a prayer, facing the icons hanging in one corner. The embers in the great woodstove were still glowing, as she had stoked the fire to cook lunch. When she was done praying, I told her how I had fallen off the horse.

You remember the chant I taught you against wolves? she asked. I nodded.

Well, here's one for snakes, she said. You've got to be ready if one bites you or your horse someday.

> On the sea-ocean, on the high hill, there stands an
> oak. On that oak are thrice nine boughs, thrice nine
> knots. Above those knots is the sentinel bed of the
> Virgin Mary herself. On that bed is the Virgin Mary's

bedding. A bed before the Virgin Mary stand three girls,
her own little sisters. They sew, they stitch, they pull
out the needle from the snake, saying: We beseech you,
Archangel Michael. Tell old snake Fenogey and old
she-snake Shkurapeya to calm their ferocious serpents,
their raspberry snakes, blackberry snakes, water and
swamp snakes, their grass, field, wood, and forest
snakes, and their under-the-roofing, behind-the-stove,
under-the-stove, honey, and flying snakes. And if you,
old snake Fenogey and old she-snake Shkurapeya,
don't call off your serpents, then under the linden bush,
under the linden leaf, Archangel Michael will stir up a
violent wind, breaking that bush, beating with thunder,
burning with lightning. And help us, God, to extract
the snake's venom from white body, clean blood.

Say that three times, Olga Ivanovna added. My father-in-law taught me the chant during the war. When it was unsafe to stay in the village, we went to live under the cover of the forest. There he said to me, Young woman, learn to ward off snakes. Anything can happen in the woods.

Tell me about the war, I said after a pause.

What do you want to know? she wondered.

Everything. The war, how you lived in the woods, how you managed afterwards.

Well, make yourself comfortable then, she replied tranquilly. And I hope you have some time.

I sat on a stool next to the stove to listen, staring into the deep orange embers of the fire as she spoke.

Just before the onset of the Great Patriotic War, she began, I had a dream. The wooden chest in my entryway stood empty with the lid open. Clothes and other belongings

THE STORKS' NEST

were strewn about on the floor. I awoke and prodded my husband, Pavel, telling him to go look. He checked and said all was well. I dreamt it again. I woke up and lit a candle to check for myself. Everything was in its place. The next day I asked one of the elder women in the village about the dream. The woman said it meant I would become a widow. I was only twenty at the time, and already pregnant with my second child, so I tried to put it out of my head.

I remember I was cleaning out the grain mill in the field with some other women when a man from the village shouted to us to hurry back. We all gathered in front of the store, where the district policeman from Suzemka awaited us.

I bear sad news, he said. Hitler has attacked us. The war has begun.

It was June 22, 1941, she continued, I was eight months pregnant.

All our able men received notice soon after and were drafted into the Soviet Red Army. Pavel went to the enlistment office and asked to be let off until our child was born. At least until I find out if it is a girl or a boy, he pleaded.

They let him stay until the third and final mobilization, on August 12, when the last of the men in the village—the old, the young, the sick, and even the authorities—were sent to war.

My daughter Nastya was born on July 12, 1941, Olga Ivanovna went on. When Pavel was enlisted a month later, we accompanied him as far as the Nerussa River. Pavel carried our newborn baby on one arm and our two-year-old girl on the other.

At the riverbank, Pavel looked at the baby sorrowfully and said, I wish God would take you from your mother to unbind her hands.

That was the last time I saw him, she said.

I turned from the dying embers of the fire to look at Olga Ivanovna and saw that her face was somber and her gaze distant. As she spoke, I sat entranced, trying to imagine what she'd been through. Over the next couple weeks, I returned each day to hear more of her tale, and I checked out books on the war and the Bryansk partisans from the Suzemka library to fill in the gaps. But it was her story that gripped me most. I wanted more than anything to know what had happened through her eyewitness account.

Olga Ivanovna and the other villagers soon learned that Hitler's army was overrunning Bryansk and the neighboring regions of Orel and Smolensk. By November 1941, the Germans had reached the outskirts of Moscow. Olga Ivanovna remembered that the Nazis first appeared in Chukhrai in the fall of 1941. Three Nazi soldiers came and took a pig from one woman, giving her five German marks in return. But the Nazis did not control Chukhrai or the surrounding countryside. Russians who had been left behind enemy lines, those who had returned home, and boys just learning to fight created a resistance movement. They formed covert partisan groups that moved under the dense cover of the Bryansk Forest. Czechs, Slovaks, and Hungarians defecting from the Nazi army joined them. The partisans raided villages and towns to remove traitors working for the Germans, called *Politsai*.

The Soviet government supported the partisan movement, hailing it as an effective way to fight behind enemy lines in occupied territories. Soviet airplanes flew over the Bryansk Forest at night, dropping thousands of parachutes with sacks of weapons, ammunition, food, and army garb. With support from Moscow and assistance from the surrounding villages, partisans (numbering more than sixty thousand by the end of the war) began to gain control of the Bryansk Forest. They ousted the enemy from significant areas, forcing them from five hundred towns and freeing more than two hundred thousand people by April 1942. They created three partisan-controlled zones in the southern, western, and northern portions of the Bryansk region.

Chukhrai and neighboring Smelizh were at the heart of the southern partisan zone. The villagers assisted the partisans in every way possible. They sewed undergarments from parachutes and jackets from burlap bags dropped from airplanes. They provided food and shelter. Olga Ivanovna recalled how twenty-two partisans spent the night on her floor. She made a pot of porridge to feed them. One was a woman. Another night a group brought a sack of flour and asked her to bake bread.

Hitler announced that any person caught aiding, supplying, or hiding partisans would be executed and all their personal property destroyed. Chukhrai and other villages in the Bryansk partisan zones came under fire. Nazi warplanes flew from the German air base in Lokot, thirty miles away. They flew over Chukhrai daily, each time dropping bombs and perforating the roofs of houses with gunfire. I could still see craters remaining in our paddock from the bombing. They filled with rainwater in the spring, and the horses would drink from them. Igor had found several bombshells on his land. Now the exploded casings lined the stoop by our front door, below a hanging display of other rusted war paraphernalia: a Nazi bayonet, a folding shovel, the blade of an axe. Stepan used one of the hollow bomb casings as an ashtray when he paused on our porch stoop after delivering the mail.

Olga Ivanovna hid with the other villagers in trenches

dug around Chukhrai during bomb raids. The eroded furrows were still visible in the meadow beyond our lake. But soon it became too dangerous for the villagers to remain near Chukhrai during daylight hours. The women took their children and elderly to the cover of the woods before dawn, returning to the village only after dark, stealing out to the garden plots they hastily tended for food. Olga Ivanovna related that one Chukhrai woman was having an affair with a partisan. She would leave her two young children in the woods with neighbors during the day while she met her lover. One evening she fetched the children and headed back to the village before it was dark. The other women begged her to stay, saying it was too early and planes could still fly overhead. She paid no heed and ran across the field to Chukhrai, taking her four-year-old son by the hand and holding her infant on her arm. She made it halfway across the field when she saw the plane. She ducked under a willow tree, but she had been noticed. The pilot directed the plane toward them, firing round after round along the ground. One bullet pierced the four-year-old's heart, killing him instantly, but she and the infant survived.

I learned from Igor that the partisans created a makeshift airfield near Smelizh, providing a connection to the Red Army stationed in areas to the east. He told me how Soviet planes remarkably landed at night in total darkness, carrying supplies and medicine from the east. The partisans lit fires to mark a dummy airstrip in Chukhrai—where our horses grazed. While the Germans bombed the field, riddling it with craters, Soviet planes landed in the dark six miles away, near Smelizh. The planes were quickly pulled under the cover of the trees, where they were unloaded and, if necessary, repaired. Filled anew with the sick and wounded, the planes departed before dawn to Soviet-controlled territory. Despite the harrowing conditions, not a single plane crash was recorded on the Smelizh airfield during the war.

On November 6, 1942, the poet Anatoly Safronov arrived in Smelizh aboard one such airplane. He delivered a song he had written with composer Sigizmund Katz for the Bryansk partisans. They understood that it couldn't be a marching song, because partisans didn't march. Nor could stealthy partisans sing loudly. The result was a song that could be sung softly in chorus, an epic song that would become well known throughout Russia and the anthem for the Bryansk Province. Safronov sang the song that November night for the partisans there to greet him. They cheered and hugged him, begging him to sing it again and again. Which he did.

The Bryansk Forest sternly stirred
A blue haze descended like a veil
And all around the pines heard
How partisans strode down the trail

Down a hidden trail amid the birch
Hurrying through the dense thickets
And swung over the shoulder each
Held a rifle loaded with cast bullets

And in the dark of night to the enemy
To the fascist command they dashed
And bullets between the tree trunks
In the Bryansk oak woods crashed

In the forest the foe finds no shelter
Grenades tear through the trees
And a commander yells to them after
"Smash the invaders, boys!"

The Bryansk Forest sternly stirred
A blue haze descended like a veil
And all around the pines heard
How partisans strode to victory

As the partisans' new war mantra filtered through the Bryansk Forest, the Nazis escalated the bombing in partisan country, demolishing villages and towns. In the spring of 1943, the villagers of Chukhrai abandoned their homes completely and moved to the woods. Olga Ivanovna gathered up her two daughters, aging mother, and in-laws. They made two trips, first taking the infant Anastasia to safety. Her father-in-law helped carry their belongings. They crossed the Nerussa River and found an isolated hummock in the middle of a swamp. They stashed their things and hung the bundled baby in a tree, then returned for the other family members. They set out for the swamp once again, but on their way, they encountered some of the villagers running toward them.

The Nazis are coming this way, they cried.

So they turned around and headed in a different direction. The baby was left suspended in the tree through the night. Worried sick, Olga Ivanovna started back for her child, but her father-in-law said it was too dangerous. The next morning, Olga Ivanovna, learning that the Nazis were gone, went to find the baby. She crossed the river and came to the hummock in the swamp. The bundle still hung from the tree. She hardly recognized her baby. Her face had swelled up like

THE STORKS' NEST

a balloon from hundreds of mosquito bites. Now fifty-six, Anastasia lived in the neighboring village of Smelizh with her husband. I had found her to be warm and welcoming, like her mother; each time we drove by her house, she tried to entice us into her kitchen for a drink of *samogon*.

To escape the Nazi bombardment, the villagers dug earthen bunkers to shelter their families in the woods. They fortified the walls and roof of each pit with logs, shoveling dirt and laying pine bows over the top to camouflage the shelters from above. They stuffed moss into slits and holes to keep the bunkers warm and to muffle the sound of children crying, in case the Nazis came near. They stashed food, weapons, and supplies in pits in the surrounding woods.

Partisans also inhabited such bunkers. Igor had shown me the remains of a bunker off the road between Chukhrai and Smelizh where a printing press was housed and an underground partisan newspaper was published. Another nearby bunker served as a partisan hospital, housing the sick and wounded. In the makeshift hospital, cots were made from poles laced together with twine and covered with beds of moss. Doctors, nurses, and even veterinarians performed hundreds of complicated operations on a square wooden platform in the corner near the door, often without medication or anesthesia. With time these structures gradually decayed, but pits from the bunkers could still be seen in the woods half a century later. The hospital had been restored recently as a historical monument. I had ducked inside many times, and I could not imagine how doctors could have operated and how wounded partisans recuperated in the dark, damp, and dirty quarters.

I learned that as the Nazi and Soviet armies prepared for what proved to be a decisive encounter and the greatest tank battle in history, at Kurskaya Duga (Kursk Arch), about one hundred miles southeast of Bryansk, the Bryansk partisans escalated their clandestine operations behind enemy lines. Coordinating with the Red Army on the front, the partisans derailed trains and blew up railroad tracks and bridges throughout the region, cutting Nazi supply lines.

The Nazis diverted five divisions from the front lines to expel the partisans from the Bryansk Forest. They formed a chain and combed the woods around Chukhrai and Smelizh, where the southern partisan zone was headquartered. The Nazis hoped to push their adversary out onto the open floodplain of the Desna, but the partisans breached the Nazi chain and headed toward the front. The people from nearby villages weren't so lucky and remained within the Nazi loop.

On May 30, 1943, the Nazis rounded up all those found in the forests near Chukhrai, driving them from their earthen bunkers. The people hastily gathered food and supplies. Olga Ivanovna told me how her family hurriedly stuffed food and bank records into a burlap bag. They wrapped extra clothes around their waists to trade for food. Those who had cows took them along. The Nazis herded them through the village and down the road to Smelizh, burning any remaining houses on the way by throwing blazing bottles filled with kerosene into the windows. Anyone who could not keep up with the column was shot.

The terrified villagers spent the night in a field near Smelizh and were joined the next day by more people evicted from the forests around that village. They then trudged the thirty miles to the German base in Lokot, walking in a guarded human column a mile long that continued to grow as they passed each partisan village. They ate raw potatoes and nibbled on flour. Women carried their infants. Older children walked, but none dared complain.

As they left partisan country and passed through a village under Nazi control, people watching the procession cried that the Nazis were executing everyone up ahead in Lokot. When the displaced villagers arrived in Lokot that evening, their captors directed them into a bathhouse where they were to be washed and rid of lice. Men were steered one way and women and children another. Families were split. There was no time for good-byes. The men and women were then driven into separate enclosures with twelve rows of barbed wire. Olga Ivanovna counted them. The Nazis seized their cows and other livestock. They slept on the ground. The Nazis gave them boiled potatoes and water. Olga Ivanovna recalled that when a German soldier brought potatoes, he personally handed them out to each individual. However, when a Russian *Politsai* delivered the potatoes, he heaved the whole pot through the fence. The prisoners shoved each other to get to the food. Children were crushed and smothered.

Sons of bitches, Olga Ivanovna said to me. The Germans treated us better than our own. Well, in terms of food at least, she added.

It was the only time I ever heard her swear.

Soon after the prisoners arrived at the camp, the Nazis ordered all the men and boys over the age of twelve executed. The *Politsai* lined them up along a pit within view of their mothers, wives, children, and grandchildren. The executioners told them, Stand with your own and you'll lie together. They fired from four machine guns. The men folded into the pit one by one. Then they were buried, some still alive. Olga Ivanovna says that the earth groaned and heaved for three days.

After nearly two months in the Lokot camp, the women and children were loaded into eighty cattle cars and taken to

Minsk, in modern-day Belarus. From Minsk, some women were sent to Germany to work in forced labor camps. Olga Ivanovna's cattle car was hitched to a locomotive with a dozen other cars filled with women and children and sent to Ukraine. When the train stopped, a stout German officer announced that they were being sent to work in the *kolkhozy* in Nazi-controlled territory.

Dozens of horse-drawn carts rolled down to the train and took them away. The Ukrainian coachmen told them to make sure they were in the same cart as their kin, or they might end up in different villages.

Olga Ivanovna, her sister, two sisters-in-law, and their fifteen children, along with nine other families from Chukhrai, ended up in a small Ukrainian village called Kruty. They lived in the school and begged for food from the other villagers. For reasons Olga Ivanovna couldn't understand, the *Politsai* collaborators didn't allow them to work in the fields for food. Perhaps the *Politsai* didn't trust them because they were from partisan country. Their only food was potatoes given to them by kindhearted villagers. They cooked them on a fire pit outside the school. One particularly malicious *Politsai* would come by each evening and spit in the kettle. A woman living with them had an infant. The *Politsai* would tear the nursing child away from its mother's breast and spit in its face, saying nastily, That's a budding partisan. The baby died eventually.

Sympathetic to the displaced families, a one-legged accountant at the *kolkhoz* hired Olga Ivanovna to press oil from sesame and poppy seeds at his home. He gave her half a quart of oil a day in lieu of pay. His wife occasionally gave her a loaf of bread, For the children, she said.

Victorious after the Nazi retreat from Kurskaya Arch on July 17, 1943, the Red Army began to push Hitler's troops out of Russia. Suzemka was freed on September 5, 1943. In October, on its push toward Berlin, the Red Army freed the Ukrainian village where the villagers from Chukhrai were living. At last they could go home.

But Olga Ivanovna and the nine other families exiled to the Ukrainian village of Kruty remained there until spring rather than return to the charred remains of Chukhrai and face the winter without a roof over their heads. Twenty-two people lived in a two-room house. They scavenged grain from the silos the partisans had bombed. The bread and porridge they made from the grain reeked of smoke.

In April 1944, Olga Ivanovna and her family arrived by train at Nerussa station, seventeen miles from Chukhrai. They hauled sacks of food to the village, where they found only the burnt timbers of the houses in which they had once lived. Barely visible were the low roofs of root cellars, probably considered by the Nazis too insignificant to destroy. A root cellar, or *pogreb*, is a deep pit fortified with wooden logs in which potatoes and other vegetables are stored for the winter. Olga Ivanovna and her family lived in a dark *pogreb* for nearly four years after the war. Sometimes, for light, Olga Ivanovna would let her daughters soak a cotton thread in vegetable oil to burn for short periods. For heat they stoked a fire on the cellar floor, letting the smoke funnel out the small opening at the top. Most of the time they were cold and their clothes were threadbare.

In those difficult times after the war, the only way Olga Ivanovna and the other women could make money was by selling bundles of bast, the inner bark of the linden tree, used primarily to weave *lapti*, the most common footwear for peasants. Olga Ivanovna would haul twenty bundles of bast on a hand-pulled sled forty miles to the plains town of Pogar, where the linden bark fetched a higher price than in Trubchevsk, which was surrounded by forests. In return, she received seventy pounds of wheat at the market. Just walking there and back, Olga Ivanovna wore out two pairs of *lapti*. Her mother made new shoes for her and prepared more strips of bark to sell while Olga Ivanovna towed the older bundles to market. As soon as her new shoes were ready, she would set out again. As *lapti* are not warm, Olga Ivanovna wrapped her feet in strips of cloth, called *portyanki*, and pulled the shoes over them. Igor used *portyanki* inside his rubber boots. He said he preferred them to socks, as they were warmer and didn't slip down.

It took Olga Ivanovna three days and two nights to walk to Pogar and back. She spent the night in the woods or with kind villagers she met on the way. She gave them one bundle of linden bark in return for a night's rest. More than fifty years later, I saw tears come to her eyes as she remembered the kindness of an old man and his wife who regularly took her in on her journey. They fed her and dried her clothes on the stove. Seeing the rags on her feet, the old man gave her new *portyanki* and a loaf of bread for the road.

In 1945 the *kolkhoz* in Chukhrai was restored, and all the villagers were put to work. The *kolkhoz*'s operation did not prevent a second famine, that of 1947. The harvest that year was poor, and most of the villagers still lived in root cellars and makeshift houses. Fifteen children in the village died that year, including Olga Ivanovna's eight-year-old daughter Antonina. She would eventually give birth to another girl, named Tamara, in 1956, fathered by Shamornoy's youngest brother, who later lost his mind and hung himself.

Still reeling from the famine, the villagers slowly rebuilt their homes. Without transportation or even horses, they could only use materials close to the village. Most of the war survivors who returned to Chukhrai were women, and construction was limited by the weight they could carry. They built traditional-style houses with log frames, but these were made with shorter logs, only as big as three or four women could haul from the forest. For this reason, all the houses in Chukhrai are the same small size: two adjoining rooms, each about twelve by twelve feet. When I first came to Chukhrai, I had been struck by how small the houses were, despite the apparent abundance of land. Only later did I learn this explanation.

After hearing about all that the villagers had been through during the war and the difficult time afterward, I was filled with respect for my neighbors, for their ability to persevere in the face of hardship and tragedy, for their dignity, and for their determination to go on.

By October the grasses beyond our lake turned yellow, the vivid earth tones having faded to the brown and white shades of winter. Kosha continued to bring mice from the field, which we fed to the owl. She didn't bother with the mice that had come into the house in search of a warm place to spend the cold months ahead. We could hear the critters scurrying in the space between the walls during the day. At night they scampered fearlessly about the room, chewing on boards and books. Kosha and Mysha would perk up their ears, but were too lazy to rise from their resting places. Igor set traps in the kitchen, and I would jump when I heard the loud *smack* in the dark. Kisa would emerge from under his blanket in a corner of the room and bark and whine, bullying the prisoner, until one of us got up and set the contraption with the writhing mouse outside on the front stoop, where the tomcat ate it.

One morning Kalkan's nephew Nikolai entered our yard to fetch water from the well. Nikolai, known as "Balyk," meaning "a cured side of meat," had come to live with his aunt and uncle a month before. His wife in Suzemka evidently had grown tired of his drunken ways and kicked him out. Since his arrival, Kalkan sent Balyk to our well for the water, but this was the first time I'd seen him in nearly a week. I heard he had been thrown into the detoxification center when he went to Suzemka to pick up his new internal passport.

I was outside when Balyk came to the well. His hair was unkempt, and his face looked tumid and rumpled. His bare feet were blackened with soot.

I heard you got put in detox, I said. Where did they pick you up?

I turned myself in, he said, laughing.

As it happened, Balyk stumbled into the passport agency at the Suzemka police station, drunk as usual, and the police sent him to detox for five days. There he was assigned community service work, during which he managed to lose his boots. When he got home, barefoot and passportless, his aunt sent him to Smelizh for *samogon* with one hundred rubles ($4) she had borrowed from the postlady. Balyk turned around and walked to Smelizh, where he bought four one-quart bottles. He drank one and started home with the other three. Somewhere along the road he lost the *samogon* and, thinking he had reached home, settled down on what he thought was his broad wooden bench to sleep. He woke up shivering from the cold and climbed up onto what he thought was the stove and went back to sleep. The next morning, Balyk found himself clinging to a pine, wedged in the crook of the tree six feet off the ground. He climbed down and tottered home, only realizing that he had lost the booze when he saw his aunt. So he walked back down the road, found the booze, and returned home. That evening the postlady came to deliver the monthly pensions and settle the debt. She found all three of them, Kalkan, his wife, and their nephew, sprawled on the floor. Not a one was sober enough to sign for the pension money.

The next day, while Kalkan's wife and nephew were nursing their hangovers with the remaining *samogon*, Kalkan wobbled across the way to our house, swinging each of his long thin legs first out to the side then forward. He complained to Igor that he couldn't hear out of his right ear and asked to be taken to the hospital.

Vasily, I am not taking you to the hospital, Igor said.

Igor would never call him Kalkan to his face. Many of the villagers' nicknames were derogatory or had a veiled meaning. Kalkan never actually accepted his nickname. He was a bastard child. His mother's first husband died of tuberculosis. She became pregnant with Vasily after sleeping around, but wouldn't reveal the father's identity. When Vasily was born, everyone said he looked like Kalkan, the stable hand at the *kolkhoz*. So he inherited the nickname. Kalkan is the word for the pine sap that male wild boars rub on their shoulders to form a protective armor when sparring with other males for mates.

Igor knew that taking Kalkan to the hospital would mean leading him around like a child and sitting there with him all day. Rather than do that, Igor decided to try to heal Kalkan himself. He took the big black Russian medical encyclopedia from the bookshelf in our kitchen. It was the kind of book that no matter what ailment you looked up, you came away convinced you had it and, likely, the consequences were fatal.

Foreign object in ear, Igor read to me. Foreign objects in the ear are most often observed in children, who stick various objects in the external ear canal (paper, fruit pits, peas, sunflower seeds, beads, etc.). Adults typically have pieces of cotton, broken matchsticks, etc. Various insects (bedbugs, cockroaches, flies, etc.) can also end up in the ear canal. Treatment: Flush the ear with water or fish out the object with the aid of a small hook.

I don't think earwax is a foreign object, I said. Or is it?

Okay, he flipped the page. Here we go. Earwax plug. Accumulation of earwax in the external ear canal as a result of excess secretion of glands found in the ear. Earwax can build up and cause obstruction because of its viscosity, or the narrowness and sinuosity of the ear canal, or if cement or flour dust gets into the ear. The earwax plug is first soft, then becomes hard, even rocklike. The plug can cause other problems if it puts pressure on the eardrum, such as coughing, buzzing in the ear, dizziness, and even death. Treatment: Flush the ear with warm water using a syringe.

Igor directed Kalkan to lie down on the bench outside. He used a syringe to rinse Kalkan's ear with what appeared to be half a bucket of warm water. Slowly, a wax protrusion began to emerge in the stream of water. Igor continued to flush, and a two-inch-long wax cork slid out.

When's the last time you washed your ears? Igor asked.

Probably the last time I had a bath, Kalkan said, grinning like he always does.

And when was that?

Can't remember, Kalkan replied, pleased as a schoolboy that he could finally hear. He took the plug across the way to show to his wife, but she was too drunk to care.

October 14 in Russia is Pokrov, the Feast of the Intercession of the Holy Virgin. Pokrov and Nikola (for Saint Nikola, celebrated December 19) are Chukhrai's Patron Saint Days. The two celebrations were traditionally hosted here, when Chukhrai was a bustling village before the war, and for some time after. People would flock to Chukhrai from neighboring villages to mark the two holidays. Other villages had different Patron Saint Days: the Feast of the Assumption of the Holy Virgin was celebrated in Smelizh, Ivan Kupala (John the Baptist Day) was held in Yamnoye, and so on.

Pokrov is the most important religious holiday for Chukhrai, and one of the twelve significant Orthodox holidays in the year. According to Orthodox tradition, the Virgin Mary was honored on Pokrov as the protector of the earth and the people. But in rural Russia, Pokrov is largely personified as a male protector, dissociated from its original meaning. Pokrov marks the end of the harvest, when all has been reaped from the fields and the work is done.

The word *pokrov* comes from the word for shelter or roof. On this day, which straddles fall and winter (fall in the morning, winter in the afternoon, the villagers say), snow covers the earth to shelter it and keep it warm in the winter. In the days leading up to Pokrov, the villagers make repairs to keep themselves warm as well, fixing the roofs and caulking holes in the timber frames with moss and clay to keep out winter's chill.

In the olden days, young couples often held weddings

after Pokrov, deciding whether to make them lavish or modest depending on the bounty of that year. It took more than a month to plan a wedding. *Samogon* had to be made, funds had to be collected, a dress fashioned. When everything was ready, the wedding day was set. On the morning of the wedding, the groom went to the bride's house to steal his betrothed and take her eight miles to the church in Krasnaya Sloboda.

Following the wedding ceremony, the groom took the bride to his house, where his parents greeted her with bread and salt, holding an icon. The entire wedding party filed into the house to celebrate. Inside, the hosts hung embroidered cloths on the walls and windows and laid a feast on the table. The bride's girlfriends cut down a small spruce tree to grace the table. They had to chop it down with one blow of an axe; two blows meant the bride would be married twice. The sapling was inserted into a large loaf of bread and placed in the center of the table. The women decorated it with ornaments made of cloth and red berries, to signify the bride's chastity, and the men fashioned candles to illuminate the tree.

While the couple's families celebrated through the night, the friends of the bride put the newlyweds to bed and waited in the next room. The groom had to prove that his new bride was a virgin by showing them her nightgown with blood on it. In the morning, the nightgown was presented to the mother-in-law. If the bride was truly a virgin, her in-laws put *pryaniki* (spice cake) on the breakfast table for her. If there was no blood on the bride's nightgown, the in-laws put manure on her plate and removed the red ornaments from the tree. It is not clear to me what transpired next in this situation and whether or not the wedding celebration continued. I suspect an extra supply of blood was often kept available.

Later that day, at the invitation of the newlyweds, the

THE STORKS' NEST

entire wedding party moved to another relative's house, and the next day to another's, and so it continued, for three days to a week, going from house to house, giving the new hosts time to prepare another feast.

What a glorious occasion a village wedding must have been! I was sorry there were no longer any young people in Chukhrai to carry on the tradition. Maybe Igor would ask me to marry him the old-fashioned way.

After three weeks, my hip was mostly healed. We worked on the house before winter came. Igor asked his father and two others to help lift a dozen iron rails he had found on abandoned train tracks. The rails reached from the top of one wall to the top of the opposite wall and would serve as joists to support the ceiling for the first story and the floor for the second story. Igor placed temporary boards under the rails, supported by posts from below, and covered them with tar paper. He mixed dry cement with sand dug by the river while I pumped water from the well. I helped him spread the wet cement, inserting iron rods to reinforce the bond and smoothing the mixture between the rails with a trowel. When the cement dried, we removed the posts and boards, leaving only the reinforced cement ceiling. We had planned the garage, bathroom, and spare bedroom for the first floor. For the second floor, we planned a living room combined with a small kitchen, a sun room, and another bedroom. Our plans eventually changed and we decided to build a separate garage, freeing up space on the first floor for the kitchen. But all that would come much later. For now, we boarded up the windows and covered the temporary top of the house with tar paper and planks, sealing it for winter.

Liberated from my crutches, I walked to the Nerussa to see if the red and orange foliage of fall still flanked the river. Most of the leaves had fallen, but some still clung to the maples, reflecting gold in the tranquil water. At the crossing to the ranger station, I found willow branches beavers had gnawed strewn along the shore. Impressions along the river's edge showed the beavers had dragged more of the boughs under-water, in anticipation of winter's ice. They anchored them to the riverbed with sand to ensure an ample supply of food for the coming cold months.

That night two of the old poacher Lepen's sons navigated up the Nerussa River from Trubchevsk in a motorboat. His health failing, eighty-one-year-old Lepen had left Chukhrai and moved in with family in Trubchevsk a month before. His sons, however, apparently weren't ready to relinquish the family's poaching grounds. They fired shots at game as they motored upriver. Igor's father, Pyotr Nikitich, heard the gunfire as he was readying for bed in the ranger station. Igor and I also heard the shots two miles away in Chukhrai. Pyotr Nikitich ran to the river with his rifle. The poachers came around the bend in the river and headed for the ranger station. Pyotr Nikitich recognized their voices immediately. They shone a spotlight along the bank and when they saw his face, they fired shots at him. He jumped behind a tree, and the bullets whistled past. The poachers turned around and headed back downriver. The next day Pyotr Nikitich radioed Igor to come see what had transpired in the night. I joined them, and we found two bullet marks in the tree behind which his father had taken cover. We walked downstream and found blood in several places along the bank where the poachers had killed beavers. Even though Pyotr Nikitich had seen the perpetrators, under Russian law, the poachers couldn't be brought to trial without additional witnesses. We were furious and frustrated that we could not prevent this killing. For the week afterwards, Igor and his father waited on the riverbank in ambush nightly, but the poachers didn't return.

Olga Ivanovna and I were talking one day when she asked me if I knew about the hidden gold left by my great-great-grandfather.

What? I asked, stunned. My great-great-grandfather was a slate miner in Wales. I was sure he didn't leave any gold in Chukhrai.

No, not your real one, she said. I mean the grandfather that everyone thinks you're related to. She chuckled, and then explained.

There used to be a house where my kitchen garden grew. An affluent (for Chukhrai) man named Matvey lived there with his wife and children, two sons and a daughter. When the Communists accused him of being a *kulak* and stripped him of his riches, Matvey gave a pot of gold coins to his daughter, telling her to hide it. She buried it in her yard. Ten years later, when the villagers returned to Chukhrai after the war, she couldn't find where she had buried the gold. She eventually moved away, but her son, the drunkard Kiset's father, built a house near the trove. He made wooden barrels to sell at the market in Trubchevsk. He would bury the wood shavings in the yard, digging a new hole each time. One day his wife, Kiset's mother, was cleaning up the yard and found the gold coins.

Supposedly, one of Matvey's sons, Vasily, went to America after he was freed from a prison camp in the war. There, they say, he got rich and started a family. Eventually, the villagers alleged, Vasily sent his granddaughter to Chukhrai to regain his family's land and build a house. Many believed that I was that granddaughter and had returned to claim the gold and my ancestral land.

My neighbor Evdokiya Balakhonova, known by her patronymic Trofimovna, died on November 7, 1997. But no one noticed that day. A blizzard, the first of the coming winter, raged over Chukhrai for two days. All tracks were swept away or buried in the snow. Three days later, when the sun came out, Igor went for a walk in the woods. As he passed Trofimovna's house, he found it strange that no smoke was coming from the chimney. Then he realized that he hadn't seen any smoke the day before either. She usually stoked the stove in the early morning, just before dawn, when from our window we could see wisps of smoke drifting skyward.

Igor went next door to Kalkan's house to ask when he had seen his neighbor last. Two, maybe three days ago, Kalkan guessed. So Igor and Kalkan went to have a look.

They knocked on the door, locked from within, but no one answered. Igor peered in the window. The overstuffed bed with overstuffed pillows, where she usually slept, was empty, the covers pulled back. Silence. Suddenly, a cat appeared in the window and scratched feverishly as if trying to get out. Igor bent back the nails holding in one of the small glass panes, and the cat shot out, disappearing behind the house. That's when he came to tell me that Trofimovna was dead.

I just know, he said. She hasn't come to get water out of our well in a couple of days. No smoke from her chimney. And the cat. Clearly it hadn't eaten in days.

Igor radioed to the reserve office, asking them to call the police in Suzemka. When I asked why, he said that maybe somebody had killed her, and, in any case, we didn't want the police to think that we did it. The police said not to touch anything and they would be there shortly. We waited all day. But they never came. The road was too difficult for them, we guessed. Or perhaps they had no gas, as was often the case.

That evening a handful of villagers gathered outside her house. What to do? The Forester said that usually they took care of these things without the police. He added that when Stepanovna (the old lady who used to live next door to Igor) died, they went in through the window and buried her themselves. No police. No funeral parlor. No church service. Just a brief procession from the house to the graveyard. That's what we've always done, he said.

Darkness fell, and the villagers decided that there was no point going in there at night. Might as well wait until the morning comes.

Rats is all, the Forester said. Rats can get to them if you don't get in there quick.

Not a week earlier, I had watched Trofimovna sawing wood from my window. She heaved a large log onto a sawhorse and began to ply at it with her two-handled saw, pushing forward and back. The saw was made from a length of metal about three feet long and eight inches high. Dozens of teeth on the blade were missing, so in places the gullets converged into dull edges that would catch on the log as she sawed. The blade had rusted red from years of use. Each end had a wooden handle, dark and smooth from sweat and wear. The long saw bent and shuddered as Trofimovna pushed, then grew taut as she pulled. Several times I started across the road with the thought of taking up the second handle, but then I would turn back, uncertain. I wasn't sure if she would appreciate my help or would feel indebted. Moreover, I wasn't sure my inexperienced hands would be of much use to her.

Kudinyonok hobbled briskly to our end of the village on hearing of Trofimovna's passing. His wife was Trofimovna's first cousin, and he was her *kum*, meaning he was the god-father and she was the godmother of the same child. Years ago they had christened a child together, and although that child was long gone, they were bound in the eyes of God forever. Being of the Balakhonov kin, Trofimovna was related to about half of the villagers in one way or another, although there was really no one she could call family. Trofimovna's brother had hung himself in Trubchevsk a couple years back. She hadn't been on speaking terms with him anyway. She couldn't stand his two children. She had told Kudinyonok a few months before that he was not to let her niece stand over her coffin when she died.

Trofimovna didn't like people in her house. I had been inside perhaps a dozen times, to borrow a cup of sugar or to bring her bread from town, and she always seemed a bit uncomfortable. I was shocked by how plain her house was. The rectangular log frame housed two small rooms. One was a dark foyer that was cold and used only for storage. Here she stacked pots, buckets, bottles, barrels, and other receptacles. The other room served as her bedroom, her kitchen, and her living room. A large brick woodstove stood to the right of the door, stuccoed with clay and coated with a pale blue wash. Here she piled logs each morning and lit a fire to heat her house. This was also where she cooked her meals, and, even in the heat of summer, she would stoke it about every other day to bake bread, cook soup, or boil water for tea. I remember watching as she took up a long stick with a rounded metal prong on the end to remove a cast-iron pot from the coals to cool or as she took a fresh round loaf of dark rye bread from the oven. The room always smelled of rye bread and wood smoke. In with those agreeable smells mingled unpleasant odors of stale food, rat droppings, and rotting tailings for the chickens and cow.

A small round table covered with a layer of newspapers stood in the opposite corner. Although she couldn't read, she subscribed to the Suzemka newspaper. She used it for lighting fires or wrapping up wedges of *salo*. I had seen her *salo* wrapped in the pages of my insert, the *Zapovednik Scroll*. In the corner above the table, a white cloth with embroidered flowers hung from the ceiling, framing a small shelf with two or three icons and candles. Under the table and in every possible nook and cranny were burlap bags holding sugar, flour, rags, soap, and other bundles. The floor was dusted with flour around several of the bags. Windows on either side of a wardrobe faced our house across the way and let light into the otherwise dark room. At night I rarely saw the bare lightbulb shine out from the two windows. A third window opened onto her small, cluttered yard, enclosed by a high tumbledown fence.

It was through this window that Kudinyonok entered her home after the snowstorm to find out if she was dead. He took Kalkan with him as a witness. Drunk and wobbly, Kalkan wasn't much use for anything else. Kudinyonok bent back the nails holding in the window frame and gently lifted out the window. He set it on the ground as Kalkan watched, gurgling and cooing to himself. They climbed in the window.

There was no sign of Trofimovna in the main room, although the bed had been slept in and was unmade. The room was cold. They opened the door to the foyer. At first the door didn't budge, then Kudinyonok rammed his shoulder against it. Slowly it gave way, shifting a heavy weight behind it. A terrible smell filled the dark entryway, and Kudinyonok pinched his nose. Kalkan seemed not to mind. They turned on the light and gasped in horror.

Trofimovna lay on her back on the floor of the entryway, her stockinged feet wedged up against the door. Her thick tights were pulled partway down. Her arms were splayed out to the sides. But what kept their gaze was her face, or what was left of it anyway. Her long gray hair fanned out around her head, surrounding her face like rays of the sun. One eye stared up to the low ceiling; the other was gone. One cheek had wrinkled skin pulled over the bone, the other had none. Her teeth and jaws were exposed where her lips and chin should have been. For the three days she had been lying there, rats had slowly gnawed away at her face, her scalp, her neck, and part of her shoulder.

The two men pulled her carefully into the main room and laid her on the floor. They went out the front door to get some fresh air, having seen more than they could take. The villagers gathered to hear the news.

Dead, Kudinyonok said.

Kalkan prattled in agreement. Definitely dead. And half eaten, too.

The villagers gasped, covering their mouths. Kalkan's wife began to cry, although everyone knew she and Trofimovna hated each other. As she and Kalkan were usually drunk, Trofimovna had no desire to associate with the lot of them.

Several offered theories as to what had happened. Maybe

she got up in the night to pee in a bucket in the corridor (it had been too cold and blizzardy to make it to the outhouse) and fell and hit her head. Or maybe she had a heart attack.

Whatever it was, Kudinyonok said, we've got to get her washed and buried. While there's still something left to bury.

The villagers agreed.

I'll go to Smelizh to see about a coffin, he added.

They went separate ways to make preparations for the burial. Some went into her house to see the body. Others stayed away.

Olga Ivanovna helped Kudinyonok's wife wash the body. They stoked Trofimovna's stove one last time. Trofimovna's scrawny white cat ran out of the house as they came in. The cat had been feeding on her left shoulder and what was left of her neck.

Darn cat, the old women hissed, kicking it as it scurried between their legs and out the door.

They put a blanket under the body and began to undress it. Olga Ivanovna set a pail on the stove to heat some water. She found clean towels in the bottom of the wardrobe and a big sack filled with bars of pungent brown household soap under the bed. When the water was warm, they washed the body, running the damp towels along the deep creases of her weary skin. Olga Ivanovna washed her thin gray hair in a metal basin and wound it in a neat bun to dry. Finally, they rinsed the blood from the bones of her face and neck, patting what used to be her cheek and mouth dry. Trofimovna's one eye glared up at them, and her exposed yellow teeth pressed tightly together, as if with loathing.

They found a dark blue suit, clean and pressed, in the wardrobe. Like most of the clothing within, it looked as though it had never been worn. She always wore old, ragged clothes, torn or patched and mended a dozen times. In cool weather, she dressed in a black men's suit jacket, ripped at the elbows, the pockets hanging from their seams. She had sewn one shoulder back on with thick brown thread. The dirty jacket hung loosely over her bony, humped back, nearly to her knees, over a long, wide skirt, a piece of colored fabric wrapped around her small waist. In summer she wore a yellow or blue polyester men's shirt, which slid down her sloping shoulders, exposing her bare, sagging breasts when she leaned over. On her feet she wore shin-high rubber boots or short rubber galoshes. In winter she pulled warm *valenki*, made of pressed felt encased in rubber galoshes, over her feet.

Given Trofimovna's usually sparse attire, the two women were surprised to find neatly stacked piles of brand-new sweaters, shirts, skirts, and the dark blue suit. But before they could dress her, they needed to do something about her neck. All that was left was the backbone and a thin layer of flesh wrapped around the protruding vertebrae. So Olga Ivanovna wrapped scarves around the bone until it grew to the size of a neck. They covered her face and head with a clean white scarf and tucked it into the neck scarves. Then they stretched new nylon stockings over her bowed, intricately veined legs and carefully wrapped a clean white shirt around her torso, pulling her muscular hands through the sleeves. They pulled the dark blue skirt up over her waist and wrapped the jacket around her shoulders. They found a pair of black dress shoes that had hardly been worn and strapped them onto her feet. She looked the nicest she had looked in years, if not for her face. They tidied up the house and put everything away. Before they left, they covered the body with a thick blanket to deter rats and cats.

The next day, Kudinyonok took his horse to pick up the

coffin he had ordered in Smelizh. The two village drunks, Khovryach and Kiset, now joined by Balyk, were commandeered to dig the grave. Kudinyonok's wife came to our door, not willing to knock but too fearful of our barking dogs to enter. She was a small old woman with a kind face. She walked folded over a wooden walking cane that was fashioned out of a stick nearly as crooked as she. I opened the door, and she burst into tears.

What? What is it? Come in, come in. Don't stand there and cry, I pleaded.

She brushed the snow off her *valenki* with a broom on our stoop and came into the entryway. We don't know where to have the wake, she sobbed. Trofimovna's house is small, and we'd have to stoke the stove, and who is going to make the food there anyway? Laura, Lorochka, maybe you will help? You can make the food and have the people over just for one drink. Just one drink. Then everyone goes home. She burst into tears afresh.

All right, okay, don't cry. We'll do it, I offered. What time? What should we make?

We'll bury her whenever you are ready, she said. Ivan will be back any minute now with the coffin and some sausages and *samogon*. We will all come to your house after the burial. Usually we make *borsch*, *bliny*, boiled potatoes, and *kisel* to drink. But just make whatever you have on hand, she said.

Okay, okay. We'll tell you when we're ready, I replied.

I enlisted Igor to help make the *bliny* and cranberry *kisel*, a drink made with fruit, sugar, and starch. Igor's son Petya, who was visiting for the weekend, assembled tables and chairs from the house and yard in our small kitchen. I made the *borsch*.

Three hours later, the food was ready. I threw on my coat

and went outside to join Igor, who was already standing in front of Trofimovna's house with the rest of the villagers.

We're ready, I told Kudinyonok's wife.

As we approached Trofimovna's house, I heard a wailing from within. A woman was screaming in grief.

Who is that? I asked someone standing next to me.

Her niece, I was told. She came from Trubchevsk just now. They must have explained why Trofimovna's face was covered.

This is the niece that wasn't supposed to stand over her coffin, I thought. The portly niece, who looked to be about sixty, then exited the house, accompanied by a man who must have been her husband. He was trying to calm her. She wiped away her tears with a wrinkled kerchief.

How could you have let this happen?!?! she suddenly screamed upon seeing Igor and me.

Igor and I looked at each other in disbelief. We had never seen this woman before. We were the ones who had found Trofimovna, I thought. Igor was the one who informed her that her aunt had died.

Why didn't you find her earlier? Why weren't you looking after her? She's a human, for God's sake! You let the rats get her! She broke into tears again, wailing at the top of her lungs.

The villagers looked at her in disgust, probably thinking, Where were you for the past forty years?

Four men carried the coffin out of the house. The coffin, a plain box of pine boards crudely nailed together, seemed so small and narrow, just enough room for Trofimovna's body, shrunken with age and pulled down by gravity. They placed the box on a sleigh pulled by two of the men. Olga Iva-novna handed out clean scarves and towels from Trofimovna's wardrobe to people to drape over their forearms. Someone asked me to get the wreath, so I ran into the house and took the large oval of fake flowers from the floor. I was directed to the front of the procession, just behind Glukhaya, who held an icon wrapped in a white cloth. Igor took up one side of the wreath and I held the other as we walked toward the small graveyard at the center of the village. Behind us, the men heaved and jerked the sleigh forward with its dead weight. Two others walked directly behind the coffin to make sure it didn't fall off. The rest of the village followed. At the end of the procession, someone tossed spruce bows along the way to the graveyard to help the soul find its way home. The soul is said to remain near until the ninth day, when it departs for heaven, or hell.

I could hear the niece wailing somewhere behind us. Glukhaya, deaf and oblivious, trotted ahead with the icon in one hand and her walking stick in the other. Her stick kicked up snow as she widened the gap, leaving the procession behind. At first Igor and I tried to keep up with her, but then decided we should slow down and stay with the others.

We arrived at the graveyard, enclosed by a rickety picket fence. The drunk grave diggers were there waiting. I said hello, but no one responded. Then Olga Ivanovna whispered to me that you didn't greet people at a burial. The usual way to say hello, *zdravstvyuite*, implies wishing someone health and is inappropriate at a funeral. I walked over to the freshly dug pit and set the wreath next to a tree. The hole was about six feet deep and just big enough for the narrow coffin. The mound of dirt to one side of the pit showed dark against the white snow. Bones stuck out of the pile of earth, and a cracked skull sat next to it.

I pointed the bones out to Olga Ivanovna. Seeing my

THE STORKS' NEST

concerned look, she said not to worry. These were the bones of Trofimovna's relatives, and she would be buried in the same place as her ancestors. She pointed to Trofimovna's father's grave next to hers, saying this was probably the skull of her grandmother or grandfather. Each family had its own corner in the graveyard, so no one had to rest eternally with the bones of someone not of their kin. People have been buried here for three hundred years, she explained, and the graveyard has always been the same size. We just keep burying one on top of the other. That's the tradition.

I pondered what I had just heard and thought that, environmentally, it seemed like a wise approach. Abruptly, I was jerked back to the moment by the wailing of the niece. They had taken the top off the coffin for one last farewell. The niece kissed the white cloth over Trofimovna's face and crossed herself. Some of the other villagers approached the coffin, quietly saying, May you rest in peace, may heaven be bright and the earth as soft as feathers. They crossed themselves and moved away. I took a few steps toward the coffin, debating whether or not to say good-bye. Afraid I might do something wrong, I stopped about ten feet away.

All I could see were her hands. They had been placed together on her stomach, the fingers of one hand cupping the fingers of the other. I couldn't take my eyes off them. They didn't look like the hands of a dead person. They were not pale or blue, as I would have expected, but seemingly full of blood, full of life. They were muscular yet bony. The fingers were crooked, yet graceful in the way they arched. These were the hands that she lived by for more than seventy years, the hands that sowed seeds, plucked weeds, kneaded bread, chopped firewood, milked the cow. At last, her hands had come to rest.

The men banged nails into the lid of the coffin and carried it over to the pit. Igor guided two ropes under the coffin, and the men lowered it slowly into the ground.

I turned to Olga Ivanovna. Now what do we do? Do we say a prayer?

Nothing, she whispered. Who is going to say anything for this poor old woman?

The men shoveled the dirt onto the plain wooden box, tossing the bones back into the pit as they went. The empty eye sockets of the skull filled with dirt, likely for the last time, as there was no one left to bury in this corner of the grave-yard. The men thrust an old cross into the earthen mound. The cross was made of thick oak beams. It had been someone else's cross.

Soon a low, elongated mound covered the pit. Someone placed the wreath and remaining spruce bows on it. The Forester's wife, Tatiana, started talking to me about the rats and how they had eaten her eye. She went on and on. I shushed her, begging her to have some respect.

We filed out of the graveyard to our house for the wake. This was the moment the men had been waiting for. The booze would flow to honor the dead woman. One by one, the villagers funneled into our small kitchen and packed them-selves around the three tables placed end to end. Twenty-two in all, I had counted: the now seventeen villagers, the niece and her husband, plus Igor, Petya, and me. I took their coats. Most were damp, dirty, and smelled of wood smoke and God knows what else. A musty odor began to take over the kitchen, snuffing out the sweet smell of *borsch*.

Petya dished out the *borsch*, one ladle for each to make

sure there was enough. I placed sliced smoked sausages and bread on the tables. Igor poured the *samogon* Kudinyonok brought from Smelizh. The men drank without a word.

Then Igor proposed a toast: To Trofimovna—she was a hard worker. Everyone lifted their tumblers, but no one clinked glasses. This is the custom when drinking to the deceased.

Yes, agreed Kalinyonok. She was a difficult woman, but she was a hard worker. I'll give her that.

The men nodded and drained their glasses, mopping their mouths with bread.

The niece sat in the corner and didn't say a word, nor did she touch her soup or her glass. Perhaps she was still angry that we could not have prevented Trofimovna's death. When the villagers finished the *borsch*, Olga Ivanovna said that next they usually ate potatoes.

I apologized, saying I hadn't made potatoes, feeling horrible for my omission and break with tradition.

It's okay, she said.

The villagers proceeded to eat *bliny* and drink cranberry *kisel*. Slowly, they began to leave, and I handed them their coats. A couple of the men were too drunk to put them on, so I hung them over their shoulders. Kiset fell into the kitchen window on the way out, nearly shattering the glass.

How did they get so drunk so fast? I asked Igor.

They started days ago, he said.

One of them demanded the rest of the *samogon*, so Igor handed him the remaining two bottles along with a plate of bread and sausages. They went across the way to Trofimovna's house to continue drinking. The niece left our house without a word.

I cleaned up, then walked over to Trofimovna's to return the scarf I had carried on my forearm in the procession. Five of the villagers were sitting on her bed and a small purple sofa, draining the bottles. The niece was sorting through piles of clothes in the wardrobe while Olga Ivanovna looked on from the sofa.

Seven skirts, six sweaters, look at all this, the women counted in disbelief.

The niece handed me a shirt, saying, Look at all these clothes she never wore. Do you want this?

I shook my head. All I could think was that I hoped no one would count how many sweaters and skirts I had when I died. I wondered if I should get rid of some of them now.

The Forester held up a wad of useless Soviet rubles from his seat on the couch. Or take some of these as souvenirs, he said, laughing.

No thanks, I said. What do I do with this scarf?

Keep it, Olga Ivanovna said. It's yours to remember her by.

Then Kalkan's wife, who had been sitting in the corner on the bed, her eyes bloodshot with drink, bolted out the door with something under her arm.

Stop her, cried the niece to her husband in the yard. He grabbed her and yanked a sack of laundry soap from under her arm and escorted her to the gate, shoving her out of the yard.

That's the third time she's tried to take something, Olga Ivanovna laughed. First she hid jars of butter from the foyer in the snow, and then she stole pots, and now the soap.

The niece and her husband packed plastic bags of clothes into the jeep they had hired and captured Trofimovna's one hen with the blue streak. Trofimovna had painted the poor bird blue because it refused to remain alone and always mingled with our identical hens. Trofimovna had sold her cow a year before, saying she no longer had the strength to cut hay for it.

THE STORKS' NEST

The cat, what of the cat? I asked the husband as he watched his wife stuff the bags of clothes into the car.

We have enough of our own, he said. Shoot it.

The niece kicked the villagers out of Trofimovna's house, and, before she locked it, I went back in to collect my plate.

Nearly a week passed, and Kudinyonok's wife stood outside our door again. Bent over her walking stick, she burst into tears when I opened the door. Her husband hadn't gotten up since drinking too much at the wake. He was lying on the stove, dying. He's got to get to the hospital, she pleaded. He hasn't had a bowel movement in a week, and he won't eat a thing.

Okay, I said. I'll talk to Igor.

And tomorrow is nine days since Trofimovna died, when the soul departs from its home and loved ones, she added. We have to have another wake. Who's going to do it? Laura, will you do it again? Tears welled up in her eyes.

Oh no, I said. Once was enough. I did it the first time out of respect for Trofimovna, I told her, but now I see that most don't give a darn about her. All they want is drink.

The tears spilled down her cheeks, and she said that she couldn't do it either, with her husband sick and all.

Let's hold it at the graveyard, I offered, next to her grave.

She stopped sobbing, and her face lit up. She agreed that it was a good idea. Then she took a small kerchief out of her pocket and began to unwrap it, revealing several hundred-ruble notes.

This is money we found in Trofimovna's house, she said. Take it and buy some food and moonshine for tomorrow. And here, she pushed more bills at me, this is for your troubles.

No, no, I couldn't, I said, taking only enough to cover the groceries.

That afternoon Igor drove Kudinyonok to the hospital, where he would remain for a week, and then he bought food for the wake. The next morning, the ninth day after Trofimovna's death, when the soul is said to depart the earth to wait for God's judgment, we held the second wake by her grave. The air was chilly, and snowflakes drifted leisurely from the sky. We took two cardboard boxes of bread, smoked sausages, sardines, candies, and liquor to the graveyard. I spread a tablecloth over the wooden bench next to Trofimovna's father's grave and cut bread and sausages. The Forester opened two cans of sardines with a knife, and his wife put little piles of candies on each corner of our makeshift table. We only had three glasses for the whole village. Igor and I held on to one for our family. They were our glasses, after all. The second glass was for soda for the handful of women who didn't drink, and the third was for *samogon*. So the men, the Forester's wife, and Kalkan's wife drank *samogon* one at a time, extinguishing the liquid fire with bread and sausages. No words were said. Each waited his or her turn in silence. Igor and I left after a while, and they kept on. It saddened me that most of the villagers had come not to remember Trofimovna, but to drink at her expense.

The third time to mark Trofimovna's death was after forty days, when the soul is said to leave the earth and enter either heaven or hell. Igor and I made ourselves scarce that day, although we raised our glasses to Trofimovna in the evening.

She fetched her own water and chopped her own wood to the very last day. No one took care of her. She didn't spend a day of her life in the hospital and never took any medicine for her ills.

THE STORKS' NEST

That's how I want it to be, Igor said to me. I don't want to be a burden to anyone in my old age. He paused. Except to you, of course, he said, smiling.

I want a real Thanksgiving, I told Igor. I have missed Thanksgiving and the Fourth of July for four years. Humor me.

As the fourth Thursday in November drew near, I began to make holiday preparations. I extended an invitation to Igor's family to join us. I planned the menu. I had the makings for cranberry sauce in the freezer from cranberries I had collected in the swamp. I never really liked pumpkin pie anyway, so apple would do fine. Potatoes were easy to come by, and for stuffing I could invent something. The problem was the big Butterball turkey that was so critical to upholding this timeless American tradition. Desperately seeking turkey, I begged Igor to do something.

How can I possibly have Thanksgiving without a turkey? I cried.

On the Wednesday before Thanksgiving, Igor set out in the jeep in search of a turkey. He stopped in Smelizh at the house of the father-in-law of a ranger from the nature reserve. Everyone called him "Test," meaning "father-in-law."

Test, he called to the old man, where can I find a turkey?

Try Krasnaya Sloboda. Test pointed in the direction of the next village. Amayev has some geese. Maybe he's got turkeys, too.

Amayev was the most influential person in that village, a man from Dagestan who had privatized the *kolkhoz* and its cattle and then became mayor.

Igor thanked the old man and drove on. He came to Amayev's house. He knocked on the high gate to the yard, but there was no answer. Igor opened the gate and walked into the yard to look around. He found the henhouse and peeked inside.

Geese. No turkeys, just geese, he noted.

Igor drove on. He came to the next village of Berio-zovka, where the house I once lived in stood abandoned. He stopped at the home of Semyon, the father of one of the maintenance men at the nature reserve.

Turkeys!? the old man laughed loudly. I haven't had any turkeys in over seven years. There's a fellow in the next village of Stuzhenka who used to raise turkeys, but he doesn't keep them any more either. He roared with laugher, practically doubling over, as if the request had been for unicorns. Igor punched the gas and drove off.

And so Igor continued from village to village. Finally he came to the village of Krupets, thirty miles from Chukh-rai. Krupets served the Nazis during the war, and the other villages in the region still held a grudge against descendents of the *Politsai* who lived there. Igor stopped at the town council's office to ask if anyone in the village kept turkeys.

Ask the girl in the store, the secretary said. She knows everybody.

Igor went to the store.

Maria Ivanovna has a few turkeys, the storekeeper offered. Go down the main road about half a mile, turn left on the dirt road just past a big haystack. Hers is the fourth house on the left.

Igor parked in front of the lady's house and knocked on the gate. Hearing no reply, he opened the gate and looked inside. Seven turkeys waddled around the yard with a dozen chickens. Igor walked around the house and found the woman milking a cow.

THE STORKS' NEST

Are those your turkeys? he asked.

The woman said they were and asked guardedly why he wanted to know.

I want to buy a turkey, he said.

The turkeys aren't for sale, she snapped. Buy my calf. He's for sale.

I don't want to buy a calf, Igor replied. I need a turkey.

How about a ram? I can sell you a ram. You can make some mighty tasty *shashlyki*, she insisted.

Please, Igor pleaded, I don't need a ram. I need a turkey.

Why the heck do you need a turkey so bad? she asked.

You see, Igor explained, my wife is American, and tomorrow is a very important American holiday, Thanksgiving. They eat a turkey as part of the tradition.

In that case, all right. Last year I sold a turkey to a fellow for one hundred rubles ($4). Okay with you? she asked.

Yes, he said, fine. I'll pick up the bird on my way back from town. I need to run a few errands first.

Igor drove to the next town to get gasoline and some produce from the store. He bought bread, wine, and three Snickers bars—presents for me—spending all the money he had with him except the one hundred rubles for the turkey. He returned to the turkey lady's house. She had put on a coat and was heading out the gate.

I told three people that I was going sell you a turkey for one hundred rubles, and they all laughed and said I should've asked for more, she said defensively.

Well, how much do you want? Igor asked.

At least 130 rubles ($5), I reckon.

I only have one hundred rubles left, Igor said. I spent the rest of my money in town and set aside only what we agreed on.

THE STORKS' NEST

The lady stood on her tiptoes to peer into the jeep. She caught a glimpse of the Snickers bars lying on the passenger seat. Well, how about one hundred rubles and those Snickers bars you got there? she haggled.

Okay, you've got a deal. Igor handed over the Snickers and one hundred rubles.

The bird's just inside the gate, in the small pen there on the right. You can go get him yourself. I'm in a hurry.

Wait! Igor cried to the lady as she headed off down the road. Aren't you going to kill it for me?

No time, sonny. Why can't you kill it yourself? She looked at him strangely. You're a man after all!

Igor sighed and opened the gate. He caught the big bird, which shrieked in despair, and closed it in a large cardboard box in the back of the jeep.

The sun had already set, and I was worried about Igor. I wondered if he had found a turkey. Would we have to call off Thanksgiving? Just after 10 P.M. I heard the jeep approaching the house. Igor came inside, stomping the snow off his feet on the stoop.

Happy Thanksgiving! he said, beaming.

I smiled and gave him a big hug.

Where is it? I asked.

When he told me it was still in the back of the jeep, I hesitated for a moment and then asked, Is it still going "gobble gobble," or is it dead?

In Russian we say "gob gob," he replied, and if the bird hasn't frozen to death, then it's still alive.

I started outside to see the turkey. Then I decided that if it had to die, I had better not get to know the creature personally. I asked Igor where we should put it for the night.

In the henhouse? In the barn?

Just leave it in the jeep, he said.

What if the poor thing freezes to death? I asked. The weather forecast called for temperatures to drop to -15°F.

Then we won't have to kill it, he answered.

Then I worried that if the turkey froze to death, I wouldn't have time to defrost it.

We went to bed, discussing how we would have to kill the turkey in the morning. We'll ask the postlady's husband, Stepan, to kill it for a glass of *samogon*, we decided. But then we remembered that the next day was Stepan's birthday. If we gave the bird to him to kill, he could mistake it for a birthday present, or he might be offended if it wasn't.

That night I had a dream that I was together with Mom and Chas and my brother, Mark, for Thanksgiving. I didn't know how to tell them that the bird they were about to feast on for the holiday was still running around outside. When I finally got up the courage to tell them, Mark, a movie producer in Hollywood, jumped at the chance to be the hatchet man.

Come on, I'll do it, Mark said in the dream. What's the big deal?

The next morning all I could think about was the dumb bird.

Igor, I said, maybe we should let it live until next Thanksgiving and then eat it.

Then you will get attached to it and you won't ever want to kill it, he replied. We could just let it live with the chickens, he offered.

Does it have any purpose? I asked. I mean, does it lay eggs or eat weeds or anything like that? I was searching for a way to let the bird live.

No, nothing. Besides, it's a male, how could it lay eggs?

Then let's do it, I said decisively. Let's just get it over with. I'll even chop off his head if you'll hold him for me.

Igor stoked the *banya*, as we would need to dunk the dead bird into a pail of boiling water to get the feathers off. I went to the jeep to get the turkey. I opened the trunk and peered into the box. The turkey glared out at me suspiciously, his beady eyes shining in the dark box. His head was bare, while his body was covered with a thick layer of brownish gray feathers, which hung longer from his neck. I grabbed him with both hands, and he gave in without a fight. As I approached the chopping block behind the *banya*, the bird, evidently sensing that something was about to happen, let out a loud squawk.

The water was ready. The axe was on the chopping block. Igor took the large, fluffy bird from me.

Maybe we should let him live? Igor considered, giving it one last chance.

With the dogs, the cats, the stork, the owl, the horses, and the mice, I said, we have enough freeloaders.

Igor grabbed the bird by the legs and took up the axe, determined to keep my conscience clean. The bird willingly offered its head on the stump. I closed my eyes. The axe swung and, without a sound, the head was severed. Blood spilled down the stump and stained the white snow red. The bird flinched. The beak on its severed head opened and closed. The headless body flapped its wings and twitched its legs for several minutes. I couldn't watch. We left the bird and checked the *banya*. I prepared the necessary implements for the next step: a pail, a knife, a plastic bag for the feathers.

Now a hardened executioner, I went about the mundane task of cleaning the bird. I immersed the limp body briefly into the pail of boiling water and then pulled out the feathers in clumps. Soon the bird was bald and looking several times smaller. Next I cut off its feet and neck. I had no idea where to cut, but I imagined the size of a drumstick and, when the knife sliced through, I knew I had guessed right. The once-living creature was quickly transforming into a piece of meat before my eyes. I began to imagine that I had just picked up a turkey at the grocery store and was about to dress the bird. Next I cleaned out the smelly insides and packed all the feathers and entrails into a plastic bag.

The turkey was looking as plain and plump as a Butterball. In the kitchen, I slathered butter and spices onto its white, pockmarked skin and crammed rice stuffing with celery and dried apricots into the stomach cavity. I tied up the legs with an uncoiled paper clip and shoved the big bird—which must have weighed twelve pounds—into my tiny freestanding box oven, which I had purchased a week earlier in Suzemka for the occasion. I decided it would need a couple of hours to cook, but I was just guessing; there were no instructions attached to this bird and no temperature gauge on my oven.

While the turkey was baking and delicious smells filled the kitchen, I thought about how we had sacrificed a life to uphold an American tradition. I hoped that we were doing the right thing and that this bird had not died in vain.

Igor's parents and brother Nikolai arrived. By now they knew that Igor and I were together, although he never told them directly. They seemed happy for us and interested in getting to know me better. I explained to them the meaning of Thanksgiving, how the Indians aided the Pilgrims after their arrival to America on the *Mayflower*. Igor interjected that the settlers then killed the Indians, but I refused to be disheartened or diverted. As we heaped turkey shavings, stuffing, cranberry sauce, and potatoes onto our plates, I knew that this was the best and hardest-earned Thanksgiving I had ever celebrated. Although my family and my country were far away, they were in my thoughts as I realized all that I had to be thankful for.

241
THE STORKS' NEST

242
THE STORKS' NEST

WINTER

THE DECEMBER air was crisp and a white frost covered the land, the trees, and even the horses' thick coats. The tree branches were brittle and snapped at the slightest touch. Tiny ice crystals clung to blades of grass. The crystals were delicate and intricate, seeming to mimic the leaves of the plant. The landscape looked heavenly in its whiteness, yet fragile and cold. For a few days, the Nerussa River turned into a giant Slurpee: crushed ice floated on the surface until it was finally brought to a standstill by a deep freeze.

The sun hovered above the horizon for a scant seven hours each day as the nights grew longer. During the extended evening hours, Igor and I would sit by the fire and read or watch whatever was being broadcast on ORT, the one national television station that reached our lonely expanse of forest. Like the sun, we went to bed early and woke up late, catching up on sleep lost in the brevity of summer's nights.

When the sun rose at about 9 A.M., we would rush outside to take advantage of the few hours of daylight. We traveled to the reserve office to meet school groups for winter excursions. We hauled dry snags from the forest to replenish our firewood stores. We took long walks along the river's icy expanse to photograph the snowy wilderness. In places where streams joined the river, the water remained unfrozen for a time. We found the handlike prints of beavers there. The food stores they gathered in autumn must have been running low, because the beavers had gnawed on willow shoots along the shore. Paw prints of otters showed that those lively creatures had been frolicking on the ice. Roe deer had ventured across the river into newly accessible areas, leaving tiny spadelike tracks. The double-wedged prints of wild boars demonstrated that these animals behaved more cautiously. They took tufts of dried grasses in their mouths and scattered them over the slippery surface to improve their footing.

A mile downstream from Chukhrai, we found signs of a drama that had unfolded the night before. A pack of wolves pushed a boar out onto the ice. Without proper traction, the animal slipped, and the wolves closed in for the kill. By morning, only wiry clumps of dark hair remained, caught in a pool of frozen blood.

Igor wanted to teach Orlik to pull the sleigh. We hooked him in the harness and piled hay on the wooden slats of the broad, low sleigh. Orlik watched warily as Igor kneeled in the sleigh and took up the long reins. I stood at Orlik's head and urged him forward with my hand on the bridle. He nudged ahead and, feeling the unfamiliar weight behind him, suddenly bolted out of the paddock and across the field. The sleigh bumped along behind him, sailing over hummocks and stirring up clouds of powdery snow. Igor crouched low, clinging to the long wooden rails on either side. Finally, Orlik came to a stop. Igor pulled him around toward home. Foaming with sweat, Orlik walked slowly back, sleigh in tow.

Soon Orlik mastered the sleigh. Igor took us on a night-time safari. While in Africa, we had discovered the "night drive," venturing out in open jeeps with rangers whose powerful spotlights allowed us to catch glimpses of leopards, hyenas, and other nocturnal creatures. Orlik drew the sleigh almost noiselessly across the snowy fields as Igor scanned the forest edge with a spotlight. Eyes glimmered in the darkness, and we made out a herd of deer staring down the beam. Roe deer bounded across the wintry field, the white of their rumps glaring back at us. Wild boars scurried along deep trails in the snow, which they had formed with their broad chests. Back home, Igor and I rekindled our idea of developing ecotourism around the reserve, taking visitors on nighttime safaris. It could bring in funds for conservation activities, we reasoned.

On Christmas Eve, we took the sleigh to search for a spruce tree. Igor picked out a tree he said wouldn't make it due to competition for light and resources. We chopped down the six-foot spruce and laid it in the sleigh. We returned home after dark to find the electricity was out. I lit candles. Igor used a length of wire to hang the tree from a hook on the kitchen ceiling, a trick I never would have thought of. I placed a bowl of water under the dangling trunk. We decorated the tree with ornaments made from colored paper, ribbons, and tinfoil. Soon the little spruce resembled a proper Christmas tree. Most Russians wouldn't put up their trees for another week, until just before New Year's. Russian Orthodox Christmas isn't celebrated until January 7, according to the Old Russian calendar. We had dinner by candlelight, and Igor opened a bottle of Georgian red wine, Kinzmarauli. Stalin's favorite, he said. We were about to call it a night when the electricity came back on, but we pretended we didn't notice and went to bed.

We woke up early Christmas morning. I looked at the thermometer outside on my way to the outhouse. It was -15°F. When I went back inside to wash up, I discovered that there was no water. The pipes from the tank above the *banya* had apparently frozen. Igor took a heating panel to the attic above the *banya* and plugged it in, putting it in the box filled with sawdust insulating the water tank. He stoked the *banya* to produce heat from below and then brought two buckets of water from the well into the house to tide us over. By late afternoon, the ice plug had melted, and we had running water to make dinner. I made roasted chicken and mashed potatoes and put marinated cabbage, pickles, and other preserves on the table. Igor opened a bottle of wine.

To your first Christmas in Chukhrai, Igor said, lifting his glass. He leaned toward me and our lips met. Then he pulled me over to the couch, not caring that the food was getting cold. We went to the *banya* after we ate, where we took off our clothes and sat on the bench in the steamy *parnoye*. Igor tossed water on the hot rocks piled in a niche in the stove. Steam hissed and rose to the ceiling, then wafted down over us. We breathed in the penetrating mist and relaxed.

Igor glanced out the small window and saw a red glow on the snow. He wiped the steam away from the window for a better look. Suddenly, he ran out of the *banya*. I followed. We went behind the *banya* to see flames leaping from its attic. We raced back inside the *banya*, threw on our robes, and filled two buckets with water. Igor climbed the rickety wooden ladder to the attic. I handed him the buckets, and I couldn't help but laugh when I saw his bare bottom under the wind-flapped robe.

A light! he cried. Go get a light!

I ran into the house and, not finding the flashlight, grabbed the lamp by our bed and an extension cord and sprinted back to the *banya*. Igor got more water while I plugged in the lamp and directed the light into the attic.

More water, he said, tossing the buckets down.

How about the hose from the pump in the well? I asked.

Go get it!

I dashed to the well and hooked up the hose. I dragged it over to the *banya* but was stopped short. The hose wasn't long enough. So I filled buckets from the hose and passed them up to Igor.

In another ten minutes, the fire was extinguished. We returned to the heat of the *banya*. Igor's face was black from the smoke. As our bones warmed, we analyzed what had happened. Igor had left the heating panel on, and evidently the sawdust insulating the vat caught on fire.

I felt light-headed after the unplanned contrasting sessions of hot and cold. Having averted catastrophe, our moods were lifted as we headed back to the house to open one present each, having decided to save the rest of our gifts for New Year's Eve. But I felt I had already received mine— a Christmas to remember.

The next morning, I walked to the other end of the village to find out why Stepan hadn't brought the mail by for nearly a week. Surely I must have had some Christmas cards or packages waiting. I knocked on the gate in the high fence surrounding his yard. Stepan opened it, inviting me into the house. I sat on the broad bench in the hallway. Stepan handed me two scanty issues of the Suzemka newspaper, which came out twice a week, but no letters. My Christmas cards would not arrive for months. Then he pulled a little tin from his coat pocket and put a pinch of something in his palm.

What's that? I asked.

Makhorka, he said. Homegrown tobacco.

You grow it yourself? I asked, surprised.

Kuda denus? he replied, meaning, What choice do I have?

He took an old, yellowed newspaper from the shelf and tore off a two-inch-square piece. He put a little of the tobacco in the middle of the paper and rolled it up, licking the edge to make it stick.

You're going to smoke that? I asked.

Yes. Why?

Newspaper has lead in it! I said. That's bad for you.

No one dies healthy anyway, he retorted.

Let me try one, I said.

So he gave me a scoop of tobacco and a section of newspaper. He offered to roll it up for me, but since I didn't want to smoke his spit, I carefully rolled it and sealed it with my own. He lit a match, and I inhaled. I coughed immediately and stubbed the thing out.

How can you smoke that? I cried.

That's what all the men here smoke, he said. After *makhorka*, all other cigarettes seem weak.

His stained yellow teeth and fingers attested to a lifelong devotion to *makhorka*. I heard a loud squeal from the next room. I looked through the doorway and saw nothing but two narrow beds and the stove.

It's the swine, he said. We keep him in the box by the stove in the winter.

I stepped inside the room to take a look. There was a tall, narrow wooden box painted blue standing next to the stove. It had a diamond-shaped peephole in a small door at one end. I looked inside and could barely make out the dark form of a large pig. The smell, however, left no doubt in my mind.

Do all the villagers keep their pigs inside in winter? I asked.

Of course, he said, or else they'd freeze and we wouldn't have any *salo*. After a pause he added, Then we'd freeze!

My black cat, Kosha, asked to be let out one cold night, then never returned. Olga Ivanovna said that Kalkan's nephew Balyk probably ate her. Maybe he wanted some meat to go with his *samogon*. I was angry and confronted Balyk, but he just stared in disbelief, not bothering to deny my accusation.

What can I do? I asked Igor, wanting to get back at the drunkard somehow.

Igor shrugged. One less mouth to feed, he said.

Igor never warmed to Kosha, mostly because she was an "it." Most Russians don't care for "its." They consider it cruel to spay or neuter animals, to take away their sexuality. On the other hand, they seem to have no qualms about drowning a sackful of unwanted kittens. It always seemed a little strange to me. Igor, however, explained the philosophy simply.

Humans are predators. We kill. We eat meat. God gave us that right. But he did not give us the right to change things, to alter the essence of their being.

I defended Kosha, saying she wasn't a complete "it," as she had had one litter of kittens. It was my own moral compromise across the two cultures. I would let her experience her sexuality and then rid the world of unwanted kittens.

Now Kosha, my faithful companion through my first five years in Russia, was gone. She had traveled with me to every nature reserve I visited within driving distance of Moscow, watching out the rear window and never getting lost once we got there. She had a gift for healing. If I had a stomachache, she would lie on my belly and the pain would quickly subside. I was overcome with sadness and cuddled her daughter Mysha in my arms. She purred loudly and didn't seem to notice that her mother was gone.

Petya arrived the week before New Year's to spend winter vacation with us. He was sympathetic about my loss, expressing his condolences about Kosha. I had noticed that Petya was a very considerate and caring young man. He would make a good husband and father someday. Tikhon, Igor's older son, arrived soon after, also on vacation, from his forestry institute in Bryansk. Tikhon was more outgoing than his younger brother, and less sensitive, but fun to be around all the same. I was happy that Igor's boys seemed to have accepted that their father had chosen to be with me. I worried, however, that if Igor and I were married, I would instantly become stepmother to two nearly grown boys, only eleven and fifteen years my junior. I thought back to how difficult it must have been for my stepparents to embrace my brother and me. Unexpectedly, I found myself full of regard for my stepmom, Pat, and my stepdad, Chas, for having played a major role in my life. I vowed to do the same for Igor's children to the extent that I was able.

With three continually hungry males in the house and the road temporarily impassable, I was at pains to put enough food on the table. Igor and I took the horse and sleigh to the small store in Smelizh to stock up on groceries before New Year's. Very occasionally, a tractor from the village store in Smelizh would grind its way to Chukhrai and deliver basic goods such as bread and flour, but not when the road was impassable. Now the ice covering the large potholes and depressions in the road was not thick enough to hold vehicles, but was too solid to allow them to pass unhindered. Even Aza, who weighed nearly half a ton, fell through in places, and the broad sleigh barely made it across the broken patches of ice through which murky water bled.

As we coasted through the snowy woods at a steady trot, I lay on my back in the soft mattress of hay and gazed up at the trees as they appeared to move across the pale blue sky. The bright sun glistened on snow-covered branches. A thick layer of snow muffled the sound of Aza's hooves. Occasionally Aza kicked up cold bursts of snow that sprayed my face. If I was not careful, low branches would whip past and scratch my cheeks, rosy from the frost. We were bundled in thick pants and government-issue down camouflage jackets, with *valenki* pulled over our feet.

As we climbed the low rise from the floodplain of the Nerussa, tall Scotch pines replaced the moisture-tolerant alder and oak trees. The straight reddish orange trunks of the pines were dotted with white clumps of snow, which clung to little knobs where lower branches once hung and formed a colorful mosaic of orange bands with white spots as they flew by.

Igor stood in the sleigh holding the long reins firmly in his gloved hands. I watched his tall figure above me as we traversed low hills in the terrain, occasionally hitting bumps and falling into pits. He braced himself for each rise and fall, for each bump and pit. He put his arms out for balance occasionally, but mostly just leaned this way or that to counteract the jerking movement of the sleigh. My previous few attempts to stand while driving the sleigh had ended in my heavily bundled form falling back into the hay or careening out of the sleigh altogether into the mercifully soft snow.

Igor almost always drove the sleigh standing up, a habit that gained him respect among the elders of Chukhrai. Shamornoy once told Igor that if you want to know how a man works, watch how he drives a sleigh. According to the old man, men who lie down in the sleigh and hardly look where they're going are lazy and lack initiative. Men who stand in the sleigh while observing their surroundings are energetic and tireless workers. Men who sit in the sleigh are *ni ryba ni myaso* (neither fish nor fowl). I was not sure how these observations applied to women. We probably earned extra credit for driving a sleigh at all.

We arrived in Smelizh and pulled up in front of the store only to find that it was closed. It was Friday, and usually the store was open on Tuesdays and Fridays, but, with the holiday approaching, the schedule was erratic. We went down the road to the storekeeper's house and knocked on her door.

We came all the way from Chukhrai, we told her. Can you open the store for us, please?

Sure, she said, just let me get my coat.

We all piled into the sleigh and returned to the store. Inside we bought smoked sausages, cans of corn and peas, mayonnaise, salt, tea, cookies, sweetened condensed milk, bread, and toilet paper. We put the groceries in a large canvas backpack and headed for Chukhrai.

Igor stopped at the first long trough on the road home and broke the ice with a shovel. He took a bucket from under the hay and scooped up cold, slushy water, pouring it along the ruts in the road where the ice was thin.

If I can just get another half inch of water to freeze on the road, he said, it may be passable by car.

After repeating this chore in four large, ice-covered

depressions with several dozen buckets of water, we arrived home, cold and tired. We released Aza to Orlik and went inside to warm our bones and make dinner.

That night it snowed several inches, nullifying Igor's work on the semifrozen pits that day. The snow's blanket would insulate them, keeping them from freezing solid. Now even the horse and sleigh would not make it through the sodden floodplain.

It is on New Year's Eve that Russians decorate a tree and open presents brought by Ded moroz (Father Frost) and his assistant, his granddaughter Snegurochka (Snow Maiden). Children dress up in costume, and families gather to bring in the new year. Christmas, celebrated on January 7, was banned under Communism and remains primarily a religious holiday.

We invited Igor's parents and Igor's brother Nikolai and his wife, Natasha, to join us on New Year's Eve. Igor's mother came early to help cook, and Igor and the boys pitched in as well. We sat down to eat at about 11 P.M., as is the custom. The table was decked with spruce boughs, pinecones, candles, and twelve different dishes of food, one for each month of the year. Pickled cucumbers and tomatoes, marinated cabbage with cranberries, sliced ham and cheese, salads, mashed potatoes, pork chops, baked mushrooms with *smetana*, and *olivye*—no holiday feast would be complete without this traditional Russian potato salad.

Olivye Potato Salad
(sometimes called Stolichny)

*5 medium potatoes, boiled in their skins until easily
    pierced with a fork*
*2 medium carrots, boiled in their skins until easily pierced
    with a fork*
4 hard-boiled eggs
8 oz. chicken, pork, or beef, boiled or baked
1 small onion
1 large cucumber
3 medium pickles
1 C. canned or frozen peas, cooked
1 C. fresh dill and parsley leaves
1 C. mayonnaise or more, as needed
Salt and pepper
Thinly sliced oranges and parsley sprig for garnish

Prepare potatoes, carrots, eggs, and meat and allow to cool.
Potatoes and carrots should be tender yet firm, not crumbly
when pierced with a fork. Remove skins from cooked
potatoes and carrots and cut the peeled vegetables into small
cubes. Peel eggs and dice. Cut meat into cubes, discarding
skin and fat. Dice onion. Cut cucumber and pickles into
small cubes. Drain peas. Chop parsley and dill. Combine all
ingredients. Add mayonnaise, and salt and pepper to taste. Toss
ingredients gently. Chill before serving. Decorate with orange
slices and a parsley sprig.

We piled the food onto our plates. First we bid farewell to the passing year, leaving all that was undesirable behind us. The men drank vodka, and the women drank wine. We raised our glasses as each person said a toast (one is not supposed to put the glass down until the toast is finished and everyone drinks). As midnight drew near, Igor opened two bottles of champagne and refilled the glasses. The TV was broadcasting a traditional holiday concert, and, as the countdown began, the screen showed the clock on the bell tower in the Kremlin wall. When the clock struck twelve, we clinked glasses and rejoiced, dancing around the room and hugging each other. Now we could welcome in the new year, so another round of toasts began. We put on music and danced, shaking the floorboards and windows of our small house. By 2 A.M. we were exhausted. Igor's parents invited Nikolai and Natasha to spend the night at the ranger station at Staroye Yamnoye. They all climbed into the sleigh led by the old mare Anfisa and disappeared into the night. Petya and Tikhon crashed on the couch, which unfolded into a double bed, and Igor and I fell into bed behind the bookshelf partition.

The next day the festivities continued. Leftovers were taken from the fridge and new dishes hastily put together to feed guests who poured in throughout the day. Igor's younger brother, Dima, and wife, Vita, arrived with their son, Nikita, from Bryansk. They stopped by on their way to the ranger station. The absence of a road didn't deter other visitors, who made a special effort to hike in with food and gifts for the holiday. Petya and Tikhon left that evening to spend the rest of their break with their mother, who lived about fifteen miles away, near the reserve headquarters.

Alone at last, Igor and I took a walk that night under the clear, starry sky. The moon was out and the air was chilly. We came across the carcass of a wild boar that had died not long before. A strange feeling came over me, and I wondered what it meant. Igor took my hand, and we walked home.

At first light, Igor and I ventured out in the sleigh to find the bison. We pulled into the enclosure where the gate was left open and found fresh tracks around the hay. The grain that the ranger left for them every few days had been eaten. We continued on through the woods and headed to the northern part of the reserve.

Suddenly a gunshot rang out in the cold air, rebounding off the tall pines. Poachers. We pulled around a bend in the path and saw a group of men walking down the forest road that extended along the northern boundary of the reserve. Igor counted thirteen. One carried the limp body of a large gray wolf slung over his shoulders. Fresh blood dripped from the carcass. Evidently they had formed a human chain and combed the forest, flushing the normally wily wolf out into the open, where they shot it. Hearing our horse, they turned around to look at us. They didn't run. Igor recognized several of them. They were police officers from Trubchevsk.

Although surely the men knew who he was, Igor identified himself as head ranger and director of the Bryansk Forest Zapovednik and said that by killing an animal in the protected reserve, they had committed a federal offense.

The men claimed they had a license to kill the wolf and shot it outside the reserve. Igor said that he could still prosecute them for having unsheathed rifles in the buffer zone.

Ha! interjected one of the policeman. A store was just robbed in Trubchevsk, and you match the description of the man who robbed it perfectly, he said threateningly to Igor. We can take you into the station and hold you for twenty-four hours until we determine that it wasn't you.

Igor laughed, undaunted by the remark. He took out a pen and paper and calmly wrote a protocol on all the men, as was required when prosecuting violators. The men refused to sign the paper or provide identification. I signed as a witness. Igor knew three of the men, and with a witness he would be able to initiate court proceedings against them. In normal circumstances, we would have taken the whole group into the police station for identification and prosecution. But they were the police. We could do nothing but let them go with the wolf, although we made sure they headed for Trubchevsk and not back toward the *zapovednik*.

The next day we found blood and entrails from a wild boar shot in the reserve near where we ran into the policemen. Igor filed the papers on the three men he could identify, accusing them of carrying unsheathed rifles in the reserve and killing the wolf. One of them was near retirement age, and, if forced to resign, he would lose his pension. Igor would spend the next two years in a court battle trying to prosecute the men, but to no avail. The system was too corrupt, and evidently rules didn't apply to those charged with enforcing them.

Rozhdestvo (Russian Orthodox Christmas) passes largely unnoticed in Chukhrai, as it has ever since the Communists stamped out the religious holiday. Old Russian New Year's Eve is celebrated on the night of January 13, according the Old Russian calendar. Traditionally, children would dress in costume and go from door to door to collect treats and money. When the head of the house opened the door to receive them, they tossed grain over the threshold, chanting,

257

Sow, sow, I will sow, Happy New Year I wish thou.

The real Russian winter only kicks in after January 19, when the Russian Orthodox holiday known as Kreschenie (or Epiphany, in the West) is celebrated. Temperatures drop well below zero and stay that way for a week or more. I woke up one morning to find it –25°F outside. Igor and I lingered in bed, not wanting to leave the warmth of the blankets and each other. Igor finally rose to stoke the stove. While the house was heating, I went for a walk to see if the foxhole in the glade by the river was occupied. The hairs inside my nose froze from the cold, and I held a gloved hand over my nose to breathe. I found the fox den inhabited. Fresh tracks marked the snow around three of the entrances on the small knoll. I would return in spring to observe and photograph the fox kits after they were born. I continued to the river and found the Forester ice fishing with his son, Dima, the only schoolboy in Chukhrai, who walked eight miles to class. He was glad for the cold, because school had been canceled. Heavily bundled, the Forester wielded a large hand drill to carve a hole in the ice. Dima dropped a fishing line into the hole, using worms dug up from a manure pile as bait. The fish were hungry and took the bait. Dima pulled them out one by one and let them flop around on the ice until they froze or otherwise expired. I asked if I could take a couple of the smaller fish for the stork chick, and they kindly obliged. I was cold and left after a couple minutes with the fish flopping around in a small plastic bag in my pocket. Father and son stayed on until dark.

In a few days, the weather warmed slightly and snow fell, covering the land with a fresh white blanket. We piled hay into the feeder for the horses, but it remained untouched. They preferred to dig for last year's grasses under the snow in the field on the other side of the lake. Each afternoon a wild boar dug for roots in the same field. He was thin, and in my binoculars I could see the outline of his ribs through his shaggy pelt. Between the horses and the boars, all the snow was quickly overturned until the next snowfall.

Olga Ivanovna came to visit, leaving her cane outside on the stoop. We drank tea, and I treated her to homemade chocolate-chunk cookies. Kisa begged for a treat, and she willingly broke off a piece of cookie and gave it to the dog.

Good cookies, she noted. They must be American. I've never had ones like these before.

We sat and talked for a while.

What do you think of Americans? I asked.

They're the same as us, she said. They're white, good-looking. They just don't talk like us. I've heard they're friendly.

Not all Americans are white, I explained. Have you ever met any besides me? I asked.

No, she said. And I don't consider you an American, Lorochka. You're one of us. You're a Chukhrai girl.

We sat in silence for a while, then she told me about the time her daughter Anastasia, or "Nastya" for short, the same one who spent the night hanging in a tree as a baby during the war, suffered from what she thought was a curse. Nastya, who was five at the time, had stopped walking and began to whither away. She refused to eat, and her stomach bloated. Olga Ivanovna took her to one of the village medicine women, an old lady named Polina. Polina said she could cure the girl in twelve days. The next day Olga Ivanovna brought Nastya to Polina's house, along with goods to pay for the treatment: hemp seeds, fish, and flour. The old woman laid the child on a blanket in front of the stove and began to chant quietly. She melted beeswax over the stove, then let it drip into a dish of cold water held over the child's head. She poured the wax into the water three times, each time saying a prayer. The wax hardened, and when the two women looked closely, they saw that the wax had congealed into the form of a calf.

It's *ispug* (fright), the old woman said, meaning that Nastya's illness had been caused by fright. A calf has frightened her, she continued. That's what she's suffering from.

Olga Ivanovna brought Nastya back each day, carrying fish her father-in-law caught in the river and other gifts as payment. Each time the woman chanted and said prayers. She gave Olga Ivanovna a bottle of water and told her to take it home and sprinkle it in the form of a cross on their doorstep, then rub it on the girl's hair, face, arms, and legs every morning at dawn for six days. On the sixth day, the old woman boiled an egg and Nastya ate it. It was the first food she'd eaten in days. On the eighth day of treatment, the little girl got up and walked across Polina's room. She hadn't walked for three months. The last three days, Nastya walked to the medicine woman's house unaided. She was cured.

I asked Olga Ivanovna if she has ever put a *sglaz* (literally "the evil eye," or "curse") on anyone.

No, no, she shook her head. That's the devil's work. I've only helped break *sglaz* and healed people when they are sick. I fear *sglaz* more than anything, she continued. If someone is jealous of you or makes fun of you, that's *sglaz* too. I get a fever and fall ill. That's why I always wear this safety pin fastened to the inside of my shirt, she said, turning out her collar to show me the pin. It protects me. And, of course, my cross. I don't feel right without a cross around my neck. I pray several times a day, when I get up in the morning, before and after every meal, and when I go to bed at night. Do you know *Otche nash* (The Lord's Prayer)? she asked. That's our main prayer.

I recited it to her in English, Our Father, who art in heaven, hallowed be thy name, retrieving the prayer from the depths of my mind and Sunday school when I was eight.

She laughed, saying it sounded nothing like *Otche nash*. She paused, then asked me timidly when Igor and I were going to buy a baby.

Buy a baby? I asked questioningly.

She chuckled. That's what we say, she explained. When people have a baby, they buy it, so to speak. Or sometimes we say that we found a baby in the garden under the cabbage leaves.

Oh, I see. We say that storks bring babies, I told her. I hope to have children some day, I continued, but we haven't really thought about it yet.

Don't wait too long. You'll never be young again. She paused, then said, That reminds me of a song. She began to hum, closing her eyes. With her mind somewhere far away, she started to sing.

> There stands a high knoll,
> And below the knoll a wood, wood,
> A green wood, a dense wood,
> Unspoiled as God's paradise
>
> In that wood runs a river,
> Like glass the water glows, glows,
> Down through the wide valley,
> Where the water flows

Flowing from the river's bank
Where they bind skiffs, skiffs,
Three willows have grown weak,
And they do despair, oh yes

Do not despair, Old Willows,
Yet to arrive is spring, spring
But youth shall not return,
The years shall not return

I set off to visit the United States for two weeks in the beginning of February. I was sad to leave Igor behind but excited to see my family. We piled my suitcases onto the sleigh and hooked Orlik into the harness after determining that the ice on the road would hold us. As we pulled out of our barnyard, our neighbor Glukhaya came running out of her house, shouting, Stop them! Stop the electricians!

Igor stopped Orlik in front of her gate. Two men were standing on her doorstep.

We are trying to cut off the old lady's electricity, one of the men said, because she hasn't burned a single kilowatt in four years.

Petrovich, Glukhaya appealed to Igor, using his patronymic, please don't let them do it, please. I want to have electricity when I die.

Igor raised his hand, gesturing to the deaf woman not to worry. He walked up to the men and explained to them that the old woman couldn't hear. He said that he would make sure she turned on her light every now and then.

They agreed to keep the electricity on, and then said they needed to check our meter and collect payment. So Igor and I returned to the house to fetch our booklet. Igor wrote down the reading on the meter and paid them the few dollars we owed for the last two months. They seemed pleased. After all, with the kettle, the space heaters, and other electronic equipment, we consumed more wattage than anyone in the village. Before we left, I glanced in the mirror to stave off the bad luck that comes from having to return home just after one has set out on a long journey.

We hopped back on the sleigh, and Igor urged Orlik into a fast trot down the road to civilization. In Smelizh a driver from the reserve met me in my old Russian Lada to take me to the Suzemka train station. Useless to me in Chukhrai, I had given my old car—one of the last reminders of my former city-self—over to the *zapovednik*, only occasionally reclaiming it when the jeep was stranded in Chukhrai. In the car, I changed from cold-weather country clothes to city garb. Igor and I kissed and said good-bye, pausing to look into each other's eyes. As the Lada whisked me away, I watched out the rear window while Igor pulled Orlik around and headed for home, kicking up a powdery trail of snow.

In Moscow the next morning I took a taxi from the Kievsky train station to the airport and boarded the ten-hour flight to JFK. I couldn't sleep. I stared out the window at the blue expanse of sky above and the cold ocean below. The world seemed so huge, so empty, so lonely. Then I thought of Igor, and I felt grounded. I was certain that life was too short for us to be apart. I collected my bags at JFK and walked through the opaque sliding glass doors to America. I looked up to see a man with a moustache wearing a cowboy hat and holding a hand-drawn sign reading Williams. Because of the sign, I hardly recognized my dad. Always the comedian. Pat greeted me and gave me a hug. We climbed into the Ford Explorer, plush and cozy compared to the Russian UAZ with its rough edges and cold drafts. We drove four hours to their home near Glens Falls in upstate New York, where they had moved shortly after I graduated from Cornell. I spent a week with them and visited other family members; my grandparents and two aunts lived nearby, as this was where Dad grew up.

I indulged in all the foods I had been craving: bagels and cream cheese, pizza, Reese's peanut butter cups, and chocolate ice cream. Then I began to miss the familiar tastes of my Russian home: homemade cranberry juice, *borsch*, *bliny*. When I went into a bookstore, the cashier asked me what country I was from. Did I have an accent in English? I wondered. I felt like a stranger in my own country. I took reusable bags to the grocery store, as everyone did in Russia. The man bagging the groceries looked at me strangely and asked, Are you from Greenpeace or something?

Later, talking to Dad and Pat, I fished for words and could only come up with Russian expressions. When I tried to translate them into English, they stared at me blankly. The meaning was lost, and I couldn't think of an English equivalent. They laughed at the habits I'd picked up, the Russian superstitions I observed. When someone tried to shake hands with me over the threshold, I took a step back, forcing them to come through the door so our hands wouldn't meet in the doorway. I turned the guest bed around so my feet weren't facing the door: dead people are carried out of rooms feet first.

When the week was over, I flew from Albany to Denver, where Mom and Chas met me. As always, we drove by the old house where I grew up, on the corner of Severn and Locust streets, then we headed for the condominium where they now lived, on the eighteenth floor above Washington Park. The view from the balcony at sunset was spectacular: the Rocky Mountains were awash in a red glow and snowy peaks reached to the sky. The thing I missed most. The mountains. Igor once told me that if the lack of mountains ever kept me from staying in Chukhrai, he would raise some.

I drove to Boulder to visit my girlfriends from boarding school, Mandy and Caroline. They never questioned my decision to move to Russia and were always fascinated by my stories about our life in the village. They introduced me to music I had never heard, although it had been around for five years, and were surprised I hadn't seen any of the latest movies.

By the end of my trip, I was anxious to return to Igor and the village I had grown to love. Back in Moscow, I boarded the day train for home after calling Igor at the reserve to tell him when to meet me. As the train pulled into Suzemka station after dark, I saw Igor run down the platform to catch up to my car, only to be thwarted by border guards in uniforms. Suzemka is the last stop before Ukraine, so all continuing passengers must clear customs. Igor waited impatiently for me to appear, then ran to me and threw his arms around me.

I missed you so much, he whispered into my ear, hugging me so hard my feet lifted off the ground. Let's never be apart again.

He took my bags, and we walked to the jeep, where the driver from the reserve was waiting. On the ride to Smelizh he told me how all our animals were faring. Kisa went down a foxhole and could be heard barking at a fox deep underground. Then his eyes swelled up from the sand. The horses crossed the river and didn't return for days. The owl flew into the house one night and got into a spat with my cat Mysha. The rooster attacked the stork. But in the end, all were well.

We pulled into Smelizh, where Orlik was patiently waiting, munching hay from the sleigh. I wrapped my arms around his neck, and he flared his nostrils to smell my coat. Igor put my warm *fufaika*, the gift from the governor, around my shoulders as I climbed into the sleigh, and we took off into the darkness. Orlik was eager to get home to his mare and barreled through the darkness, zigzagging between the trees. Igor and I held on to each other tightly, trusting that Orlik's night vision was better than ours.

In the morning, I walked out to the outhouse and took in the cold fresh air. I smiled when I saw the familiar storks' nest in the tall willow in our yard. Only a thick layer of snow occupied the nest, and the stork pair wouldn't arrive for two months. I glanced the other way and was startled by the empty plot before me. Trofimovna's house was gone. Only the solid brick stove with its pale blue wash was left standing in a snowbank. As no one had claimed the house after her death, the villagers had taken it apart for firewood while I was away. I walked over to the stove. A gaping hole in one side was where wood once burned. Suddenly Mysha jumped out of the dark cavity, scaring me so that my heart leapt into my throat. Her mostly white coat was blackened with soot. It saddened me that Trofimovna's house was gone, yet it seemed symbolic that only the stove remained. It was her stronghold, the very center of her existence. Now it stood alone, looking like a small fortress with its several square stories, the tall chimney, and windowlike cubbyholes in the side. Igor said he'd break it apart in the spring to fill potholes in the road.

266
THE STORKS' NEST

Back in the 1950s, abandoned houses had signaled the beginning of the end for Chukhrai. Before the war, there were 124 households in the village, but when people returned to rebuild houses, the number dropped to 85. The village shrank further when the Soviet government recruited people to settle Siberia, the Russian Far East, and East Prussia (primarily Kaliningrad) in three different waves. Several dozen young families and single men were lured from Chukhrai by the offer of lucrative salaries, traveling expenses, and housing. Some worked for a year and then returned, but most stayed away.

Due to its diminished size, Chukhrai's *kolkhoz* was merged with Krasnaya Sloboda's in 1952. Olga Ivanovna, who had worked as an accountant at the *kolkhoz* since 1945, became the village storekeeper in 1955. She showed me the bricks, lying in a mound by the graveyard, where the store once stood. Goods there were always scarce. Food was rationed according to lists. The villagers paid for goods, but could only purchase them in limited quantities, depending on how many members were in each family. Each person was allotted a pound of sugar a month and forty pounds of flour, to make bread. Rarely, the store would receive a limited supply of specialty items such as oilcloth, used for tablecloths, and the women in the village would literally beat each other up to get them.

After the *kolkhoz* was scaled back, many of those remaining left in search of work opportunities and a better life. Young people moved to Suzemka, Trubchevsk, and beyond, and their parents followed them if they could. By the 1960s, the bustling village of Chukhrai was no longer. When I walked among the rotting houses in the village, I thought about how much effort people had put into building their homes and how heartbroken they must have been when they had to move on. While I wished I could have seen the village back in its glory days, when there was a store, a club, and the *kolkhoz*, I was sure I would like it better now.

Igor woke me early one morning before the sun was up.

I want to take you to a place I used to explore a lot when I was a kid, he said. Come on, the horses are ready.

Over coffee he told me the place was about an hour's ride from Chukhrai, where the wide band of forest known as the Bryansk Forest crossed into Ukraine. He and his colleagues at the reserve had created the Skripkino Zakaznik on the Russian side three years before. He reminded me of the conference I had attended, while still working at WWF, about creating a Russian–Ukrainian transboundary park. Skripkino was the sanctuary on the Russian side of that proposed park.

I would love to see it, I replied.

I had always admired transboundary reserves as examples of international cooperation in nature conservation. And I loved that Igor wanted to share with me the places that were special to him.

We rode out of the village toward the river, crossing where the ice was solid. We turned down an old logging road, abandoned since the *zapovednik* was created ten years before. The road narrowed in places, so we had to duck our heads to pass under tree branches. With all the saplings coming up beneath us, soon it wouldn't be recognizable as a road at all, except for the deep ruts that would take decades to erode. We passed a large hole on one side, and Igor said that a bomb had carved the depression during the war. On the other side of the road, the remains of an underground bunker from the war could be seen on the forest floor. The square pit had a fifty-year-old pine tree growing from its center.

We rode past the *zapovednik* boundary and crossed the muddy, wet road that had for centuries served as the only route between the two district centers of Suzemka and Trubchevsk. In half an hour, Igor shouted back to me that we'd crossed into the Skripkino Zakaznik. We explored the sanctuary, taking note of the terrain and tracks in the snow. I suggested to Igor that one of the Trubchevsk schools might be interested in adopting this *zakaznik*, but he replied that the area was not accessible by road. We followed the boundary for a bit, then turned in toward the center of the sanctuary.

After about half a mile, we came to an open glade filled with bare young birch trees growing beyond the shadows cast by the tall pine forest. In the middle of the clearing, a huge dark green spruce tree towered to the sky. Its broad branches hung like enormous fans, swaying and creaking in the wind. We dismounted and tied the horses. We walked toward the spruce tree, and Igor pointed to a broad pit underneath it. The roots of the tree spanned the pit, and remains of a wooden frame poked out from beneath the snow in places.

Igor told me he first came to these parts with his father when he was ten years old. His father had just bought a Jupiter motorcycle with a sidecar. He was anxious to try it out, so he put Igor on the seat behind him and drove down the forest road leading from the town of Belaya Beriozka, where they lived. After about fifteen miles, they came to the Skripkino Woods, where we were now. They spent more time pushing and pulling the motorcycle through the sand and mud that day than they did riding it. They got lost deep in the forest. They followed the sun south, thinking they would come to the Ukrainian town of Znob, from where a well-traveled road led to Belaya Beriozka. The sun had nearly set when they saw the outline of a lean, old woman walking on the forest road ahead, her crooked body bent over almost to the ground. She carried a large sack over her shoulder.

Is this the way to Znob? Igor's father asked the old woman without turning off the motorcycle.

Yes, the old woman replied.

Get in, we'll give you a ride, he said, casting the cover off of the sidecar, sure the old woman would be glad of the offer.

Thank you, young folk, but I'm in a hurry, she replied.

Puzzled by her response, they drove on.

In about a mile, they came to a bridge made of logs spanning a swampy brook. As they drove over the bridge, the front wheel of the motorcycle got stuck between two of the logs. They tried to push the motorcycle out, and it became wedged even further. Soon the old woman caught up to them. She looked at them sympathetically and walked on. Igor and his father worked late into the night prying the logs apart to free the wheel. They got home as the sun was coming up.

Four years later, after finishing his exams in eighth grade, Igor decided to explore the Skripkino Woods. He took the two-car steam engine train from Belaya Beriozka to a small forest village. From there, he continued by foot along a creek. The unassuming creek formed the boundary between Russia and the Ukraine. Throughout the entire day, Igor didn't see a single border post or barrier. In fact, he didn't meet a single person. He must have crossed the creek a hundred times that day, jumping from one bank to the other, crossing from Russia to the Ukraine, from the Ukraine to Russia.

As Igor tired, he searched for the road that would lead him home, but the forest seemed endless. Mosquitoes swarmed around him as the light began to dim. Then he saw a gap in the woods up ahead. The smell of smoke reached his nose. When he arrived in the clearing, the very spot where we were standing, he saw the tall spruce tree with drooping branches. Smoke rose into the air, encircling the giant tree. He drew closer and saw that the smoke came from five or six smoldering fires of rotten logs. More than twenty cows lay in the grass among the fires, chewing their cud and lazily brushing off mosquitoes and flies, which numbered fewer near the fires than in the woods. One of the cows stood while a black piglet suckled her udder, perhaps a wild boar or a hybrid.

Igor guessed that he had stumbled upon the residence of the *dikaya babka* (wild old woman) he had heard about many times. He had not believed the stories. He could see the door to an underground dwelling under the roots of the spruce tree. The pit we were standing in front of twenty years later was all that remained. The dwelling had probably been built several decades before Igor's childhood discovery of it, since the roots encircled the entrance, becoming entwined with the logs beneath it. The roof formed a level plane with the ground, hidden under a thick blanket of peat and moss. Beyond the tree, he could see well-kept rows of vegetables in a garden that sloped down to a creek. A fence fashioned of piles of dead trees, snags, and crooked branches protected the garden plot from the cows and wild animals.

Then he noticed a little old woman sitting with her back to him near the garden. Her clothes were tattered and black with grime. Tufts of gray hair stuck out from under the scrap of fabric wrapped around her head. Igor approached her and saw that she was peeling beets on a stump. Next to her, smoke wafted from a fire pit made of a few bricks. Blackened kettles hung from crooks on a branch wedged into the ground next to the crude stove. A chicken, the only one to be seen in the

THE STORKS' NEST

secluded clearing, sat comfortably on the woman's shoulder. The old woman hadn't noticed Igor, so he walked around the garden and up to her from the other side, where she could see him from afar. He greeted her loudly, and she responded in a kind voice and stood up, looking him over.

The chicken remained on her shoulder. The swarm of mosquitoes that had followed Igor into the clearing from the woods quickly enveloped the old woman. The chicken began to peck them off her shoulders and headscarf. The old woman threw a pile of wilted grass onto the fire and a cloud of smoke rose, causing the mosquitoes to vanish. Igor studied her face and recognized her as the woman who had refused the lift on the motorcycle four years earlier.

Can you tell me the way to Znob? Igor asked.

She explained plainly, then asked, Where are you from, boy? And why are you wandering the woods in mosquito season?

Igor told her he was looking for black storks, and she nodded. She didn't appear to think it was a silly thing for a boy to do, as so many others did when they heard his mission.

Later Igor learned that the woman's name was Matryona Pavlovna Kasha. Like many others, she fled her village on the Russian-Ukrainian border in 1941 to escape the Germans. She excavated a pit in the forest and fortified it with logs to wait out the invasion. Most of her loved ones died during the war. Perhaps it was the unbearable pain of her loss that kept the woman from leaving the forest with the others when the war was finally over. She remained in the decrepit bunker with no heat for the rest of her long life. In the winter, during severe freezing spells, she brought two of her cows into the dwelling and lay down to sleep between them. She had nearly thirty cows, but as she didn't cut hay to feed them, some would die each winter and new ones would be born each spring.

In 1942 she saved the life of a Russian pilot whose fighter plane went down not far from her meadow. She healed his wounds with herbal tonics, fed him, and sent him back to civilization with the partisans. The pilot survived the war and became the head of a factory in Kiev. He returned to the forest to check on the woman several times, on each occasion offering to help her move to the Ukrainian town of Znob, about seven miles from her meadow. But Matryona Pavlovna never consented.

Igor heard she died in the late 1970s, having lived a solitary life in the wilderness for nearly thirty years.

In the clearing, Igor and I mounted the horses to return home. I looked back at the big spruce tree, imagining the stories it could tell if only it could talk. Yet somehow the tree spoke of the peacefulness of this meadow in the woods and the life it had nurtured. Then I understood that Matryona Pavlovna had been happy here among her animal friends. Somehow they had given her what people could not: solace, splendor, and independence.

Igor was asked to teach at a training seminar in Moscow for rangers from the entire *zapovednik* system. The State Committee on the Environment, which managed the *zapovedniki*, had received funds from the World Bank to conduct system-wide seminars and increase staff qualifications as a part of the international effort to support the *zapovedniki* during difficult economic and political times. A week before the seminar, Igor had his brother Dima shoot a video on methods for catching poachers. Igor recruited his two sons and his father to act as rangers with him in the video and some of the villagers to act as poachers. We went to the Nerussa River, where the ice had cleared in areas, and enacted scenes illustrating innovative techniques for catching poachers, such as extending a fishing net across the river to entangle the motor on a poacher's boat. The film would become known as *The Shpilenoks Go to Battle* and was a great hit at the seminar.

Igor departed for Moscow for three days, and I stayed home. I didn't clean the house that day, although it was messy, abiding by the Russian superstition not to sweep the man out of the house the day he left. I missed Igor immensely and found myself counting the hours until his return.

I received a radio message from the *zapovednik* that a group of sixth graders from Trubchevsk wanted to visit. They couldn't make it to the visitor's center in the Suzemka District, because the school bus was unable to maneuver the muddy road from Trubchevsk to Suzemka. The teacher wanted to know if I could meet them on the cement bridge over the Nerussa River in the reserve's buffer zone, only a few miles from Trubchevsk. We set up a time to meet the next day. I saddled Orlik and rode north to the bridge, trotting through the reserve along the river. I was pleased that snow had fallen in the night, leaving a fresh slate on the ground on which to point out animal tracks to the children. About half a mile before the bridge, I tied Orlik securely to a tree and walked the rest of the way.

Soon a small school bus appeared, driving down the narrow dirt road to the bridge. The children piled out, and I greeted them. I could tell they were fascinated to be speaking with an American, but they were too shy to question me about my country. They may have wondered why I was in Russia or what it was like to live in America, but they didn't ask. I checked to make sure their footwear was warm and waterproof. We crossed the bridge and walked down to the river. Trash and candy wrappers littered the area under the bridge, where fishermen often fished in the buffer zone. I picked up the wrappers, putting them in my pocket. Some of them followed my example and picked up wrappers on the trail.

We walked along the river toward the reserve. I pointed out beaver tracks in the snow and freshly gnawed branches the animals had left on the bank. I could now identify all the trees, so I tested the children, and by the end of the excursion, they knew them all. I showed them the blue paint on the trunks that marked the border of the *zapovednik* and told them that visitors were not allowed to go into the strictly protected reserve unaccompanied by a ranger. I explained about the *zapovednik*'s federally protected status, and that it was one of one hundred in Russia. I told them that I was envious of their unique protected area system, adding that the National Park System in the United States, while splendid in its own right, did not have near the level of protection afforded *zapovedniki*.

I guess it's something to be proud of, one child said.

You are absolutely right, I replied.

Entering the reserve, some of the children jumped for joy, crying, We're in the *zapovednik*, we're in the *zapovednik*! Evidently the forbidden aspect of the reserve had intrigued them. Perhaps some of their fathers had poached here. At the end of the walk, I handed out informational booklets and pocket calendars and said good-bye. The teacher asked if she could bring another group sometime, and I said fine.

I found Orlik waiting patiently in the woods. On the way home, I wondered if the children would go home and tell their parents about their experience in the reserve. I thought that one of the best ways to build support for the *zapovednik* among adults, poachers even, was through their children.

At the river across from the ranger station, I decided to visit Igor's parents. I tied Orlik again and found the two kayaks strapped together, "the catamaran," as Igor's father called it. The ice was breaking apart, so it was too risky to walk. I got in the catamaran and took up the oar. Half pushing the boats over the ice, half rowing through the water, I struggled to the other side. I pulled the boats up the opposite bank and walked the last three hundred yards to the station. The branches of the apple trees in the orchard were bare except for the fresh covering of snow. I approached the house, and the little dog Charlie first barked, then wagged his tail in greeting. I opened the door to the cold foyer and then entered the warm main room, pushing aside the thick insulating blanket hanging over the door.

Lidya Mikhailovna said hello and told me not to take my boots off. I took them off anyway, and she shoved slippers under my feet. I sat by the woodstove to warm for a minute while she plugged in the teakettle.

Tea? Pyotr Nikitich exclaimed. In this weather, you should try some of my homemade apple wine.

He pulled a five-gallon glass jug from under the counter along the wall and uncorked the narrow neck. He poured the murky golden liquid into three tumblers and offered one to me. I took the cup and sipped the wine. It was pungent yet sweet, like strong apple cider. I drained the glass and soon felt it warm my insides. He poured another.

That's enough, I said, or I won't be able to climb back on the horse.

We sat and drank the wine and talked. As the light began to fade, Pyotr Nikitich walked me to the river and took me across in the catamaran. I waved good-bye from the bank, then climbed onto Orlik and trotted home. The house was cold, so I brought some firewood in from the shed and sat by the opening in the stove to warm my hands. Too tired to cook, I ate sliced cheese and bread and went to sleep.

Igor arrived home the next morning and gave me an account of his trip as I made breakfast of eggs and *salo*. I told him about the excursion and my visit to the ranger station and his father's apple wine. He was angry that I had ventured across the melting river ice on my own.

You could have drowned, he said.

He who doesn't take risks, doesn't drink champagne, I replied, reciting a Russian saying.

Or apple wine, he corrected me.

We read in the Suzemka newspaper that the German government decided to compensate families who had suffered at the hands of the Nazis through a foundation for assistance and reconciliation. Anyone who spent time in a Nazi prison camp during the war was eligible. The residents of Chukhrai and neighboring villages scrambled to collect signatures of witnesses who were held with them in the prison camps in Lokot and elsewhere decades earlier. They sent in the required forms and, a couple of months later, my neighbor Kalkan and his wife were the first in our village to receive over $1,700 each in compensation, enough to provide them with drink for the remainder of their lives four times over. A man from Smelizh bought several liters of *samogon* with his money and got so drunk he fell off the shelf above the stove and cracked his head. He died in the Suzemka hospital the next day. The villagers claimed that this was the Germans' way of getting back at them half a century later.

Belik, a resident of Smelizh, drafted a letter to German Chancellor Kohl. He wrote of the toll the war took on the village and complained that the village was so devastated that the Russian government had never paved the road to it. All the other villagers signed the letter, and they sent it to Bonn. After a month, authorities in the Suzemka District received word that the German government would finance extension of the paved road from Krasnaya Sloboda to Smelizh, meaning that the asphalt path to the outside world would creep two miles closer to Chukhrai. While construction of the road was underway, the mayor of Suzemka called Igor at the *zapovednik* office and said that he might be able to continue the road the rest of the way to Chukhrai. Igor declined, reasoning that the paved road would make the reserve more accessible to poachers.

Igor decided that instead of a better road, we needed a bigger and better vehicle.

A way out, he said to me, in case of an emergency. What if something happens to you?

Winter ice lingered on the water engulfing the forest road. Even the diligent late-winter sun could not penetrate the dense evergreen canopy. Our UAZ jeep stood helpless in the yard, unable to traverse even the first ice-covered expanse on the road. After some research, Igor found what he was looking for. He took the commuter train to Bryansk one morning while I worked at the visitor's center drafting the winter issue of the *Zapovednik Scroll* for the Suzemka and Trubchevsk newspapers.

Late that evening, Igor pulled up in a monstrous truck,

a Russian army GAZ-66 with a big square box on the back. The vehicle was akin to a large tin shed on enormous wheels reaching waist-high. My mouth was agape as I walked out to meet him. I climbed into the truck's cab with difficulty, having to pull myself up by the door handle to put my foot on the sideboard. Igor borrowed some tools from the reserve's garage and put them in the back of the truck.

Inside, we sat comfortably on two large seats with a near orchard of gear sticks between them.

One is the gearshift, Igor explained. One is for high and low gears. One is to turn on four-wheel drive. One is the parking brake. And I don't know what this one is, he said, pointing to a short stick. And you know what else? I can deflate and reinflate the wheels automatically. So if we're driving across a swamp, for example, I can reduce the pressure in the tires so we have a wider base and greater traction.

Why would we want to drive across a swamp? I asked.

You never know.

The big tin box behind us was not accessible from the cab. You had to get out and go around to the back, where there was a ladder that pulled down so you could climb up to the door. Igor said it was empty now, but he envisioned installing a double bed, a kitchen unit, and maybe even a toilet. He said it would be our home on wheels, our expedition vehicle.

Someday, he said, when I'm no longer director of the reserve and can spend more time on photography and with you, we'll travel in this truck to *zapovedniki* all over Russia.

A Russian Winnebago! I exclaimed.

Yes, but this Winnebago can go anywhere, he said. Even to Chukhrai!

Well, I said, let's see.

So he turned the key in the ignition, and the engine

roared to life. He pulled at one of the many gearshifts and, after some jerking and leaping, we were off.

The GAZ-66 could only go forty miles an hour on the highway, so we crawled along the paved road to where the asphalt ended. Then Igor shifted to low gear and we lurched up a snowy incline. Cresting it, we turned down the forest road to Chukhrai. When we reached the first big frozen trough, we looked at each other with anticipation. Igor put the vehicle into low, checked that four-wheel drive was engaged, and urged the truck slowly forward.

The ice cracked and heaved under us. The GAZ-66 plowed right through it, shoving huge, four-foot chunks of thick ice before it. The slabs of ice collected under the bumper, and, when we reached the end of the trough, they formed a veritable mountain of ice that we had to ascend. The vehicle bucked and pulled, climbing over the mountain. Igor stuck out his palm and I smacked it.

Pothole number two. This one engulfed a full three hundred yards of the road. We plowed through the ice, breaking it up and pushing the chunks ahead of us. In the deepest part of the depression, the water submerged the headlights and reached the hood of the truck, over five feet deep. The engine didn't even sputter or gasp. By the end of the water-filled depression, we had scooped up such a large mountain of ice slabs that even the monster machine couldn't surmount it. The truck bucked and heaved, but its bottom became grounded on the ice and the huge tires spun powerlessly. We climbed down from the sharply angled truck and walked around to the front. There was nothing to do but remove the ice. Igor broke it up with the long ice pick he had taken from the reserve office. We grabbed hold of the huge, cold slabs and moved them to the side of the narrow road. When two mountains of ice had formed on either side of the truck, we climbed back in, and Igor revved up the engine. With a roar, the truck lurched over the remaining ice onto firm ground.

Another three hundred yards and we saw something on the road ahead. A tractor was stuck firmly in giant pothole number three. Apparently the driver had abandoned it that morning, and now it was frozen fast in the ice. Igor guessed the tractor was from the electric company. They must have been checking the power line to Chukhrai. We got out to seek an alternate route. The only option was to try to traverse the boggy swamp that flanked the right side of the road. Igor took an axe from the back of the truck to chop down a young tree and open an entrance to the swamp. Taking a mighty swing, he slipped on the ice and missed the tree, sinking the axe firmly into his foot, protected only by a rubber boot and a thick *portyanka* wrapped around a sock.

Arrrgh! he screamed. My foot!

We couldn't see the damage in the darkness, so I helped him climb into the front seat of the truck and turned on the light. The boot had a three-inch slash just above the toe, and blood was starting to seep through. I pulled off the boot and ripped the *portyanka* into strips. The gash was thankfully less than half an inch deep and didn't appear to have reached bone. I wrapped the cloth strips tightly around his foot, and he kept it elevated for a few minutes.

Under normal circumstances, I said, you would need stitches.

Yes, but we don't live in normal circumstances. It'll heal.

He pulled the boot back on and chopped down the tree.

That was nature's way of punishing me for chopping down this tree, he said.

Using a lever attached to each wheel, Igor deflated the

tires slightly and then eased the machine into the opening. We slowly crawled about twenty feet, feeling the frozen bog give way beneath us, then the truck abruptly sank into a depression.

There must be a current here that's keeping the swamp from freezing, Igor said.

He ground the truck into low gear and rocked it gently back and forth, but the wheels only sank further into the mire.

Plan B, said Igor.

He got out and made his way around to the front of the truck, where an enormous winch was fastened to the front bumper. He pulled out the cord and instructed me to pull it to a large birch tree on a hummock in the middle of the swamp. He let the steel cord out, and I dragged it across the bog to the hummock. I wrapped it around the tree and secured the hook on the end to the cord. Igor handed me the controls for the winch, which was attached to a long wire. He showed me how to wind it up and got behind the wheel.

I waited for him to honk, my signal to wind the cord. He honked and slowly engaged the engine while I wound. The truck moved two inches forward, and the cord kept it from slipping back. I looked up at the tall birch tree and thought it had tilted slightly. He honked again, I wound, and he inched forward. Slowly but surely, the truck made its way across the swamp, literally pulling itself out by holding on to the tree. After about thirty minutes, the truck reached the birch and I let out the cord a bit to unhook it. Igor maneuvered the truck around the hummock onto firmer ground and slowly drove the rest of the way out of the bog. I climbed into the front seat, and we pulled back out onto the road. The truck careened to one side as we dipped down into the depression of the road, and I grabbed on to Igor, thinking for a moment we would tip over.

We made it the rest of the way home without incident. The truck was truly unstoppable, but we decided not to abuse it. Adventures like that would reduce its life expectancy, and possibly ours.

The next day, a car met us in Smelizh and took us to the *zapovednik* office. There we learned that the Suzemka state road building enterprise was logging trees in the reserve's buffer zone. Apparently, after enduring centuries of mud, the government was finally going to pave the road from Suzemka to Trubchevsk. Logging and road building is prohibited in the buffer zone, as are other destructive forms of economic exploitation. Furious, Igor and I drove to Suzemka to meet with the director of the road building enterprise. After some negotiation, Igor and the director reached an agreement by which the state company would trade a parcel of land adjacent to the buffer zone for the area they wanted to use for the road. In the end, Igor said it worked out better, because the new, larger parcel of land would help round out the buffer zone along its western boundary.

Economic pressure to use protected forest resources was on the rise. Soon thereafter, a forestry enterprise from Trubchevsk began illegally logging a plot in the northern part of the buffer zone. We took the sleigh to the spot and discovered that they had cut down century-old pine trees. On the ground, we found pellets from a colony of rare bats that lived in hollow tree trunks. Igor pointed out that several hundred more of the trees had been marked with an axe for felling.

When I was younger, Igor told me, I took radical

methods to stop this kind of thing.

He explained how, before the *zapovednik* was created, he had hammered dozens of nails in old-growth trees marked for felling. Several of the trees held black stork nests. The nails had a negligible impact on the trees, but stopped logging companies from logging them further. After the lumberjacks broke the first chain saw on the nails, they were forced to call the operation to a halt.

Now that Igor was director of the *zapovednik*, he had to work through official channels to stop the logging. Later, at the *zapovednik* office, Igor phoned Governor Lodkin in Bryansk to request his help in canceling the operation. Igor hoped that, in a show of his support for the reserve, the governor would put a stop to the illegal logging, saving hundreds of old-growth pines.

I received a telegram at the *zapovednik* office that the parents of the baby I had helped deliver in the commuter train just over a year before wanted to meet me. A week later, Igor and I made a trip to Bryansk to begin organizing a festival to build support for the *zapovednik* in the capital city. We were planning the environmental holiday for April, to coincide with the annual March for Parks celebration. On the way back, we decided to stop in and see the girl I had helped bring into the world. The road to the village was nearly as treacherous as the one to Chukhrai. They lived along the railroad, in a tiny village one stop from the district center of Navlya, which was about halfway between Suzemka and Bryansk.

We found them at home in their small house of dull gray bricks along the tracks. The man worked for the railroad. They greeted us warmly and invited us into their small kitchen.

THE STORKS' NEST

There was barely enough room for the four of us to sit on low stools around the stove. I pulled some toys and fruit from a bag and placed them on a small table under the window.

Thank you, the woman said. The baby is napping. We named her Katya.

How ever did you find us? I asked.

A journalist from Bryansk sent us a letter, the man said, and told us you work at the *zapovednik*. We were sorry you couldn't join us for the May holidays last year. We sent a telegram to you through the railroad.

We never received the message, Igor replied.

We had prepared a feast. Now, he continued apologetically, gesturing around the sparse kitchen, we have nothing.

The woman looked at me and said, We had hoped you would be our daughter's godmother. But hearing no reply, we went ahead and christened her.

I'm flattered, I said, but I'm not Russian Orthodox. Not yet, anyway.

The man and woman related the events of the day their baby was born. When the woman's contractions started, the couple waited all afternoon for a train to stop and take them to Navlya, where the nearest hospital was located. The man waved down every cargo and passenger train that passed, but none stopped at the tiny platform. With no other means of transportation, they were forced to wait until the evening commuter train. The woman told us that she could feel the baby's head crowning by the time they finally boarded.

How far is it from here to Navlya? I asked.

Ten minutes, the man said.

Unbelievable, Igor said.

Can I take a peek at the baby? I asked.

Sure, the woman said, motioning to a door leading to

another room, the only other one in the tiny house.

The little girl lay on her stomach, stretched out diagonally across a crib, which occupied nearly half of the tiny room. Her clothing was dirty and tattered. But that was not what struck me. I admired her beautiful blond curls and pale, sweet sleeping face. I couldn't believe that this large tot was the same tiny, naked infant I had held in my hands that cold January night in the train.

Sometimes I would think that all rainbows must end in Chukhrai with the amount of gold supposedly buried here. Indeed, on several occasions I had seen double and even triple rainbows spanning the sky above our paddock after a rainstorm. Perhaps they led to the pot of gold of my purported great-grandfather Matvey or the buried treasure Olga Ivanovna had told me about on the bank of the river. Or maybe, if I followed them, the brilliant arcs would curve around and end right back here, somewhere in our yard, where the relatives of my neighbors Lepen and Glukhaya were said to have buried the cursed Presnyakov gold.

As the story goes, twelve generations ago a man and his two sons from Chukhrai's Presnyakov family, of which Lepen and Glukhaya are descendents, went to Trubchevsk one winter to earn money repairing wooden barrels and doing other odd jobs. There the three men met a rich merchant who paid them well for their services. He came to trust them and let them spend the night in his house. One day when he went out, he left the keys and told them they could stay. The Presnyakov men found a locked wooden chest in one of the rooms. They turned it over, broke out the bottom, and found a sack of gold. They took the gold and put the trunk

286
THE STORKS' NEST

back without touching the lock so the merchant wouldn't notice. They packed their things, and, as soon as the merchant returned, they started off.

Wait, join me for lunch, he said to the men. What's the hurry?

But they refused and quickly departed. The merchant thought this odd, since normally the men ate with him before they left. He opened the trunk and found the gold missing. He and his men pursued the thieves on horseback. They caught them in the woods on the way to Chukhrai, but the Presnyakovs opened their bags and showed the merchant that they had nothing. Later, the merchant came to Chukhrai and asked them to give the gold back, like honest men. He offered to split it with them and said that no one would have to know, that there would be enough for everybody.

We didn't take it, the men said, and that's that.

So the merchant said that if they were telling the truth, they should come with him to the church and swear that they hadn't taken the gold. They agreed and went to the church in Krasnaya Sloboda. They swore in front of the priest on the Pyotr's Grave Holy Book, one of the holiest books in the Russian Orthodox Church. If they were lying, the merchant said, anyone in their family who touched the gold would be cursed, for twelve generations.

The Presnyakov men later went to the woods to dig up the gold they had buried. They brought it home, and all three of them died almost immediately. Every member of the family who touched the gold fell ill. Some died, some went mad, others got tuberculosis. Three generations of Presnyakovs died in the three years after they stole the gold. Only those who refused to touch it survived. For many years, none of the other villagers wanted to build on their land. No one would marry their daughters and granddaughters.

Two of the Presnyakov brothers used to live in a house on what was now Igor's land. It was said that they buried the gold somewhere on the plot. The villagers were certain it was still there somewhere. They speculated whether Igor had discovered it when he dug the pit for our foundation, or perhaps I found it while poking around in my garden.

Maslenitsa, marking the arrival of spring, arrived early that year, at the end of February. I made traditional *bliny* and *paskha* during the week. Shrove Sunday, literally "Forgiveness Sunday" in Russian, marks the last day of Maslenitsa. On this day, all are to forgive each other, and Igor even forgave Stepan for bringing the mail two weeks late.

A group of students from Moscow spent Maslenitsa week at the reserve doing fieldwork. I went to the reserve with them on several occasions to help them identify birds and set traps for the field mice they were studying. They turned an old cabin in Chukhrai into their base camp. On Sunday they invited us to join their Maslenitsa celebration. They fashioned a scarecrow out of straw to symbolize Old Man Winter, then set it ablaze, carrying it on a stick through the village. That evening we made a bonfire outside the cabin and sat around and sang songs accompanied by the strumming of an old guitar. I was amazed that at gatherings like these there was always someone who played guitar and everyone knew the words to the songs. Sitting in a circle on logs half buried in snow and warming our hands over the fire while our backs absorbed the chill, we were pleased to have orchestrated a proper welcome for spring.

Spring, unfortunately, wasn't ready to arrive. For the next

few days, snow continued to fall and the temperature dipped to well below freezing. Meltwater in the village turned into a smooth sheet of ice. Yet when the sun peeked out late one morning, warming my face and the back of my neck, I could sense that spring was not far off. A little flutter of excitement, hardly perceptible, buzzed through me as I basked in the late winter sun. The few birds—bullfinches, sparrows, and jays—that braved the winter were also more active, flitting from bough to bough, rejoicing that warmer days were soon to come.

THE STORKS' NEST

SPRING

PATCHES OF bare ground peeked through the melting blanket of snow, and the Nerussa's waters finally flowed free. Ice still remained on the submerged forest road, however, and Igor said it wouldn't clear until the beginning of April. But it appeared that the three white horses of December, January, and February, according to the Russian folk song, had reared their heads and reluctantly galloped away.

I was busy during March organizing the environmental festival in Bryansk, which we were calling "Long Live the Bryansk Forest." The festival would coincide with the March for Parks celebration in April. My assistant, Natasha, and I traveled to the provincial capital nearly every week, and I reluctantly tore myself away from Igor and from the sanctuary of Chukhrai and the *zapovednik*. We arranged for a band to play at the opening ceremony and a youth comedy club to perform an act with an environmental theme. Governor Lodkin agreed to open the festival. We involved schoolteachers in the process and organized drawing contests in the schools. The *Bryansk Worker* wanted to sponsor a drawing contest as well, regularly publishing children's pictures in the newspaper. Natasha and I composed questions for quizzes on nature in the Bryansk Forest and procured prizes for the winners. When all the arrangements had been made, I took a few days off to help Igor build blinds in the woods before the black storks arrived from Africa.

We hauled boards and plywood for three blinds on two horse-drawn sleighs deep into the woods. At one point, Igor knew of twenty-four occupied black stork nests within a twenty-mile radius of Chukhrai. Twenty-four pairs. That was forty-eight black storks, plus their young, more than the entire nesting population of many European countries. Since Igor made the black stork the symbol of the reserve, the bird had become a symbol for conservation of the entire Bryansk Forest. No wonder he needed more photographs of the elusive bird.

I was at the reins behind Orlik, and Igor drove Aza. Kisa hopped in my lap and grabbed the reins with his teeth, nearly steering my sleigh into a tree. We first headed north to the Hunchback Bridge, then turned along an overgrown logging road into the reserve. A mile within its boundary, I noticed a deftly laid circle of supple birch branches on the ground next to the road. Wild boars had fashioned a soft bed for themselves where they piled together to keep warm. They must have abandoned the nest upon hearing us only moments before, because soon we spotted a chain of tiny brown piglets with white spots and stripes tearing through the woods after their startled mother.

A thirty-foot ice-covered pothole yawned ahead on the road. Aza and Igor made it across in their sleigh, but the thin ice began to crack under the weight. When I drove Orlik forward into the middle of the pothole, the cracked ice gave way and Orlik fell through. The sleigh with me aboard still rested firmly on the ice behind Orlik, its broad base lending it support. Although the water was only three feet deep, the ground underneath was slippery, and Orlik couldn't get his footing in the puddle. He frantically tried to stand, thrashing his legs. Igor jumped from his sleigh to push us from behind while I pulled at the reins.

After a few minutes, Orlik gave in and lay down in the cold water. Kisa barked at him excitedly, jumping into the water and grabbing Orlik's mane with his teeth, trying to pull him up. I lifted the wet dog out of the cold water and tossed him into the hay on my sleigh.

Now I was frantic. My horse would freeze to death if we couldn't get him out.

Igor quickly removed the harness, and we pulled the sleigh out of the way. We grabbed Orlik's bridle on either side and pulled his head up, trying not to fall into the water ourselves.

Come on, Orlik, get up! I pleaded.

Нииии, stand up! Igor yelled.

Orlik tried again, putting his legs out in front of him. He slipped, then tried again and got one hoof onto solid ice. He pulled himself up and jumped out of the water onto the ice and then the nearby embankment of the road. The bridle had come off from our pulling, so I put it back on and took some hay and rubbed Orlik's wet coat.

Come on, let's go, Igor said. The best way for him to get warm is to pull the sleigh.

We dragged the sleigh the rest of the way through the icy water and put Orlik back in the harness.

Igor wiped the tears from my cheeks. Don't worry, he said, he'll be fine.

I urged Orlik into a trot and kept him running to the first black storks' nest. After another mile and a half, we pulled into a swamp and tied the horses to trees. We carried the boards across the swamp to a hummock with a towering oak, making several trips. A large storks' nest nestled in a crook of the huge oak tree. Igor scouted the area around the tree and found the perfect spot from which to photograph the storks, considering the relative positions of the morning sun and his camera. I dragged branches over while Igor assembled the blind. He had already cut the wood to size and drilled holes for the bolts. He had painted the boards dark green to camouflage them in the forest. The resulting box was cramped, just big enough to accommodate Igor hunched over his camera. It contained a low bench for him to sit on. With a small handsaw, he had carved out a round hole for his camera lens. I tried the blind, imagining how he would have to sit here motionless from before dawn until after dusk, when he could leave without the birds seeing him.

How will you sit here for hours on end, I asked, with all the mosquitoes swarming around you?

That's not the biggest problem, Igor said. Where am I going to pee?

The weather warmed, and the ice on the forest road to Smelizh melted in early April. For a few weeks, the potholes filled with meltwater and merged, transforming the road into a river. Then the water slowly drained across the boggy forest to the floodplain and the Nerussa's waters began to rise. The tips of the willows turned red, and buds on the trees swelled.

I heard Kisa howling outside the gate one night, so I stepped out to let him in the yard. Suddenly, I was struck by the loud honking of hundreds, maybe thousands, of geese.

THE STORKS' NEST

I looked up to see them flying low over Chukhrai on their way north under a clear night sky with a million stars. The honking was music to my ears. Spring had finally arrived! So many geese could not be mistaken. I ran home to tell Igor, and his face lit upon seeing my excitement.

See all that you missed living in the city? he said.

The jeep turned into a boat as we made our way out of Chukhrai, with the road a gushing river. We were to meet a potential sponsor for the reserve at the visitor's center, a businessman from Moscow escorted by an official from the State Committee on the Environment in Bryansk.

We greeted the official and his two guests: the businessman, small, nearly bald, and dressed in an expensive Italian suit, and a slender young woman. She was perhaps half his age, wearing a miniskirt and a low-cut top. We showed them around the visitor's center and had tea. The man seemed interested in photos of the bison release on the wall.

Sensing an opportunity, Igor told them about the bison program. He said that the *zapovednik* now had two female bison, but only one male, who didn't seem to be doing his job. Neither of the females was pregnant, he explained, and we were worried about the fate of the herd. We still hadn't received the second batch of bison we had been promised, and we were not sure when we would.

How much does a bison cost? the man inquired.

About $800 for a healthy male, Igor replied, including the cost of transportation from the breeding center.

The man pulled out his wallet and unflinchingly counted off six hundred-dollar bills. Then he turned to his female friend and whispered something in her ear. She reached into

295

THE STORKS' NEST

her pocket and gave him $200, probably pocket money he had given her.

Here, the man said, pushing the money across the table to Igor. But make sure it's a big strong bull.

The more things were changing in the new Russia, the more they stayed the same in Chukhrai. Elsewhere political and economic reforms, speculation, and corruption were wreaking havoc in the country, and uncertainty was the name of the game. On the streets of distant Moscow, businesses came and went in a matter of weeks, and drive-by shootings often took care of the competition. Currency devaluations and reforms meant that new ruble notes appeared and old ones vanished, along with their value. People who had trusted the one state bank with their savings suddenly found themselves with nothing. Others got rich from overnight speculation and corrupt pyramid schemes.

None of this affected Chukhrai, however. Each year the villagers hauled manure and sowed the land as they always had. Their investments—potatoes, beets, cows, and pigs— continued to grow.

Like mushrooms after the rain, politicians from Suzemka popped up in Smelizh and even Chukhrai. They posed with shovels to spread manure, hoping to win votes.

What do you need, *babushki*? one of the candidates asked. Medicine? I'll make sure you get what you need.

We don't need anything, they replied. We are used to getting by without.

Television brought new diversions on the one state-owned channel that reached Chukhrai. Through a window, I saw Shamornoy watching his television's reflection in the

THE STORKS' NEST

mirror. All the garbage on TV comes from the devil, he said. Many of the villagers believed that if they watched TV in the mirror, the devil couldn't reach them.

The only real difference between then and now, Olga Ivanovna told me, is before we had money, but there was nothing to buy. Now the city stores have everything, but we have no money.

The result was that the villagers still had nothing. There were no signs of political or economic change in Chukhrai, just the repetitions of the seasons as they came and went.

Thinking that businesses in Bryansk might be in a position to sponsor reserve activities, I traveled to the city to meet with the directors of several large companies. They seemed puzzled that an American was asking for money for nature protection in the Bryansk Forest, but in time, I won small contributions for the *zapovednik*—probably only because they were intrigued by my efforts. A computer manufacturer donated computers and software, a printing company offered a free print run for our informational brochure, and a liquor factory provided funds to purchase grain for the bison.

But we were unprepared for the phone call we received one day from a woman named Elena Postalateva offering her assistance. Thus far, we had only been able to round up nominal contributions by exerting a great deal of effort. And here was someone calling us to volunteer support.

My husband and I are small farmers in the Trubchevsk region, the woman told Igor over the phone. We don't have much, but we want to support what you're doing.

That's wonderful, said Igor. Let's arrange a meeting.

Elena invited Igor to visit her farm. A few days later,

Igor drove to Trubchevsk and then north along the Desna to the property.

He found the house without difficulty. It was a collection of old train cars haphazardly placed together and surrounded by several dozen acres of farmland. Elena, an attractive, pleasantly plump woman of about forty, introduced him to her husband, Sergei, a cheerful, thin man with a bushel of disheveled blond hair on his head and deep lines on his face. Within a few minutes, Elena elaborately set the table in the small kitchen. Roasted chicken—her own, she said—potatoes, preserved vegetables, and salted herring—*seliodka*—Igor's favorite. And, of course, vodka.

Igor drank sparingly as they talked about the *zapovednik*. They explained how they had followed the bison reintroduction program in the papers and wanted to help in some way. Elena asked if the reserve needed grain or hay to feed the animals.

Igor could see that they were struggling as farmers. Aging farm equipment littered the yard. The makeshift house was modest and its furnishings old and torn. There were holes in the kitchen floor through which a black-and-white cat poked its head during the meal.

Igor told them that any contribution would be greatly appreciated, and he invited them to visit the reserve.

The next weekend I prepared lunch while Igor met the farmers in Smelizh. When they arrived in Chukhrai, they piled out of the jeep bearing baskets of gifts: a freshly plucked goose, jars of pickles, homemade liquor, *seliodka*, and much more. They brought two of their three teenage daughters with them. The girls were not related, being from previous marriages, yet they all seemed to interact easily as a family.

Before lunch we drove to the enclosure to show them where the bison had been released. Elena and Sergei took a sack of oats from the back of the jeep and poured the contents into the feeding trough while Igor snapped pictures. Igor told them that the bison would probably come after dark to check the troughs. Afterward, I saddled Aza and took the girls for a ride. It was the first time they had been on a horse. Spirits were high as we sat down in our small kitchen for lunch.

Elena was gracious and commented on my carrot salad, asking for the recipe. I served brownies for dessert and offered tea. Igor produced a strong balsam liqueur made from pine buds and other herbs from the Bryansk Forest.

Elena turned to Igor and remarked, You are very lucky to have such a good cook.

All she feeds me is carrot salad and brownies, Igor complained, when what I really want is good Russian *salo* and *seliodka*!

We all laughed. Igor poured a round of the balsam liqueur, and we toasted the bison.

Then Elena proposed a toast. Let's toast to us, she said, to the beginning of a friendship.

She was right. We would become the best of friends.

More than two thousand people attended the "Long Live the Bryansk Forest" festival in the provincial capital on April 22, about half of them schoolchildren. The concert, games, and performances ran smoothly. All the region's newspapers and television stations publicized the event. Our new friends Elena and Sergei and their daughters came to show their support. At the end of the day, the reserve staff came away exhausted but triumphant. We had lifted the *zapovednik* to a whole new level of awareness in the region. New sponsors proposed to fund reserve activities, and groups of school-children and older students from Bryansk soon began to pour into our visitor's center.

Back home, in the calm of Chukhrai, the noisy events of our hectic day in the city quickly faded from my mind. Here it was the holiday of Saint George the Victorious, which marks the beginning of the growing season for the villagers. Saint George, astride a mighty steed and having conquered the "snake" of paganism, as pictured in Russian icons and tsarist coins, is revered in Russia for tirelessly professing the Christian faith. The saint, known more simply as Egorye to the Russian peasants, is closely associated with peasant life. The two holidays for the saint, celebrated April 23 and November 26, mark the beginning and the end of the growing season.

Many traditions in Chukhrai are associated with the vernal holiday, also known as Egorye. The villagers begin to plow their fields and sow seeds after Egorye. If there is frost on Egorye, it is said that oats and millet will grow well that year. The dew that falls on this day is thought to have healing powers. The villagers used to take clean tablecloths and soak them in the dew, then rub them over their cattle to protect them.

After Egorye the villagers, no matter what squabbles they may have had and how many decades old their feuds, turn to the fields and help each other plow their plots and plant potatoes. That is how it has been done for generations.

I crept slowly and soundlessly toward the foxhole I had scouted out in winter. Fewer than one hundred yards away, I saw three-week-old fox kits bounding recklessly up and down on the low mound pitted with the multiple entrances to their den. The mother was evidently away. She would not let them be so careless in plain sight. I hid behind trees rimming the clearing as I inched closer to the unsuspecting kits. I crouched behind a fallen oak not fifty feet from the den, and I watched the comic creatures through my binoculars. They jumped around as if on pogo sticks, pouncing on imaginary mice. They broadsided each other and tumbled in the sand, nipping and scratching.

They were oblivious to my presence. I crawled closer to the mound on my hands and knees, hiding behind small hummocks and tufts of grass. I lay with my stomach flat to the ground when I reached the edge of the broad mound, only ten feet from the noisily frolicking foxes. The wind was blowing in my face, steering my scent and sound away from the animals. Yet even if they could have smelled or heard me, their senses had not yet been tuned to such danger. I slowly took Igor's cast-off Nikon camera from its case and set the exposure. With Igor and Nikolai, there were already two accomplished wildlife photographers in the reserve, but I nonetheless took pleasure in honing my skills. Just for fun, I would tell Igor after getting fuzzy photos back.

I centered one of the fox kits in my lens. I snapped his profile when he stood still for a moment, his ears cocked at something in the distance. Hearing the click of the shutter, he abruptly turned toward me. I snapped his portrait again. His green eyes sparkled in the sunshine as he looked down my lens. He was not afraid. He stood motionlessly and watched me. The other two kits, sensing his intent gaze, stopped their cavorting and sniffed the air. My photogenic fox slowly inched toward me, pausing with each step to extend his nose, rigidly holding one front paw in the air. When he was four feet from me, I unhurriedly put down the camera and stared him in the face. He stared back, transfixed.

Just then, I heard a single loud yelp from the edge of the glade. The fox kits jumped into the air and dove into the safety of their den. The mother fox was returning from a hunting foray. Either her warning call had caused them to seek shelter or they realized they would be in trouble for being so reckless while she had been away. I saw her approaching the den about 150 yards away, and I slowly retreated, not wanting to alarm her. As she neared the mound, she stopped for a moment to study my lingering scent.

During the next two weeks, I returned to the foxhole daily and had repeated success observing and photographing the kits. I learned the mother's routine and respectfully left before her return. The fox kits quickly became accustomed to my unthreatening company, romping and playing in front of me. I enjoyed my time with the foxes, watching them as they watched me.

Weeks later I developed the film. Igor, impressed with the photos, praised my work.

I just pushed the button, I said. The foxes were the real stars.

Thinking of the foxes' home, I realized that Igor's village had become mine in just a year's time. I loved that here I could observe baby foxes grow, walk out my front door to the sound of cranes greeting the dawn, or watch as a startled boar across the lake ran for the safety of the trees. I felt fully immersed in nature, something I had always dreamed of. And I wholly appreciated it, having spent much of my life in cities.

I was amazed how when one motorcycle scooted by, the smell of its exhaust lingered, irritating my nose and making me sneeze. I hoped never to live in the city again.

In four short seasons, one cycle of life, I had become one with nature. So much of what I had learned, I owed to Igor. I had mastered the stealthy walk of a partisan moving through the woods, freezing when I heard the slightest shifting of an animal ahead. I had learned to identify trees in the forest and decipher animal tracks in the soft earth. I was fearless in the woods, certain that a strange sound would quickly become identifiable as the flapping of a wood grouse's wings or the screeching of two entwined pines bending in the wind. I knew the uses of the herbs growing in the meadow, and I dried them to make medicinal teas for when I developed a cough. I could coax food from the garden and eggs from the hens.

All that I gained in one year made my efforts with Igor to preserve the Bryansk Forest and my desire to appreciate the timeless local traditions seem worthy endeavors.

I was sitting on the broad bench in Olga Ivanovna's main room. We had just finished planting potatoes in her garden, now diminished from an enormous plot in the field to the bounds of her fenced-in yard. With her health waning, it was all she could handle. She was teaching me how to weave round throw rugs from strips of cloth. She pulled out a plastic bag with the material: old dresses, robes, towels, stockings, and other fabric that she had saved for this purpose. She had ripped each garment into thin strips and sewed the strips together, rolling them up into balls of fabric now ready to use. She took up a thin metal rod with a hook on one end that

Khovryach had fashioned for her out of a nail. She looped a length of light blue cloth around the hook, then pulled another loop through it, and another, and another. Soon she held a flat circle that would be the center of the rug.

She picked up a ball of pink fabric in her small, wrinkled hands. My old nightgown, she said shyly, handing it to me. Here, you try.

The cloth smelled of fragrant Russian household soap, bars of which the villagers often stored between stacks of sheets and clothing to keep them smelling fresh. She guided me as I looped the fabric over the hook. After several dozen loops, my pink ring surrounded her blue circle. We continued until the rug was nearly ten inches in diameter.

Enough, she said. I'll work on it later.

A few days later, Olga Ivanovna came over with a plastic bag in one hand and her cane in the other. This is for you, she said, handing me the bag.

I opened it and unrolled the fabric rug, now a full four feet in diameter. It was beautiful. Colorful rings of tightly knitted fabric. Fabric with a history. Each ring, like the rings on a tree, told a story about a point in her life, in the life of Chukhrai.

Taking my clue from the villagers, I began to work the soil in my garden. The previous year's preserves were gone, and I was eager to taste fresh vegetables. On the ground on my hands and knees, I churned the soil with my trowel, making shallow furrows in which to sow carrot, radish, lettuce, and parsley seeds.

I looked up upon hearing a clattering and batting of wings and saw a white stork arriving to claim the nest in our yard. It was probably the male, staking out his territory. Likely the same one as last year, and the year before. Soon its mate arrived. They threw their heads over their backs, cocking their wings, beating a drumroll in their elation of being joined once again. The male jumped up on his mate's back and flapped his wings to lighten his load as the pair copulated. The female tossed her head and rattled her beak in accord. The birds had not seen each other for nearly eight months. Males and females winter in different locations, perhaps growing weary of each other's company in the close quarters of their summer abode. They parted ways last August to fly to their respective wintering grounds, only to meet again the following spring, same time, same place. I wondered if they knew to worry, to hope that nothing would happen to the other on the long flight to Africa, during the winter there, or on the long flight back. Perhaps they just flew, not knowing why or what would draw them back to the same place over and over. I didn't know how long this pair had been together, but storks are monogamous and can live thirty years or more. Now they returned each year to our backyard, their meeting place, their summer home. Reuniting to re-create their family. Was it my imagination or did they truly rejoice in seeing each other for the first time this year, just moments ago, knowing that all is well and their kin would go on?

I walked over to our unfinished house to rest in the shade for a moment, my back against the cool bricks. While we would soon renew the construction project, I had come to realize that with the road to Chukhrai rutted as it was, it would take us several more years to finish the house. Fortunately, I was in no hurry to leave Igor's side.

I stood for a few moments, peacefully thinking about

the storks, the house, Igor. Then I was startled by Orlik as he abruptly came around the corner of the house, galloping from the pasture to the barn. He whinnied loudly to Aza, who was returning from the woods with Igor. Igor's long legs were wrapped around Aza's expanding belly, heavy with foal. Igor smiled and waved to me as I walked back to the garden.

I took a moist clump of soil in my hands. It felt warm from the midday sun. It felt alive. Suddenly I knew this was my home. Maybe the villagers were right. I had found gold.

I walked over to the well and slid the bucket on the long wooden pole into the cool water below. I pulled the brimming bucket up and poured the water into two smaller pails. I carried them over to my freshly planted rows. Slowly, so the water wouldn't slosh over the sides.

THE VILLAGERS

Forester Vasily Ermolaevich Kopylov, born 1961. Came to Chukhrai from Riga in 1993 with his wife, Tatiana, born 1960, and son, Dima, born 1987. Tatiana's mother was originally from the village before being resettled during the war. Tatiana's great-grandfather and Trofimovna's father were brothers. Vasily secured one of the two jobs in the village, as the resident forester, hence his nickname. Their son, Dima, the only child in the village, walks eight miles to school in Krasnaya Sloboda twice a week and spends the rest of his time fishing on the Nerussa River with his father.

Glukhaya Maria Vasilevna Presnya-kova, born 1930. Our next-door neighbor. She and Kalkan are first cousins. Has been deaf since she bumped her head sliding under a train to cross the tracks as a girl. Glukhaya means "deaf woman."

Kalinyonok Ivan Mikhailovich Balakhonov, born 1934. Lives with his wife, Anna Mikhailovna, born 1933, at the far end of the village from us. Ivan's grandfather and Olga Ivanovna's uncle were brothers. His wife is Kalkan's half-sister. He is the only one in Chukhrai who still knows how to shape wooden runners for horse-drawn sleighs. His nickname comes from his great-grandfather's moniker "Kalina," meaning "arrow wood."

Kalkan Vasily Mikhailovich Balakhonov, born 1936, and wife, Maria Ivanovna (Kalkanikha), born 1930. Kalinyonok's grandfather and Olga Ivanovna's uncle were Kalkan's great-uncles. The couple lives in a tumbledown cabin with a leaky roof across the way from us. Both are avid drinkers. *Kalkan* is the word for the pine sap that male wild boars rub on their shoulders to form a protective armor when sparring with other males for mates. He inherited the name from a stable hand at the *kolkhoz* suspected of being his father. Their nephew Nikolai, known as "Balyk" (meaning "a cured side of meat or fish"), periodically comes from Suzemka to live with them and go on drinking binges.

Khovryach Vasily Ivanovich Balakhonov, born 1960. One of the two village drunks. His father (who was also the postlady's father) was Olga Ivanovna's first cousin once removed. Lives alone since his mother died. His house, which flanks one of the depressions that connects to the Nerussa River in spring, is often flooded. He inherited the nickname "Khovryach," Old Russian for "swine," from his forefathers. ***Kiset***, Nikolai Nikolaevich Balakhonov, born 1959, is inseparable from drinking pal Khovryach (their great-grandfathers were brothers). Lives at the other end of the village with his aging mother, Anna Andreevna. Often seen with Khovryach lying on the road between Smelizh and Chukhrai. Has invalid status due to a plastic plate in his head, installed after the front part of his skull was smashed by a metal part that flew from a lathe. The nickname "Kiset," inherited from his father, means a small tobacco pouch.

Kudinyonok Ivan Mikhailovich Balakhonov, born 1934. Lives with his wife, Anastasia Yakovlevna, born 1929, next door to Kalinyonok (who has the exact same name). Known to be frugal, yet resourceful. Comes to collect the cows from pasture each evening. His nickname is the diminutive of his stumpy stepfather's: "Kudik," meaning "stumpy or runtlike."

Lepen Stepan Andreevich Presnyakov, born 1916. One of the two patriarchs in the village and a notorious poacher. His father and Glukhaya's grandfather were brothers. Lepen's house stands back-to-back with Igor's. But for creating a potential fire danger to his own house, Lepen might have burned down Igor's to avenge being caught poaching in the nature reserve numerous times. The name, which he inherited from his father, is thought to mean "wet snowflakes."

Olga Ivanovna Olga Ivanovna Balakhonova, born 1920. My friend and source for much of the folklore and village history recounted in this book. A first cousin of Kalinyonok's father, Kudinyonok's father-in-law, Trofimovna's mother, and Khovryach's grandmother. Believed by some of the villagers to be a witch because she can heal with herbs and break curses. Has lived alone since her husband, Pavel, died in the war. Has two surviving daughters, one in Smelizh and one in Trubchevsk. A third died in the Chukhrai famine of 1947.

Igor Petrovich Shpilenok, born 1960. Naturalist, photographer, and environmental activist. Moved to a house on the only lake in Chukhrai in 1991 to be closer to the Bryansk Forest Zapovednik, which he founded in 1987. Originally from Belaya Beriozka, twenty miles from Chukhrai as the crow flies and on the border with Ukraine, Igor spent his youth exploring the Bryansk Forest in search of the black stork. Most of the villagers call him by his patronymic, Petrovich.

Shamornoy Mikhail Feodorovich Presnyakov, born 1910. The infamous old poacher, village patriarch, and Igor's archnemesis. Likely distantly related to Lepen and Glukhaya. Lives alone at the opposite end of the village since his wife died. Raised five sons and three daughters. His nickname comes from the hellebore plant, which drives livestock mad when they accidentally eat it.

Stepan Stepan Aleksandrovich Trotsenko, born 1937. Came from the Ukraine in 1991 to live with a woman in Krasnaya Sloboda. After she died two years later, he moved in with Chukhrai's postlady. Occasionally the villagers call him Khokhol, meaning "a tuft of hair" (from the old Ukrainian custom of shaving the head except for a single tuft of hair on the top). The **postlady**, Antonina (Tonka) Ivanovna Balakhonova, born 1948, walks the six miles to Smelizh twice a week to fetch the village mail. Being deathly afraid of the dogs all the villagers keep, she gives it to Stepan. Half-sister of Khovryach.

Trofimovna Evdokiya (Dunya) Trofimovna Balakhonova, born 1923. Lives alone across from us. Never married and not on speaking terms with many of the villagers or even her own family members.

The Storks' Nest

RUSSIAN WORDS, NAMES, AND PLACES

amerikanka   American girl or woman. Also an invasive weed that overruns the villagers' gardens. The weed and the Colorado potato beetle keep Russian farmers occupied all summer. Some blame me, an American from Colorado, for both banes.

babushka   grandmother, old woman.

babye leto   Old Wives' summer or Indian summer.

banya   steam bath. Sweating in the *banya* is a favorite Russian pastime. *Banyas* are more common in northern regions of Russia and often provide the only means of getting clean in the countryside.

bednyak(i)   poor peasant(s), many of whom were promoted to high-ranking positions as part of Stalin's repression of merchants and prosperous peasants at the end of the 1920s and early 1930s.

berioza   birch tree. The root for the names of many Russian villages, including Belaya Beriozka (White Birch), the town twenty miles from Chukhrai on the border of Ukraine, where Igor grew up, and Beriozovka (Birch

Wood), the village near the *zapovednik* headquarters where I bought a house upon moving to the reserve.

blin(y)   crepe(s). A Russian staple traditionally served on Maslenitsa to mark the arrival of spring. Recipe page 50.

borsch   beet-based soup. Tradition has it that a spoon should stand upright in a good, thick bowl of borsch. Recipe page 174.

bublik(i)   thick, ring-shaped bread roll(s). My food staple when I first came to Russia in 1990 as a vegetarian.

chornye vorony   literally "black ravens," as the black vans that took people away during the purges of the 1930s were called. A black raven took away Igor's great-grandfather, and he was never heard from again.

Chukhrai   the tiny village in the Nerussa River floodplain that Igor and I call home. The village lacks a passable road for much of the year, effectively cutting it off from civilization. In the spring of 1997, Chukhrai has twenty mostly elderly residents, down from three hundred before the war. The meaning of the word comes from the Belarussian *chukhrai*, or "working man."

Ded moroz   Father Frost. Russia's equivalent of Santa Claus, who appears on New Year's Eve with gifts and merriment.

dikaya babka   the "wild old woman" who refused to return to civilization after she lost her loved ones in the war and lived the rest of her life in a secluded meadow in the Bryansk Forest.

Egorye   Egorye the Brave, or Saint George the Victorious. Revered for professing the Christian faith in Russia and stamping out the "snake" of paganism. Holidays to honor the saint are celebrated on April 23 and November 26. Many village traditions are associated with Egorye.

fartsofshik(i)   small-time black marketeers(s) who sold souvenirs and other goods to foreigners in the early 1990s.

fufaika   a warm coat of wadded cotton worn by peasants in the countryside, and a gift to me from Governor Lodkin.

ispug   a fright or alarm, usually associated with a curse, and potentially healed by medicine women.

Ivan Kupala   John the Baptist. A religious holiday celebrated July 7 and associated with many traditions in the Russian countryside, including collecting the elusive but inspiring blossom of the flowering fern. Also the saint in honor of whom the old church at Staroye Yamnoye was named.

kisel   a drink made from fruit (usually cranberries) and thickened with starch—like liquid Jell-O.

kolhoz(y)   collective farm(s). The villagers of Chukhrai were forced to join the *kolkhoz* after the Great Famine of 1933. They had to work a certain number of workday units and were paid only in kind, with the produce the farm reaped.

koromysl   a yoke used to carry buckets of water, and, again, a gift to me from Governor Lodkin.

Krasnaya Sloboda   a village of about three hundred people located eight miles from Chukhrai and two miles beyond Smelizh, where the paved road to Suzemka begins. Its church, serving the region, was destroyed by the

Communists in the 1930s. The closest elementary school to Chukhrai is located in Krasnaya Sloboda. The name means "Red Settlement."

Kreschenie   an important religious holiday (Epiphany, in the West), celebrated January 19. Also associated with the time of year when temperatures dip to their annual lows in the Russian countryside.

kuda denus?   literally, Where will I put myself? Or, What choice do I have?

kulak(i)   rich peasant(s) persecuted under Stalin during collectivization.

kulich   a tall, round loaf of sweetbread traditionally made for Russian Easter and exchanged between neighbors and friends.

kum(ovya)   the godparent(s) of one's child, or the relationship between the two godparents of a godchild.

kurgan(y)   ancient burial mound(s), of which there are 240 at the pre-twelfth-century site of the town of Trubchevsk, making it the second largest such site in Russia.

Kurskaya Duga   Kursk Arch, in the Kursk region. The site of one of the greatest tank battles in history where the Russians defeated the Germans on July 17, 1943.

kvas   a nonalcoholic drink made from birch juice or water with fermented bread.

lapti   shoes worn by peasants woven from the inner strips of linden bark (bast).

Lokot a town about thirty miles north of Chukhrai where Nazi warplanes were based and the site of the prison camp where many of the villagers were interned during the war.

makhorka homegrown tobacco, usually smoked in rolled-up pieces of newspaper. Stronger and cheaper than regular cigarettes.

Maslenitsa Shrovetide. The religious holiday to welcome the arrival of spring, accompanied by a week of feasting, before Lent.

okroshka a cold summer soup of chopped vegetables in a *kvas* base. Recipe page 109.

olivye potato salad with meat and vegetables, named for the French chef Olivier, who invented it. Recipe page 254.

Otche nash The Lord's Prayer, recited three times to ward off curses and ensure overall health and well-being.

parnoye steam room in a *banya* where bathers are beaten with birch brooms to intensify the heat and open the pores.

paskha a fine cottage cheese (*tvorog*) with raisins, nuts, and vanilla. Traditionally served on Russian Easter, which is also called Paskha.

Petrov Den St. Peter and Paul Day. A religious holiday celebrated July 12 and traditionally accompanied by merriment and rides on a makeshift Ferris wheel in Chukhrai.

pogreb a small root cellar with an entrance through the top. Villagers lived in these cellars after the war, their homes having been destroyed by the Nazis.

Pokrov Feast of the Intercession of the Holy Virgin. An important religious holiday and the Patron Saint Day for Chukhrai, celebrated October 14. Associated with a number of traditions in the village, including the beginning of the wedding season.

Politsai Russians who collaborated with the Nazis during the war. Their descendents are still loathed in the countryside.

portyanka(-ki) strip(s) of cloth wrapped around the feet for warmth. Often mistaken for rags, but actually preferred to socks by many, as they are warmer and don't slip down inside boots.

Radonitsa, Rodichye the second Tuesday after Easter (the Tuesday of St. Thomas week, in the West) when the villagers honor their ancestors in the graveyard. Radonitsa comes from *radost*, "joy," for the joy associated with Christ's resurrection.

raskulachivanie Stalin's repression of *kulaki* to force them to join collective farms, or *kolkhozy*.

Rozhdestvo Russian Orthodox Christmas, celebrated January 7, but abolished during Soviet times. As a result, Russians exchange presents on New Year's Eve.

salo pig lard, often smoked or salted. It is said that no Russian can survive the winter without *salo*.

samogon moonshine. Often used as payment in the village, and a usual accompaniment to *salo*.

seliodka salted herring. Traditional fare served with Russian vodka.

sglaz the evil eye, a curse.

shashlyk(i) shish kebab(s). Traditionally made with mutton cooked over an open fire.

Smelizh a village of about three hundred people located six miles from Chukhrai. Krasnaya Sloboda is two miles beyond it. During the war, the Bryansk partisans cleared an airfield near the village and set up a makeshift hospital, printing press, and other structures in bunkers in the woods. The name comes from the Russian *smyely*, or "brave."

smetana similar to sour cream, but sweeter. Made by skimming the cream from fresh milk and letting it thicken.

Snegurochka Snow Maiden, Ded moroz's granddaughter.

Spas Feast of the Transfiguration. A religious holiday celebrated August 19. It is a sin to work on this day, to sew, to chop with an axe, or to use a hammer.

Staroye Yamnoye a spit of land on the opposite side of the Nerussa River from Chukhrai where a monastery of the same name once stood more than two hundred years ago. Igor found an abandoned forester's cabin there in 1980 while searching the neighboring woods for signs of the black stork. He later moved to the cabin, fixed it up, and eventually succeeded in creating a sanctuary and then a federal protected area, or *zapovednik*, on the lands around the cabin. Today the site is home to a ranger station, where Igor's father works. The name means "old hollow," probably for the botwed lake that flanks he spit of land.

Suzemka   a town of seven thousand about twenty-five
    miles from Chukhrai on the road through Smelizh,
    Krasnaya Sloboda, and Beriozovka. Where Igor
    and I do most of our shopping at outdoor markets
    and a handful of stores. The name comes from
    the Old Russian word *suzem*—"dense forest."

Trubchevsk   an ancient town of about sixteen thousand
    situated on the high west bank of the Desna River and
    reachable from Chukhrai by car only by crossing the
    broad Desna River and floodplain, either over the perma-
    nent cement bridge via the paved road through Suzemka
    (fifty miles), or more directly by old logging roads and
    across the seasonal pontoon bridge (twelve miles), or by
    boat on the winding Nerussa River, which flows near
    our house and into the Desna (twenty-five miles). The
    name of the town comes from *truba* (pipe), originally
    the word for "a stream or river in a deep ravine."

Ukraine   formerly one of the fifteen republics of the
    Soviet Union that gained independence in 1991. Referred
    to as "the Ukraine" prior to 1991 and simply "Ukraine"
    following independence. Ukraine borders the Russian
    province of Bryansk only seven miles from Chukhrai.

valenki   warm boots made of thick pressed felt, sometimes
    with rubber soles. Standard footwear for the villagers in
    winter, but worn year-round by Stepan, the villager who
    brings our mail, to avoid being nipped on the heels by
    our dogs.

zakaznik   refuge or sanctuary. Has a lower level of protec-
    tion than a *zapovednik*, but where logging, drainage, and
    other destructive forms of nature use are prohibited. Igor

fought to create eleven sanctuaries in the Bryansk Forest
to protect nesting black stork populations and the old-
growth forests where they reside.

zapovednik(i) strictly protected nature reserve(s) where
human presence is discouraged. Today there are 101
zapovedniki in Russia. The first *zapovednik* (Barguzinsky)
was created in 1916 on the eastern shores of Lake Baikal
to save the rare Barguzin sable. Since then the system has
expanded to an area covering 83 million acres, or 1.4 percent of the Russian lands, despite attempts by Stalin and
Khrushchev to slash the reserve system and open the areas
for resource exploitation. *Zapovedniki* harbor such natural
wonders as the geysers and volcanoes of Kamchatka, the
mountains ringing Lake Baikal, and some of the last intact
European broadleaf forests in the Bryansk Forest. *Zapovedniki* were created to save critical habitat for endangered
species such as the Siberian tiger, saiga antelope, Russian
desman, and black stork. The Bryansk Forest Zapovednik,
established in 1987, was primarily created for protecting
important floodplain and forest habitat for the black stork.

Acknowledgments

I HAVE SO MANY people to thank. First and foremost, none of this would have been possible without my husband, Igor, who lured me from the big city to Chukhrai and whose stories about life in the Bryansk Forest inspired me to write this book. I want to honor my friend Olga Iva- novna Balakhonova, who tirelessly told and retold tales of growing up in the village. Thank you, Andrea Williams and Charles Dewey—Mom and Chas—both for understanding my choice to live in Russia and for your invaluable input in editing multiple versions of this book. Thank you, John Williams and Pat Williams—Dad and Pat—for your unfail- ing support. Thank you, Mark and Eric, my brothers, for not always doubting my "tree-hugger" convictions. Thank you, Pyotr Nikitich, Lidya Mikhailovna, Dima and Vita, and Tikhon and Petya—the Shpilenok family—for accepting me as one of your own. And special thanks to Nikolai Shpilenok, Igor's brother, for his philosophical insights and for providing the map and photos to illustrate this book. I am thankful for my two sons, Andrei and Makar, for the joy they bring to our lives and for motivating me to write this down so that they may know how their father and I fell in love.

THE STORKS' NEST

I am grateful to my good friend and Russian godmother, Elena Postalateva, who lost her life in a tragic farm accident in October 2003, for her unfading energy and enthusiasm and for helping deepen my understanding of Russian tradition.

I am also indebted to the people who created opportunities for me and, albeit unknowingly, set me on the road to Chukhrai: John Fred Bailyn, Bill Chandler, as well as Bill Eichbaum, Vladimir Krever, and other dedicated conservationists in the WWF family.

Thank you to Gary Kinder for his keen advice. Thanks to Fred Strebeigh for cheering me on and for reviewing this manuscript. And I would have been lost without the unshakable support of my dear friends Joanne Turnbull and Nikolai Formozov, my virtual encyclopedia on Russian nature, culture, and interpretation of the Russian language. I would also like to recognize my friend Margaret Williams, another *Amerikanka* who shares my love of Russian *zapovedniki* and Chukhrai. Thanks to my dear friend and fellow Russophile Michelle Schorr for sending peanut butter cups and helping me through difficult times.

I am grateful to Alexis Troubetzkoy for the information he provided on his family. Thank you to my agent, Richard Curtis, for his enthusiasm and faith that my manuscript deserved to be published. I am grateful to my publisher, Bob Baron of Fulcrum Publishing for helping this book to see the light of day. Special thanks to my editor, Faith Marcovecchio, for her input and attention to detail, as well as Ann W. Douden, Haley Berry, Erin Palmiter, Kay Baron, and the entire Fulcrum team. Finally, I thank all the villagers of Chukhrai for their will to prevail despite a lifetime of hardship.

327

THE STORKS' NEST

LAURA LYNNE WILLIAMS set up the World Wildlife Fund's first office in Russia in 1993 and for four years co-ordinated WWF's biodiversity projects throughout Russia. Since leaving Moscow for the countryside in 1997 to work for one of Russia's strictly protected nature reserves, called *zapovedniki*, she has freelanced as a nature writer, contributing articles to *National Wildlife*, *BBC Wildlife*, and other magazines. She writes the "Notes from a Russian Village" column for *Russian Life* magazine. Laura has a bachelor's degree in international environmental policy from Cornell University and a master's degree in conservation biology from the Yale School of Forestry and Environmental Studies. She grew up in Colorado where she learned to love horses and wildlife. Today she lives with her husband, award-winning nature photographer and naturalist Igor Shpilenok, in the remote Russian village of Chukhrai, whose population recently swelled to twenty-one with the birth of their second son.